Available From the American Academy of Pediatrics

Achieving a Healthy Weight for Your Child: An Action Plan for Families

ADHD: What Every Parent Needs to Know

Autism Spectrum Disorder: What Every Parent Needs to Know

Baby and Toddler Basics: Expert Answers to Parents' Top 150 Questions

Building Resilience in Children and Teens: Giving Kids Roots and Wings

Caring for Your Adopted Child: An Essential Guide for Parents

Caring for Your Baby and Young Child: Birth to Age 5*

Caring for Your School-Age Child: Ages 5–12

Dad to Dad: Parenting Like a Pro

Family Fit Plan: A 30-Day Wellness Transformation

Food Fights: Winning the Nutritional Challenges of Parenthood Armed With Insight, Humor, and a Bottle of Ketchup

Heading Home With Your Newborn: From Birth to Reality

Mama Doc Medicine: Finding Calm and Confidence in Parenting, Child Health, and Work-Life Balance

My Child Is Sick! Expert Advice for Managing Common Illnesses and Injuries

The New Baby Blueprint: Caring for You and Your Little One

Nutrition: What Every Parent Needs to Know

Parenting Through Puberty: Mood Swings, Acne, and Growing Pains

The Picky Eater Project: 6 Weeks to Happier, Healthier Family Mealtimes

Raising an Organized Child: 5 Steps to Boost Independence, Ease Frustration, and Promote Confidence

Raising Kids to Thrive: Balancing Love With Expectations and Protection With Trust

Retro Baby: Cut Back on All the Gear and Boost Your Baby's Development With More Than 100 Time-tested Activities

Retro Toddler: More Than 100 Old-School Activities to Boost Development

Sleep: What Every Parent Needs to Know

Waking Up Dry: A Guide to Help Children Overcome Bedwetting

healthychildren.org

Powered by pediatricians. Trusted by parents.
from the American Academy of Pediatrics

For additional parenting resources, visit the HealthyChildren bookstore at https://shop.aap.org/for-parents.

*This book is also available in Spanish.

Co-parenting
Through
Separation
and Divorce
PUTTING YOUR CHILDREN FIRST

Jann Blackstone, PsyD
David L. Hill, MD, FAAP

American Academy of Pediatrics
DEDICATED TO THE HEALTH OF ALL CHILDREN®

American Academy of Pediatrics Publishing Staff

Mary Lou White, *Chief Product and Services Officer/SVP, Membership, Marketing, and Publishing*

Mark Grimes, *Vice President, Publishing*

Holly Kaminski, *Editor, Consumer Publishing*

Shannan Martin, *Production Manager, Consumer Publications*

Amanda Helmholz, *Medical Copy Editor*

Sara Hoerdeman, *Marketing Manager, Consumer Products*

Published by the American Academy of Pediatrics

345 Park Blvd

Itasca, IL 60143

Telephone: 630/626-6000

Facsimile: 847/434-8000

www.aap.org

The American Academy of Pediatrics is an organization of 67,000 primary care pediatricians, pediatric medical subspecialists, and pediatric surgical specialists dedicated to the health, safety, and well-being of infants, children, adolescents, and young adults.

The information contained in this publication should not be used as a substitute for the medical care and advice of your pediatrician. There may be variations in treatment that your pediatrician may recommend based on individual facts and circumstances.

Statements and opinions expressed are those of the authors and not necessarily those of the American Academy of Pediatrics.

Any websites, brand names, products, or manufacturers are mentioned for informational and identification purposes only and do not imply an endorsement by the American Academy of Pediatrics (AAP). The AAP is not responsible for the content of external resources. Information was current at the time of publication.

The publishers have made every effort to trace the copyright holders for borrowed materials. If they have inadvertently overlooked any, they will be pleased to make the necessary arrangements at the first opportunity.

This publication has been developed by the American Academy of Pediatrics. The contributors are expert authorities in the field of pediatrics. No commercial involvement of any kind has been solicited or accepted in development of the content of this publication. Disclosures: Dr Hill disclosed an advisory board member relationship with Gerber and Before Brands, as well as an expert reviewer relationship with Marico Bangladesh.

Every effort is made to keep *Co-parenting Through Separation and Divorce* consistent with the most recent advice and information available from the American Academy of Pediatrics.

Special discounts are available for bulk purchases of this publication. Email Special Sales at aapsales@aap.org for more information.

Printed in the United States of America

9-449   1 2 3 4 5 6 7 8 9 10

CB0117

ISBN: 978-1-61002-380-1

eBook: 978-1-61002-381-8

EPUB: 978-1-61002-382-5

Kindle: 978-1-61002-383-2

PDF: 978-1-61002-384-9

Cover design by R. Scott Rattray

Publication design by LSD DESIGN, LLC

Library of Congress Control Number: 2019948059

What People Are Saying

"A direct and practical guide that talks parents through the complexities of caring for their children as families come apart, and helps them find new ways to do the best possible job as parents, going forward."

—Perri Klass, MD, FAAP, author of *Quirky Kids: Understanding and Supporting Your Child With Developmental Differences;* professor of journalism and pediatrics, New York University

"Two experts draw on their professional and personal experiences in this wise, comprehensive, and essential guide for divorced parents. Do yourself and your children a favor and keep this book handy. You will return to it often for its immensely practical advice and spot-on tips for parents from the beginning of separation through remarriage and beyond. Solid gold!"

—Dr. Richard A. Warshak, author of *Divorce Poison: How to Protect Your Family from Bad-mouthing and Brainwashing;* past clinical professor of psychiatry, University of Texas Southwestern Medical Center

"This book is a must-read for any parent going through separation and divorce. The authors provide real-world examples giving concrete, useful advice to parents that is based on their years of professional experience."

—Lauren Rosen Crosby, MD, FAAP, pediatric and adolescent medicine, Beverly Hills, CA; TV news medical expert

"I think this book should be a court-ordered read for all separating families."

—Sheila Ballin, Esq, family law facilitator, director of family court services, and family law manager, San Joaquin County Superior Court (retired); former adjunct family law professor, Humphreys College School of Law

"At last! A resource for parents who have split up and restructured their families, written by 2 phenomenally insightful experts able to bring expertise from the worlds of law, medicine, and mental health. This book is insightful, actionable, and frankly invaluable."

—Cara Natterson, MD, FAAP, pediatrician, consultant, and author of *Decoding Boys: New Science Behind the Subtle Art of Raising Sons*

Dedication

Co-parenting Through Separation and Divorce is dedicated to all the "bonusfamilies" out there—families who have adopted the philosophy of "good ex-etiquette," or good behavior after divorce or separation; understand that using the term "bonus" as a prefix is a compliment to their loved one; and continue to put their own issues aside in the best interest of their children.

I'd also like to acknowledge my family, who have always understood the time it takes to write a book and worked around my "I can't; I have a deadline."

Dr Blackstone

I dedicate this book first and foremost to my wife, Christy, and to my children's mother, Margaret, for always being willing to work together to ensure that the children we all love come first. Second, *Co-parenting Through Separation and Divorce* is for my mother, Anne Hill, for finding the most amazing "bonusfather" anyone could hope for, John Hill, my role model for all things fatherhood. Finally, this book is for my children and my "bonuschildren"—Julian, Sellers, Alex, Abby, and Emily—who have been patient and forgiving as the co-parents in their lives have worked to improve every day at understanding and meeting their needs. As they rapidly emerge into adulthood themselves, I am incredibly proud of the people they have become and are still becoming.

Dr Hill

Contents

About This Book

We knew from the start that in no way could one voice alone tell the story of co-parenting through separation and divorce. There are as many experiences as there are families, and each person's circumstances are unique. To try to reflect at least some of that diversity, *Co-parenting Through Separation and Divorce* draws on the expertise of 2 authors: Jann Blackstone, PsyD, and David L. Hill, MD, FAAP.

Drs Blackstone and Hill have a lot in common. They have both experienced divorce and remarriage, and they have both faced the hurdles of combining families and raising children with their new partners. Both are experts in their fields with decades of writing and storytelling experience. Both are intimately involved with helping families solve problems: Dr Blackstone spent years in the California family court system, where her doctorate of psychology gave her the skill set to steer families through mediation to solutions that served children's interests, and Dr Hill has practiced primary care pediatrics for more than 20 years in North Carolina, a practice serving families from diverse cultural backgrounds.

The authors know that families come in all varieties: married, never-married, opposite-sex, same-sex, fluid, young, old, and in-between. Although the experiences of the authors stem from more traditional relationships, this book is meant to include all parents and all families. Regardless of where we start, we all face the same struggles, and we all strive to put our children first.

The text in this book reflects a conversation among Dr Blackstone, Dr Hill, and the reader, with each author jumping in at different times throughout the chapters to offer her or his perspective. Their voices alternate, and their stories pour out like those at a really therapeutic dinner party. We hope that you will enjoy being a part of this conversation, and we hope that you will pass on what you learn to anyone who might need help. It is well-known that no child succeeds without the help of a caring adult, but, then, neither does any parent. Thank you for caring.

Acknowledgments

Even though a book states that specific authors write it, there are always people behind the scenes who contribute to making your project a success. I would like to thank all the people who volunteered their stories; *Co-parenting Through Separation and Divorce* has been a collaborative effort, and I would like to acknowledge the team who helped make this book possible.

First, I would like to thank David L. Hill, MD, FAAP, my coauthor. We did not know each other before we wrote this book—my background is more in the trenches of family court than his, but our pairing is a good pairing. He is a great sounding board, full of knowledge and open to discuss any topic, a trait of his that made it easy to explore and flesh out our different ideas and points of view. His openness and easy manner made the process far easier than I ever expected.

I'd also like to thank our editor, Holly Kaminski, whom I now count as a friend, for offering her patience and insight into the production of this project and making it a success. She answered panicked phone calls late at night and on Sundays, and she's probably sorry she gave me her cell phone number now.

Thank you to the American Academy of Pediatrics team, Sara Hoerdeman from Marketing and Medical Copy Editor Amanda Helmholz.

I would also like to acknowledge my colleagues at superior court in San Joaquin County, California. Thanks to the judges, the commissioner, the attorneys, and my fellow family court mediators for their knowledge and insight over the years—but special thanks to Sheila Ballin, retired director of family court services, for being the voice of reason when things got tough and always bringing the focus back to the children. Nothing like working for the court system and mediating parents from all walks of life helps you find the empathy and compassion needed to better help families in transition. Thank you.

Special thanks to my good friend Steven Claire, family law attorney, for lending his humor, knowledge, and recipes.

And, finally, to Jennifer Erwin, my pal and Bonusfamilies collaborator, for keeping me focused and my enthusiasm up.

Dr Blackstone

I must first thank my coauthor, Jann Blackstone, PsyD, whose experience, expertise, and wealth of stories make *Co-parenting Through Separation and Divorce* possible. I have learned much from her during this process as a practitioner, a parent, and a writer. Thanks to my colleagues Andrew S. Garner, MD, PhD, FAAP, and Robert A. Saul, MD, FAAP, FACMG, for their guidance in understanding and explaining the concepts of childhood trauma and resilience. Their book, *Thinking Developmentally: Nurturing Wellness in Childhood to Promote Lifelong Health,* served as the backbone of Chapter 8, Toxic Stress and Its Effect on Our Children, of this one. Family Law Attorney Steven Claire gets my thanks for walking me through the myriad legal aspects of separation and divorce. Finally, this book is the brainchild of and a labor of love for the American Academy of Pediatrics publishing staff, including Editor Holly Kaminski, who made sure that we actually wrote and published a book; Medical Copy Editor Amanda Helmholz, who literally dotted our *i*'s and crossed our *t*'s; and Marketing Manager Sara Hoerdeman, who makes sure that the people who need this book find it. Finally, thank you, the reader, for caring enough to pick up this book and seeking out ways to put your own children first.

Dr Hill

We would like to specially thank the reviewers from both the Committee on Psychosocial Aspects of Child and Family Health and the Section on Developmental and Behavioral Pediatrics of the American Academy of Pediatrics for their review of this book. We would also like to personally thank Damon Korb, MD, FAAP, and Candice W. Jones, MD, FAAP, for their peer review of this book. We greatly appreciate all of your time and guidance.

Introduction

Dr Hill's Story

"Now I see it, you do look a lot like your dad! I should have known you were John R. Hill's son!" I had just introduced myself to the speaker, a prominent pediatrician from my home state of Tennessee who knew my dad from multiple encounters over the years. And he was right, I *do* look like my dad. My walk is an exact copy of his authoritative stride through the hospital hallways, where I would trail him on weekend rounds. I dress like him, tying my tie, polishing my shoes, and carefully hooking my top blazer button just the way he taught me. When I examine kids in clinic, I copy the way he "beep-beeps" a 3-year-old's belly button and "doo-dee-doos," in singsong, through an ears, nose, and mouth examination.

The speaker, however, could be forgiven for not seeing the resemblance right away. I display none of my dad's ruddy complexion, and I don't have his bushy eyebrows or potbelly. Why would I? John R. Hill adopted me when I was 10 years old, 2 years after he married my mom. I never hesitated to call John R. Hill "Dad." Seven years had passed since my parents' divorce, and at the time, my birth father was living in his car, struggling with mental illness and doing odd jobs around the country.

I remember the toast Dad gave at my wedding. I was a 30-year-old, freshly minted pediatrician marrying another young doctor I had met in residency. He wished for us the same sort of happy and strong marriage he and my mom had shared for the previous 22 years. I never really understood how their marriage worked, and I was sure that he had undershot; we would do so much better.

If I knew one thing, it was this: my new wife and I, both children of divorce, would not repeat the mistakes our parents had made. We had done things right: waited to get married, dated for years, made sure that we really loved each other and that we wanted the same things in life. Sure, every other speaker, from the priest who married us to the baby boomers who stood up to toast, kept talking about how hard marriage was, but we had just finished medical residency. Compared with that, marriage would be a piece of cake. Cake with buttercream frosting textured to look like a basket and decorated with live flowers. Shut up and dance, people, we got this!

Until we didn't. Always the optimist, I tried hard to ignore the signs that our marriage was in trouble. The giveaway should have been when any of our 3 children would ask us about divorce. Learning that some friend's parents were separating, they would ask, "Are you and Mommy ever going to get a divorce?" For years, the answer had been, "No, sweetie, never. We are never going to get a divorce." Then, about 10 years into the marriage, their mom started to say, "If we did, we would both still love you just as much."

"But don't worry, because we won't!" I'd add, hopefully. Yeah, in the end, we would.

It's hard still to express how profoundly I felt I had failed at my marriage. I knew I was going to be the best kind of dad, the one who was always around for his kids, the one whose cheers and hugs and bedtime stories his kids would remember when they had kids of their own. I was going to make everything perfect for them. Now they weren't even with me half the time. And I knew the statistics. By allowing this thing to happen, I had doomed my children to higher risks of poor health, learning issues, attention-deficit/hyperactivity disorder, emotional and behavioral difficulties, and even emergency department visits. However, being a pediatrician, I thought these were exactly the sorts of outcomes that I would protect my children against. Although many of them happened, I can't really know what role the divorce played.

Nine years have passed since then. I regularly gather at the kitchen table with my wife and my ex-wife to hash out issues related to school, mobile phones, and summer camps, all the issues, large and small, that parents face. We save each other seats at band concerts, soccer games, and graduations. We text each other with cute pictures, homework reminders, and questions about curfews. The kids are fine, with good days and bad days, including triumphs and failures—the usual. And I have 2 stepchildren, double the chance to share the gift that John R. Hill gave me when he called me his son. They're good too.

As a pediatrician, I used to dance gingerly around issues of separation and divorce, not wanting to dwell on what might be a sore subject for the families I serve. Now I know better. If you're separated or divorced, you won't be shocked to be reminded of it. I now ask my questions directly and frankly, knowing how much the answers matter: "Does one parent have primary custody? What is the visitation schedule? Do any other adults live in either household? How does communication work between the houses? Do you have similar rules?" More than 1 million children a year face parental separation or divorce in the United States. The answers to these questions define their daily lives and therefore determine much of their health and development. They must be faced head-on.

If you're reading *Co-parenting Through Separation and Divorce*, chances are good that you're somewhere on your journey as a parent through separation or divorce. I'm sorry. I know it's hard. But I am here to tell you that you're going to be OK. Your kids are going to be OK. And be proud of yourself for taking a big step to ensure it. I don't pretend to have everything figured out, as a parent or as a doctor. But I have learned some things that worked, and I now know some things that don't, and I'm excited to share my thoughts with you. Thank you for being here.

Dr Blackstone's Story

My introduction to divorce was quite different. I married the first time too young and simply did not have the tools to maintain a healthy relationship. We divorced when our daughter was 9 months old. We shared custody, and we spoke very little, but he was a wonderful father and never missed his time with his daughter—ever.

In 1989, I married a man with 2 children and a very involved ex-wife, and that's when my journey truly began. I had no idea what *shared custody* really meant. My custody situation was rather conventional—my daughter lived with me and saw her dad every other weekend. But my husband and his ex-wife shared equal custody, a week with Mom and then a week with Dad. We had no rule books, no place to go to ask for help, back in 1989. The kids were 4 and 7 years of age, and my daughter was 6. I had no idea what I was getting into, and I certainly had no idea that the parenting plan my husband and his ex-wife had chosen would put me into contact with his ex-wife daily. Three years later, my husband and I would add another daughter, Harleigh, to the mix. We felt she united us all—she was related to us all. The only member of the family to hold that title.

As I write this, I am on an airplane flying from California to New York City with Harleigh, who is now 24, and my now ex-husband. We were married for 23 years. A midlife crisis—his, not mine—reared its ugly head and we didn't make it, but we continue to be there for our daughter. Who said co-parenting ends when your child is 18? Not even close.

So now Harleigh and her dad, Larry, are buckled in and asleep and my thoughts are sailing back to the beginning of it all.

ffffff

The first time I met Sharyl, Larry's ex-wife, the meeting was quite cordial. Because we were planning to marry, Larry thought I should meet his children's mother. We did. She was very polite, and that was it for about 6 months.

When the phone rang at 6:30 in the morning, I knew there was a problem. It was "her," and my husband was disagreeing very loudly on the phone about something she had said (they didn't communicate very well at this point). He handed me the phone and walked out of the room.

"Here," he snapped, before he left. "You talk to her. I can't anymore."

I remember thinking, *"You have got to be kidding me. I don't want to talk to your ex-wife."* But he wouldn't come back. He had walked out the back door.

There I stood, phone in hand, thinking, *"This woman is going to be so angry if someone doesn't say something, quick."* I was the only one in the room. I guess I had to answer.

When I finally said, "Hello," I expected the rants of a crazy woman. That's how my husband had presented her, but that's not what happened at all. Instead, after I said hello, she asked me in a sincere but frustrated tone, "Jann, why does he hate me so much?"

I have to admit, that threw me. By this time, Sharyl and I had grown quite tolerant of each other, but we avoided each other if we could. They had a clause in their divorce decree called "Right of First Refusal." That meant if one needed child care, one was obliged to ask the other first. She did, and I had a home office, so I said I could watch the kids after school, even on her weeks. That meant the kids were with me more than anyone else.

This did not make Sharyl happy. She was a working mom who felt guilty about getting a divorce, and her kids were being raised by her husband's second wife. The day her son called me "Mommy" right in front of her was the pièce de résistance. She looked at me as if she had been shot in the heart.

Although the adults thought we were keeping all our animosity from the children, my daughter started having nightmares and their daughter had chronic stomachaches. That's when we realized we had to come to our senses. Good behavior after divorce, something I refer to as "good ex-etiquette," is more than just positive interaction between parents who are no longer together—it's also gracefully integrating new partners into the mix. And I don't say this because it's some politically correct approach to anything. I say it because it's inevitable. Most parents who are no longer together will get involved with someone else, and the new person will have a huge impact on their children. The more the parental figures can successfully communicate for the sake of the children, the better chance the children will be well-adjusted and secure. Fight, argue, or bad-mouth the other parent or the partner and you are contributing to your children's potential future mental illness diagnosis. Plus, you aren't offering them much of an example for a successful relationship of their own.

I started to write about stepfamilies about 5 years into our combined family experiment. I was at the gym reading *Working Mother* magazine as I trucked away at the elliptical. I was reading a Question and Answer column and the question was about how a stepmother should approach a particular situation. The advice given was "Just do it. Make the decision." I started to laugh out loud right there in the gym. Although the magazine implied that the advice given was by a stepmother, I knew it was not. An active stepmother is a diplomat. She's a mediator. She promotes compromise and consults both parents before she does anything. She would never make a decision for her partner's children unless she was empowered to do so. I was so upset I called the magazine and asked to talk with the editor.

I look back now and wonder what I was thinking. How presumptuous of me to call an editor to complain in the middle of the afternoon. Much to my surprise, she got on the phone and I proceeded to tell her that I didn't think the article was written by a stepmother and that the advice given was misleading. I explained my life and my lifestyle and why I held my position on the subject, and that's when she acknowledged that the article was indeed written by a single mother! Well, of course it was! Single mothers can "Just do it. Make the decision!" I chuckled as I told her I suspected as much. That's when she suggested I write the column from a stepmother's perspective. I was so excited! I agreed, and I wrote the Family Matters column for *Working Mother* magazine for more than 5 years, when I went back to school and changed careers. I am now a family law child custody mediator for superior court in California. Over the past 10 years, I have worked with thousands of couples after separation or divorce—every couple was in conflict, every couple was struggling, and every couple said they wanted to do what was best for their children. For some, that wasn't always true. By the time they had reached my office, many had lost sight of what was in their children's best interest; they were in it to "win." It became my job to remind them if one of them were to win, it would be a sure sign their kids had lost.

I can honestly say I had no better teacher than working for superior court. It taught me a very important lesson—but it sounds very simple now. Bring it all back to the kids and you can turn it all around. When you base your decisions on your children's best interest, the right decisions are easy to make.

Before going to work for the court system, in 1999, with Sharyl's support, I started a nonprofit organization called Bonus Families (now called Bonusfamilies). I chose the term "bonus" because *step-* implies wicked or evil, and the word *step-* simply didn't apply to our family. "Bonus" is a reward for a job well done and seemed to be a kinder, gentler label that fit. Others seemed to agree. The Bonusfamilies website (https://bonusfamilies.com) soon became the most visited stepfamily website on the Web. People wanted real-life help from someone who had been through it.

I am gratified to say that this year is the Bonusfamilies 20th anniversary! And I continue to offer help and advice to divorced or separated parents in their efforts to co-parent their children. The most visited department on the Bonusfamilies website has always been Ex-etiquette; the most searched phrase, "good behavior after a breakup." Sharyl and I originally wrote it together, but it has evolved into my personal project. We have also written 3 Ex-etiquette books together, and I developed the 10 Rules of Good Ex-etiquette (https://bonusfamilies.com/ten-rules-good-ex-etiquette-parents) as a quick reference guide for co-parenting and often refer to them in my syndicated column, also called Ex-etiquette.

The kids are now grown and have kids of their own. Sharyl and I speak with each other but don't spend as much time together as we did when the kids were going back and forth. We still all spend the holidays as a family. I just saw her at "our" grandson's fifth birthday party.

That's my history. My life's work continues to be helping parents put aside their hurt, anger, and revenge, for the sake of the children they share. I will be the first to say I know it's not easy—parents who are no longer together forget they have a mutual interest, but they do—their children.

Harleigh just squeezed my hand and thanked me for being there for her. "Wake up, Dad," she said. "We are about to land."

I shook Larry's shoulder. "Lar, we're here."

He rubbed his eyes as he began to stir. "Is everything OK?"

"It is now," I said.

But it hasn't always been that way. It's been quite a journey. This book contains what I have learned over the years, and I humbly pass it on to you in hopes that it helps guide you as you make your journey as well.

No matter whether you are contemplating a separation, going through a divorce, just moved out, or were recently served papers, it is our hope you will find comfort in the pages that follow. You are not alone in this journey. We understand that separation or divorce can be one of the most difficult times in your life, especially when children are involved. We share stories, offer guidance, and arm you with some learning tools that will help make you feel stronger during this difficult time.

How to Use This Book

Creating a family takes a lifetime, and restructuring one takes just as long. You may be just considering a separation or in the beginning of a divorce and wondering what the effect might be on your children. You may have separated a while ago and now find yourself struggling with how to build healthy relationships with your children. Or you may be somewhere in between.

Co-parenting Through Separation and Divorce is organized along a timeline, starting with the important issues to take into account when contemplating a separation and ending with how separation with or without divorce can affect your family as your children become adults and even have children of their own one day. Together we walk you through the steps and address the subjects we feel would be the most helpful. Feel free to pick it up, put it down, or flip to the section that answers your most pressing questions right now.

You'll notice that some themes crop up repeatedly. The most important is "putting your children first." Separation and divorce usually start in moments of emotional turmoil, and that turmoil is likely to erupt from time to time throughout the process. There may be times that you can barely meet your own needs or even define them. But at every step in the process, with every question that arises, finding the best answer depends on understanding and responding to your children's needs. We have spent our careers serving children and their families, and our goal is to help you be the best parent you can be to ensure your children have the best possible future.

Separation and divorce are borne of anger, frustration, and helplessness, and these emotions can make it feel impossible for you to deal with your ex. But remember, the first concept is "putting your children first," before anything else. Doing that is going to require you to work through your anger and frustration and focus on solutions rather than problems. Your ex will now be your co-parent. Being in a co-parenting relationship is different from being in a romantic relationship. Your roles will now be working together in the best interest of your child. As unlikely as it may seem, you may be able to forge a positive, constructive co-parenting partnership with the person with whom you no longer want to share a home. You are the only person you control, so nothing is guaranteed, but we hope to show you that controlling your own attitude and behavior can give you the best possible chance of cooperating to help your children thrive through adversity.

The final themes are "transition" and "development." We all know that children grow and develop over time, that the mind of a teenager is very different from the mind of an infant, but we don't stop growing and developing just because we reach some random moment in time. You, too, are continuing to learn more about yourself and how to live your best life. If you're going to put your children first, you'll need to understand how they are developing and how you are developing as well. Throughout this book, we address children's developmental stages and offer techniques you can use to grow as well.

In a perfect world, no one would need this book. But we have had the experiences that led us to write it, and now you are having an experience that has led you to pick it up. We want you to know that you are not alone. You will have company throughout this journey, and you will build relationships and discover your strengths and gifts that may surprise you along the way. Just remember, we are much stronger when facing a crisis together than when facing the crisis alone.

1

Will I Get Through This?

When one door closes, another opens;
but we often look so long and so regretfully
upon the closed door that we do not see the one
that has opened for us.

ALEXANDER GRAHAM BELL
(COMMONLY ATTRIBUTED TO)

What Happened?

We got through it and so will you, but the journey wasn't easy—and although all of us feel as if our problems are unique, there are really no new problems. From infidelity to addiction, to abuse, to just not getting along—someone has faced what you are experiencing and has tried just as hard as you are now to make all the right decisions.

All find themselves rehashing what went wrong. Was it my fault? Was it my ex's? Was there anything we could have done to prevent this? Did we exhaust all avenues to fix the relationship? And, when we realize a breakup is inevitable, we all feel bad about our families, we worry what our friends will think, we worry whether we will have enough money to support ourselves and our children, and we feel terrible that the kids may have to change schools or feel the emotional upheaval associated with the fact that their parents, too, will no longer be together. We face strong feelings that some of us have never felt before—fear, jealousy, anger, or revenge—and have no idea, at first, how to navigate the pain. Rarely do any of us put our best foot forward during stressful times such as these, and we struggle with the realization that a decision we made or made for us devastated our families.

Most of all, we feel like failures. The stigma of a separation sticks to us, and when someone asks, "Well, what happened?" how do we even know where to start? Each of us had our reasons—and rarely do we grasp the magnitude of the decision to end our relationship at the time the decision is made. With that decision comes moments of confusion, when fear overtakes us, and we shake in our boots as we wonder, *"Did I do the right thing?"* only to get that welcomed reprieve by moments of clarity, when the decision seems crystal clear and we power forward.

The truth is, on all levels, fear is our greatest enemy. We have all heard the famous quotation by Franklin Roosevelt "The only thing we have to fear is fear itself." Former President Roosevelt was explaining to the nation that the fear of war (just like the fear before or after a breakup) was worsening things. He was saying if you sit in that fear, you become more concerned about the fear than the problem itself. A little-known fact is that Former President Roosevelt goes on to say in the same sentence, "nameless, unreasoning, unjustified terror which paralyzes needed efforts to convert retreat into advance."

Don't we all want to advance after a divorce? Go forward, not backward? Because retreating will hurt everyone involved, but most of all, it will hurt our children. The irony is, there may be a retreat, and on those days, we must learn to be patient and be kind to ourselves and, of all people, our ex, because the tragedy of this breakup is not only ours. It affects all the people in our lives. Some days we have a handle on things and soar through the day, rejuvenated from our decision to move on, but on the days that we limp, we must remember that our children are watching and may be limping as well, and it is our job to set the example and help them walk.

Co-parenting tip. I often caution clients, "Don't get ahead of yourself. Take it one day at a time, one foot in front of the other." Sometimes, when things seem their darkest, it's one hour at a time or even one minute at a time. The truth is, the sun will continue to rise and fall without our forcing it. When you are moving through this breakup, even though it feels as if the sun will never come up again, it will. I promise, "This, too, shall pass."

Positive Mind-set to Positive Outcome

All through *Co-parenting Through Separation and Divorce,* you will hear us talk about your mind-set and how you need the correct mental preparation to conquer a problem. We are both firm believers that what you think about a problem determines how you approach the problem. Psychologists have a simple, effective trick for people confronting discord and anxiety: reframe what you're feeling as excitement. You may think, *"What a strange thing to do when you are feeling anxious,"* but as far as your body is concerned, both emotions feel the same: your heart is racing, you're breathing fast, and your stomach feels weird. The only difference is your attitude. With anxiety, you're asking, *"What if something bad happens?"*

With excitement, you're asking, *"What if something good happens?"* So, rather than create agony that your life is changing and you have to move, the thought becomes *"What if my new apartment is decorated just the way I like?" "I'll never fall in love again"* becomes *"What if I meet someone I can actually make a life with?"* Or, as Dr Hill's therapist put before him the week he realized a divorce was imminent, "What if your relationship with your children is actually strengthened by this experience?"

This observation may seem surprising, the revelation that a father may actually become closer to his children once a divorce becomes final, but I have seen it happen quite often. We are products of our environment, and although times are changing quickly, research tells us that in a 2-parent family whose mother and father live with their children under the same roof, it is still true that mothers take on the primary responsibility of raising the children. If families have a hands-on mother doing a great job, dads tend to back off. That doesn't mean they aren't involved, but it means, for example, they may not be the parent to initiate a conversation with the teacher about missing homework or be the first one to talk with their daughter about the boy she likes—although Dad might hear "Dennis has a dentist appointment today, so would you mind taking him after school today?"

Once parents no longer live together, they often forget to keep each other informed of their children's progress. Anger, revenge, hurt, and maybe a basic insecurity about the transition from being a couple to being single contribute to keeping things to themselves. That means that if both want to stay informed, they each must take responsibility for communicating with the teachers, take turns taking the kids to the dentist, or lend an ear for first-time relationship woes.

I remember talking with a very good friend I have known since high school. The animosity between him and his ex was so extreme they could barely speak. He was very depressed about the demise of his marriage, but he openly confided the point I'm trying to make: "Please don't get me wrong here," he said. "I know this is going to sound weird, but this divorce has made me a better father." He went on to explain that he was now fully present whenever his kids were around. He depended on no one to tell him anything. He got the information firsthand from the teachers, from the doctors, and from the dentists, and he was proud of that.

Quite a few mothers have observed the same. However, as good as that sounds, if this is happening in your family, it indicates that something is wrong. Separation or divorce in this day and age requires us to change our attitude about the proper way to interact with an ex. We have to talk with each other, compare notes, and be respectful, particularly if the children are within earshot. We can't be autonomous co-parents (that's an oxymoron) and go ahead without consulting our co-parent, not if we force our children to go back and forth and live in both homes. The

"what happens here, stays here" message simply doesn't work. It scares children and checks their allegiance each time they leave one home to go to the other. People who abuse children tell children, "Don't tell." Consider that the next time you
tell them not to share something within the other home.

Co-parenting tip. Many use the "what happens here, stays here" philosophy for fear of reprisal. They don't want to be questioned or get into an argument with their co-parent, so they stop the child from sharing, thinking it will prevent the confrontation. It's not your child's job to prevent confrontation between parents. It's the parents' job to improve their communication so that they can problem-solve together and more important keep their children out of the middle.

When we are invested in our children, we are invested in our co-parent's success as a parent—not because we are codependent and think we must run defense for the other parent, thinking if we don't do it, it won't get done, but because our children need us both to be secure, well-rounded humans.

You Are Not Alone in Separation or Divorce

There is one divorce approximately every 36 seconds in the United States. That's nearly 2,400 divorces per day, 16,800 divorces per week, and 876,000 divorces a year. This doesn't include those who do not marry—and more than 40% of children in the United States are born to mothers who are unmarried.

Will My Child Be OK?

Parents facing separation and divorce all share the same concern: How will this affect my child? Lots of factors contribute to answering this question correctly, but researchers count parental separation among the adverse childhood experiences that can affect a child's behavior, development, and risk for health problems, both mental and physical, in the future. It's important to remember, however, that while their parents' separation is guaranteed to be stressful to any children involved, so is remaining in a family with high levels of ongoing conflict. On the positive side, if the separation removes the child from a dangerous or even more stressful situation, you may see positive effects, and sometimes they happen very quickly.

> 66 My friends always ask me if I'm OK because my parents divorced last year. I tell them, 'Yeah,' but they don't know I wish my parents had gotten a divorce sooner. They fought all the time. At least now I can sleep. 99

Parents often think they should stay together for the kids, but many children and teens who face continual fighting in the home feel like the 17-year-old teen in the scenario. "I wish they had gotten a divorce sooner" is a common response when kids live with battling parents. Ironically, most kids fantasize about their parents reconciling someday, but children who have witnessed severe domestic violence, also known as intimate partner violence, are not among that group. Things simply evolve to the point that wishing your parents would stay together isn't as important as stopping the chaos.

The truth is, not all relationships can or even should be saved. Situations involving emotional or physical abuse, substance use, criminal acts, severe mental illness, and infidelity are among those that can place severe stress onto a partner and onto children and may even be unsafe. You can expect to see adjustment issues in your children for an average of 2 to 3 years after the separation, when the issues are likely to resolve, for the most part, with predictable flare-ups of the child's sense of loss around holidays, birthdays, and other family events. These flare-ups can be minimized, or at least reduced in their intensity, if the parents do their best to keep each other informed when they see their children struggling.

I'm "the Best Parent"

Some divorced parents have a secret they would never admit but believe all the same. Information is power, and the parent with the most information about the children has the power and therefore believes oneself to be "the best parent."

"You don't know Johnny loves to bake? I do. We bake all the time when he is home." But inside the parent is thinking, *Obviously, I'm the best parent.*

Or "You don't know Lisa has cheerleading tryouts this Friday? She didn't tell you? She told *me*." *"Obviously, I'm the best parent."*

In actuality, the exact opposite is true. Bringing it back to the best interest of one's children, the parent who *shares* the most information, which in turn helps the co-parent be the best parent that person can be, is putting the children first. Because for these parents, it's not about "I'm better than you at this." It's "Our children need both of us to be good at this." So, yes, your children will be OK, but it's both parents who make it so. It's both parents' responsibility to keep their children healthy—emotionally, psychologically, and physically. That responsibility doesn't stop because parents split up and go their separate ways. On the contrary, divorce or separation makes that responsibility even more important than ever.

You see, children identify with both their parents, and after a divorce, it's not uncommon for kids to feel pulled in both directions. This is confusing and it forces kids to feel as if they have to take sides. Through no fault of their own, they are right in the middle of the 2 people they love the most, and it can be a very frightening experience.

Take Jeanne, Dave, and their son, Sawyer, for instance.

Jeanne and Dave had been divorced for 3 years and in a child support battle for the past two. Unable to make ends meet, Jeanne went back to court and had child support raised to an amount that Dave simply couldn't afford. Dave just kept paying the original amount, but an outstanding amount each month kept adding up. When Dave bought a new car, he knew Jeanne would be furious and decided to take a proactive approach. He explained the entire loan procedure to 10-year-old Sawyer. "Now, if your mom asks about the new car, you can just explain everything," he told Sawyer.

Thinking he would get into trouble if he didn't pass on the information, Sawyer became anxious and afraid to return to his father's house for his next scheduled visitation. To complicate things, he was faced with the rants of an angry mother over back child support and the purchase of a new car. Neither parent understood what was wrong with Sawyer. They had no idea that they were the ones creating and contributing to his anxiety.

I first heard of Sawyer's problem when I was called on to mediate Jeanne and Dave's child support disagreement. Because Dave was not paying the full child support amount, Jeanne felt it appropriate to cut Dave's time with Sawyer. This was reinforced by Sawyer telling his mother he no longer wanted to see his dad. I was called in to help the parents decide whether a new parenting plan was appropriate. During the process, certain questions were asked and Jeanne and Dave slowly realized that it wasn't that Sawyer didn't want to visit his father. His refusing to visit was his way of trying to stay out of the middle of his parents' disagreements. Jeanne and Dave left my office realizing the position they had put their son into and vowed to change things. Plus, they decided it was time for some counseling to help Sawyer, as well as co-parenting counseling for them to help them parent together even though they were divorced.

"Putting your children first" is the primary rule of co-parenting after divorce, something that Jeanne and Dave thought they were doing, but they learned the hard way they were not. Using your child as a pawn or a go-between to get back at your ex-spouse does not set the stage for successful problem-solving, nor does it teach your child positive ways to deal with conflict. The stress of these situations increases to the point that it bleeds into every aspect of your child's life. Infants who are stressed can't sleep or eat. Toddlers may regress in their developmental skills, such as using the potty, talking, or even coordination. Preschoolers may act out more, protesting and defying. You may also see signs of fear with an increased frequency in nightmares and reluctance to leave your side. The teen years are already a vulnerable time for high-risk behaviors, and family disruption can serve as an additional risk factor for delinquent behavior, withdrawal, drug and alcohol use, inappropriate sexual behavior, and problems in school.

What Can I Do?

The answer to "What can I do?" takes up most of the remainder of this book, but as we are offering you a glimpse of what's before you, you really have 2 equally important and intertwined jobs: take care of yourself and take care of your child. How your child responds to stress depends on several factors. The age of your child, as well as where your child is in development? What is your child's temperament and ability to be resilient? How much energy and time do you have to focus on your child's feelings and needs? How are you and your former partner doing emotionally and psychologically? Separation is stressful under any circumstances, and the better you take care of yourself, the better you'll be able to attend to your child's needs.

Self-care is both simpler and harder than the glossy magazines and lifestyle websites make it seem. Really, it boils down to physical needs—sleep, food, and exercise—and emotional needs—mindfulness, a support network, and, in many cases, counseling or therapy—to help you adjust to your new situation. Making the list is simple, but attending to each of those items may be quite challenging, especially if you're experiencing another stressor or two, such as moving homes and facing new financial pressures, at the same time. During the stressful times of a separation, you may not feel at all like eating, sleeping, or exercising, but your ability to do anything else depends on how well you can manage your commitment to wellness. And if separation or divorce has a silver lining at all, it's the willingness of friends and family members to support you and share their own experiences, when those are relevant.

It may start with simply taking a breath or even walking away when you get frustrated (and you're likely to get frustrated a lot). Reach out to someone you can trust who can help you take some time for yourself. Working with a licensed therapist, counselor, or psychologist can also help you develop new approaches to old problems. Many faith communities provide counseling services. Sometimes just having another perspective can help you see the way out of seemingly insoluble problems. If the issues are related to parenting, reach out to your child's pediatrician for advice. If parenting classes are available in your area, strongly consider signing up. Parenting, just like anything else, can always be done better, and you're going to need a full set of sharpened skills during this period. Even court-ordered parenting classes help all members of the family, and taking them can demonstrate to everyone how serious you are about doing the best possible job. Counseling that helps parents develop positive relationships with their children and consistent discipline practices has been shown to help children as long as 6 years later. In addition, if conflicts arise over parenting issues, you can always refer back to the classes to get on the same page.

The most important thing you can do, in most cases, is to stay involved in your child's life. If you are going through this separation because you yourself are struggling with substance use, anger issues, or violent behavior, you may need some time away from the child or children while you work through those challenges. Don't be afraid to take those challenges head-on.

The following experience comes from a mother facing an addiction to pain relievers:

> **❝** *I realized I was in way over my head when I fell sleep and forgot to pick up Becca from kindergarten. I was so afraid Bill would try to take her away from me, but he took care of her while I was in rehab, and once I got out, although I wanted to, we didn't go back to sharing her time equally for quite a while. Bill said it wasn't a good idea yet, and I didn't get the sense that he was being vindictive; he was looking out for Becca. I was furious and really went after him, but he was right. I needed time to get myself together before I could be really present for our daughter. After a few months, Becca would come over every day after school for a few hours. I'd help her with her homework, and then she would go back to Bill's. Thank goodness Bill saw how important it is for me to be in Becca's life. He never threatened to take her away from me or to go back to court. It's been a year and a half now and she is finally staying 2 nights a week with me. He has always put her first.* **❞**

It can be easy to give up, especially when the other parent seems to be erecting roadblocks to keep you away from your children, but stay with it. As with the couple in the scenario, when you both work together in the best interest of your child, the right answers are always right before you.

There's more to a story like this. The problems associated with substance use are ongoing and can't just be swept under the rug. Parents facing drug or alcohol use issues must take an active role in their sobriety. It's great when you can have a supportive co-parent to help you get over the humps of getting sober, but relapse is a very real part of recovery, and parents in this position must stay vigilant in their sobriety or the courts will eventually step in and change custody.

Custody

I Want Sole Custody!

Although statistics point to most custody arrangements as awarding primary custody to the mother, this is rapidly changing across the country. A 2018 study that compiled custody statistics state by state, done by Custody X Change, a software company that has designed an app to help parents stay organized when co-parenting their children, showed that 20 of the 50 US states generally award parents equal custody, with father and mother both receiving 50% their child's time, and approximately 6 states are not that far behind. Many other states currently have bills under review that are working toward various forms of shared parenting legislation. This is good news for our children, because it says that even the lawmaking bodies of our nation have begun to realize the importance of children having both their parents in their lives.

The following story is a firsthand accounting of an incident that happened in my office earlier this year. Truth is, it happens quite often. Stories such as this clearly depict the change in attitude around the mind-set necessary to co-parent our children.

The mother walked in with a laundry list that the father was doing wrong—starting with not cleaning their 8-month-old twins properly. "I want sole custody!" She was emphatic, one step below screaming. "They are going to get UTIs if he's not more careful. I think he needs supervised visits!"

The current parenting plan included 2 one-day visits and one overnight a week with the father. They had agreed to this at the children's birth. Now, Mom wanted supervised visits. In the world of child custody, supervised visits are the least amount of time one can be awarded with a child, short of no visits at all. The father was floored. "Supervised visits?" he protested. "These are my babies too!"

The mother continued with her laundry list: "And he doesn't know how to put the girls in their car seats properly! I take pictures when I pick them up. Look," she said with exasperation as she thumbed the pictures down before me, one by one. She stopped at one showing one of her daughters sitting in a car safety seat. "I can put my entire fist under the straps!"

I looked at his hands and I looked at hers. He was about 6 ft 3 in (190 cm) tall. She was maybe 5 ft 5 in (165 cm).

"Look at his hands. I'm sure he can't put his fist under the straps."

The father agreed, "I thought it was tight enough, but why didn't you say anything? You held all this in and took pictures to show the mediator a month later?"

The mother continued, "I try to co-parent. I really do."

"Really?" I asked. "Because nothing you just told me has anything to do with co-parenting."

Now she was floored. "What? I'm telling you everything that's wrong. I'm being honest!"

I let that sink in for a second. "That's true, but you're telling the wrong person. I don't change the children's diapers. I don't put them in the car seat. Dad does."

Getting more frustrated by the minute, the mother finally blurted, "I think he should make a doctor's appointment and have the doctor show him how to properly clean a little girl!"

I stayed calm. "Why don't you just show him?" I asked.

"What!" she said. "It's not my place! We were never really together! I barely know him!"

"Well," I said, "It's time to get to know him. 'Mom, meet Dad. Your new friend for life.'"

Mom huffed, Dad snickered, and I continued....

"You think breaking up now is just like breaking up in high school. It was fun—or it wasn't—it's over. Bye. You don't have children in high school—at least most don't—and so you have the luxury of moving on with few repercussions other than a broken heart, which hopefully mends quickly. You can't do that when you have children. Your children need both of you—no matter how you feel about each other—they love and depend on you both. Thank God. Don't you realize you have built-in help?"

Both parents looked at me bewildered.

"Here 2 people share something as miraculous as a child. They could band together in that child's name and realize that in this world, where people are struggling for connection, they have this mutual responsibility to raise and teach another human. It doesn't matter if they love each other. They are partners

in raising and teaching another human. And hopefully, they will move on to someone who loves that child and helps them raise the child too—and the child has 4 people who love and care for the child—two are biologically connected and two are heart connected. Actually, all 4 are heart connected."

I continued, *"So the next time Dad picks up the girls, may I suggest you set aside about a half hour and you show him the proper way to clean a little girl?"*

The mother sat quietly, processing what I just said. You could see her face soften when it finally sunk in.

"Of course," the mother said. *"I guess I have to change my attitude. I sincerely didn't realize."*

She turned to the father. "I am sincerely sorry."

To be honest, I was surprised at how quickly she understood my point. Rarely do people have such an immediate turnaround. That indicated to me that these children would be OK.

"Thank you," the father said with tears in his eyes.

"Good for you," I said to the parents. *"Your daughters are very lucky to have both of you.*99

This is a true story, and no change was made to the parenting plan. A change was made to the parents' attitude, however, right there in my office.

Custody Labels Explained

Because the courts recognize the importance of both parents in a child's life, in my experience, very few parents are awarded *sole custody,* unless extenuating circumstances must be considered to keep the child safe.

For example, sole custody is possible when a parent has had some issues with the law, specifically abuse of some sort of the other parent or a child, possibly ongoing drug or alcohol problems, or perhaps untreated mental illness, but even when those things are present, judges make their decisions case by case. Importantly, a serious mental health condition diagnosis, although something to be considered, is not necessarily the determiner on which custody is based. Many conditions when medicated allow the parent to live a happy, heathy life; therefore, if someone with a serious mental health condition stays "med compliant," that person very well may share equal custody of the child with the co-parent. Remember, particularly in special circumstances, custody is determined case by case.

Most often parents are granted joint custody, which means they each have equal rights to make decisions and sign legal papers for their child. This does not guarantee equal time with their child, however. The amount of time spent with their child is regarded as physical custody and is based on where the child actually resides. That designation depends on the parenting plan the parents choose. To be honest, physical custody can be a tricky designation. Parents who share an equal week-to-week parenting plan usually receive joint physical custody, but parents who have their child for a night each week have also been known to receive joint physical custody. Parents must remember that custody is awarded according to the best interest of the child, not what is most convenient for the parents.

As children get older, there are additional considerations. Things that seem small erupt into huge confrontations. Grooming, for example, becomes an important issue, for both girls and boys, and sometimes, parents are simply not ready for it. The following example is, once again, a reason for parents who share custody to look for ways to coordinate efforts and work together:

> 66 Let's be honest," said Crystal, a working mother of an 8-year-old daughter, Lorinda, "Sharing custody is impractical. Her dad can't do Lori's hair before school."
>
> "Why?" I asked. I knew the answer, or at least I suspected the answer, she was going to tell me.
>
> "Because he just can't. He can barely do his own hair, and Lori is embarrassed when she goes to school."
>
> Dad laughed. He didn't take it seriously. "You put these ideas in her head. You don't want me to have time with her. You're making a big deal out of nothing, and you're using our daughter to do it. 99

As the reader, you may not see this problem as serious, but I can assure you it's a real issue faced by co-parents today—and, in this case, it created an even bigger problem for these parents, because it was at the root of their distrust for each other. Dad simply didn't believe that something he saw as trivial as hair would be the reason his daughter didn't want to spend the night at his home during the week. As a result, he blamed Mom, and their communication broke down even further.

> If I hadn't faced the issue myself, in my own home, I may not have given the subject the attention it merited, and I explained to Dad that if he wanted his daughter to want to stay with him on school nights, it would be helpful if he learned to help her with her hair before she went to school. I explained that his daughter might

not tell him that it's a problem, but she would tell her mother. Mom would inevitably pass on this information, and a fight would surely start.

"That's exactly what happened," the mother confided. "And he thinks it's me."

It wasn't her, and it had nothing to do with how much Lori loved either parent. It had to do with her getting older, her self-esteem, the desire to fit in at school, and not being ostracized by her classmates. She wanted to look pretty. Either Dad had to take some classes (online tutorials are great!) on 8-year-old hairstyles or Mom had to show him what to do. It was no more complicated than that. Dad had an 8-year-old daughter who now took pride in her appearance. It simply snuck up on him.

Among the most important things you can do when faced with a disagreement is to not ramp up the conflict. Separation and divorce generally result from ongoing high levels of conflict, and it is at times like these when that conflict is at its worst. How in the heck are you supposed to not ramp it up?

Dad was starting to listen. "She's my baby. I wasn't expecting this yet. **99**

The message of this story is no different than that of the story prior. When parents don't live together, they must work even harder at co-parenting together in the best interest of their children, to allow their children to flourish. Each parent has individual strengths. And both parents love their child unconditionally. Teach your children to respect each of their parents and they will get the best of both of you.

Be Open to Change

It will help if you ask yourself for each issue, "How important is this one?" "Is it necessary to push this to an argument?" "Can I compromise some here in return for something somewhere else?" Focus on the issues, not the person. Setting a positive tone telegraphs to your ex that you are committed to putting your children's needs first, over and above any grievances you may have with each other. Now it's all about what the kids need to be OK.

The joy of parenting is that children grow, change, and develop over time. The way your child copes with family disruption will also change. It means that the acute pain of the moment is almost certainly going to improve. At the same time, as your child matures, your child may come back to you with increasingly sophisticated questions. We never stop maturing, however, and you, too, will have better and better answers.

Finally, it's important to remember that a separation or divorce is not an event; it's a process. At moments, the pain of this process will be almost unbearably uncomfortable for your children and for you. But there will also be other moments, hopefully times of joy, of special connection, and of acceptance and peace. Wherever you and your children are at this moment emotionally, the only thing you can be sure of is that you will all evolve and change with time.

Change is coming, to be sure, and change can be scary, but you're in control of your own actions, and you wouldn't be embracing change if not for the hope that whatever is next will be better.

2

How Do I Begin?

I hope you live a life that you're proud of,
and if you find that you're not,
I hope you have the strength to start over.

F. SCOTT FITZGERALD

So, so many steps are involved in creating an independent life for you and your child. Many of them are tedious, such as filling out new forms for almost everything that has ever required your name, address, and phone number: lease agreements or loan applications (if you are buying a new home), school registrations, health insurance forms, bank accounts, credit card accounts, sport and club memberships, utilities, taxes, car registration, doctors' offices, and more. The most important step, however, is a big one, and we encourage you to give yourself some time and space for it, because this step will drive all the others.

This step is simple but profound: envision your life when this is over. What will be better after the separation or divorce? How do you think you will feel? What will your day look like, from waking up in the morning to going to bed? What things in life are most important to you that you don't want to change, and which ones can you sacrifice when needed? What sort of relationship do you intend to have with your former partner or spouse? Will you be able to stand in the same room together one day for, say, your child's high school or college graduation ceremony, your child's future wedding, or maybe even the birth of a grandchild? You are about to make a lot of difficult, emotional decisions. When the going gets tough, try to come back to this vision, and remember the goals that you've laid out for yourself. When you're so frustrated that you just want to give up, think about your child's future graduation, your child's wedding, and that new grandchild, and hold on tight to a vision of civility.

A few times in life, we get to consciously decide who we want to be next, and they deserve not to be rushed. Enlist friends, family members, or a professional counselor to help you think. Put a big piece of paper onto the wall and write all over it if that helps. Meditate, exercise, or do whatever helps you become more in touch with your own thoughts and feelings as you work through this process. When you're done, actually write down the goals and values that you've identified. You're going to need to return to this list often over the course of this process, and it will help to have it there to serve as the lighthouse you steer by.

How Do I Get It All Done?

In moments of emotional turmoil, we can find it especially difficult to attend to the daily tasks of life. At a time when brushing our teeth and putting on our shoes can seem like impossible tasks, how in the world can we take the time to conduct a methodical top-to-bottom assessment and rearrangement of our entire lives? It's hard to reach the computer keyboard when you're in the fetal position.

That said, it is exactly the act of conducting tedious, mundane tasks that will help keep you sane. I remember the day of my separation: I had run out of shampoo. I searched through drawers and cabinets with my puffy eyes, looking for a few drops of gel left over from a hotel or something, but there was none. I was going to have to leave the house.

I drove to Target, "our" Target, where we always bought the kids' stocking stuffers for Christmas, and I had to get to aisle 15. I just wasn't sure I could do it. I wanted to sit on the tile floor and cry. But I never make it through a trip to Target without seeing someone I know, and explaining why I was crying on the floor was going to be awkward. Instead, I fell back on my memories of ninth grade marching band and literally counted off the steps in my head: *"Right, left, right, left,"* using the tiles underfoot as my guide. I knew that if I continued in this way, I'd make it to aisle 15 and then back to the register. The next morning, I showered with my first bottle of post-separation shampoo, and no red-shirted associate ever had to ask me whether I was OK.

If you're embarking on a separation or divorce, much of your life is about to become a matter of "right, left." With a little reflection, you can learn to take solace in these very moments. When you are in the midst of feeling helpless, it's reassuring to know that you can do something, anything, to control some aspect of your life. Brush your teeth, and there, you have clean teeth. Make your bed, fold your clothes, and wash the dishes—a new rhythm starts to build soon. You can't build a new life all at once anyway. It will come one bottle of shampoo at a time.

The steps you take now, even if they are baby steps, will set a direction for the next many years of your life and therefore your child's life. Where will you live? How will you afford groceries? What will you drive? Will you work? Will your child remain at the same school? On the same soccer team? One step at a time and you can start working to answer all these questions.

What Do I Need to Do First?

First, you're going to need secure, private communications. In the coming weeks and months, you are likely to have to answer difficult and very personal questions about your life. You'll want a secure email account with a password your former partner doesn't know and can't guess. Make new passwords for any social media accounts as well.

It's easy to neglect mail, but even today, much of the legal process occurs on paper and is then backed up on computer. Change your address as soon as possible, and for added security, you might want to get your own PO box, available at your nearest US Postal Service office or at most shipping stores. Possibly the most important change concerns your phone. You don't need to change the number because you will have to give your soon-to-be co-parent a number to contact you in case of emergencies; however, if your former partner has access to your voice mail, change the password. Consider setting up a free online phone number with its own voice mail and forwarding service. Don't forget to change your personal identification numbers (PINs) to access your phone and your ATM.

Here's something that happens all the time and demonstrates why changing your passwords and PINs, and possibly phone numbers, is a necessity.

> **❝** *I usually get gas at the station associated with my local supermarket. For every $100 I buy, I get $0.10 off each gallon of gas. I was saving up and knew I had about a $0.40 discount, but when I went to get gas this morning, it was back to $0. The account is still connected to the phone I used when I was married, and I suspect my ex used the $0.40 discount without my knowing. This is outrageous, and I doubt I can do anything about it.* **❞**

Is this stealing? Technically, it is. Will anyone do anything about it? Probably not. Changing your PIN won't do a thing in this case. Changing your phone number or associating another number with the account is the only surefire way to stop it.

Dividing the Assets

Dividing up assets is a part of separation that many view as distasteful but that will play a critical role in your life to come. Monetary assets such as cash, savings, and investments will play a huge role in how you and your children will be able to live in the coming months and years. Even trivial assets, however, can become surprisingly important. Replacing things you take for granted can get very expensive. Who will get the silverware? Will you have plates to eat on? Pillows and sheets? What about special keepsakes of yours and your children's?

A good start is to photograph every room, closet, and storage area in your home to create a comprehensive list of what you and your partner share. You don't have to place a monetary value on every cup and place mat, but items of value, such as antiques or jewelry, may need to be formally appraised. If you have original receipts for expensive items, such as electronics and furniture, make sure you can find them, and make copies.

Financial assets are often shared, so it is best to establish your own separate credit as soon as possible. If you don't already have your own bank account and credit card, get them now, and try to save up as much cash as you can. It's a good idea to use a new bank for this purpose, not the one you share with your current partner. If you have access to a computer, make sure it is password protected for security reasons, then scan copies of all financial statements for at least 3 to 5 years and store all files on a flash drive. You may also want to print out backup hard copies for easy access. Remember to include not only your checking account but any savings and investment accounts. If you bought a home while you were together, remember items such as your US Department of Housing and Urban Development statement. Also, remember to copy titles for boats and cars, special accounts for retirement or college savings, and last will and testament. Tax filings will be critical, so scan and save hard copies of both returns, federal and state. If you can, include pay stubs for you and your partner. You may also need to have a copy of your credit report or at least know your credit score. You can easily get this online through secure websites that offer your credit score as a way to market additional credit cards, but getting your score is free and does not require a *hard inquiry* on your report, which can actually bring your credit score down. Hard inquiries are done when you make a major purchase, such as a car or a house, and when acquiring certain credit cards. Viewing your credit report may also alert you to inaccuracies or accounts that you never knew existed. You can then contact the appropriate credit bureau and have the inaccuracies adjusted.

Division of Property

Division of property laws differ from state to state. Whether you were actually married to each other determines how a court approaches how property is divided between the parties. If you were never married, there is less protection financially, particularly if you comingled funds or bought a home together. In those cases, hopefully, you had legal help to oversee the purchase or at least had a notarized list of how the funds were invested and were to be split, if you parted ways.

If you were married to each other before your proposed split, the state in which you lived at the time of the divorce determines how your property can be divided.

In a *community property* state, anything purchased during the marriage belongs equally to both parties. In alphabetical order, although these may change, currently the community property states are

▶ Arizona   ▶ Louisiana   ▶ Texas

▶ California   ▶ New Mexico   ▶ Washington

▶ Idaho   ▶ Nevada   ▶ Wisconsin

All other states are regarded as *common-law property* states and different rules apply.

Simply explained, this means that both assets and debts acquired during the marriage belong to the party who acquired them—unless otherwise indicated by a legal document. This implies that if the parties divorce, they can both keep the property that belongs to them. But that still doesn't make things easy to divide. Couples notoriously comingle funds when married, and when that is done, it's difficult to determine who owns what. Hopefully, when the parties divorce, shared assets and debts will be divided equitably.

One other consideration to note may cause big problems in community property states. If one party owned property before marriage, normally, that property remains that person's sole property on divorce. However, if mortgage payments were made with community property funds during the marriage, both parties then have an interest in the property—not an equal interest but an interest all the same. The exact amount is determined by the percentage of community property funds invested.

It goes without saying that if you are splitting up property, particularly in a common-law property state, you may want to seek the advice of an attorney.

Making a Budget

The flip side of assets, of course, is expenses. You'll need to know how much you spend, specifically on your child or children: clothing, food, tuition, music lessons, team dues, and braces—all those expenses will continue, and negotiating how they get covered will be one important component of this process.

If you are the sort of person who has always maintained a strict budget, you're golden; keep doing what you've been doing! But if you're like most of us, the thought of making a budget spurs you to look around for anything more fun to do, such as cleaning out the freezer or bathing the cat. Your budget, however, is not just a chore; it may even play an outsized role in how and when you ultimately decide to separate or divorce.

Sharing your life with your partner until now saved you money in lots of different ways. A mortgage or rent, insurance, utilities, a phone contract, and furniture—all these things cost less when people share them. Now that things are changing, you will really need to create a new budget for yourself. Of course, housing is going to be the biggest expense. Whether you rent or own, it will be more expensive now that the responsibility is solely on you. Having an idea of your new expenses will help you figure out what you can afford on your own. You might need to consider moving in with family members to help save up some money for a little while. Or maybe you can get a roommate to help offset some costs.

Here's an easy way to create, and follow, a budget that will help you manage your expenses once you officially separate.

STATEMENT OF PERSONAL INCOME AND EXPENSES		
INCOME		
Item	**Source of Income**	**Monthly**
1	Earned Income	$
2	Spousal Support	$
3	Child Support	$
4	Other	$
	TOTAL	$
EXPENSES		
Item	**Type of Expenses**	**Monthly**
1	Mortgage	$
2	Insurance	$
3	Utilities	$
4	Car Payment	$
5	Credit Card Payment	$
6	Cell Phone	$
7	Cable	$
8	Groceries	$
9	Other	$
	TOTAL	**$**
	EQUITY	**$**

To create your personal budget, you will first want to make a list of all your monthly income. This will include your salary, spousal support, child support, and any other additional money that comes to you monthly. Next you will want to create a separate list of all your monthly expenses. This includes things such as rent and mortgage, insurance, utilities, car payments, credit card payments, cell phone bill, doctor bills, cable and internet, groceries, school activities, and any monthly spending for things such as movies, eating out, or haircuts. For this to work, and for you to get a realistic budget, you will need to make sure to include all your monthly expenditures. Don't get overwhelmed, because this step can be a real eye-opener sometimes. Until you start writing it all down, and closely examining your expenses, you forget how fast things can really add up in a months' time.

Once you have listed all your expenses, you will need to compare it with your monthly income list, side by side. If your income is higher than your expenses, you are in good shape! If your expenses are more than your income, you need to look closely at your list of expenses. One too many pumpkin spice lattes and you may find yourself over budget. You will need to look closely and consider where you can cut back so that you will be in better financial shape each month.

Making positive changes to lower your expenses can be simple but just a little time-consuming. For example, creating a grocery list using the sale circular and choosing sale items can help lower your weekly food bill. Maybe it means making coffee at home before you leave for work or reducing the number of times you eat out each month. Look closely at your cable bill and watch for promotions that can help reduce your larger monthly fees.

On the flip side, are there some creative ways you can increase your income? Depending on your time frame, consider obtaining additional job training or a degree. Anything you can do to maximize your earning potential is a worthwhile investment right now. In my case, I had to pick up some overnight shifts at the hospital where I worked and I cut back the amount of times I ate out each week to offset my expenses.

This new budget template that you create is important to look at each week. I took a picture of mine and stored it in my notes on my phone. I also kept track of my unexpected expenses in my notes to add to the expense side of my budget every night, when I get home from work. Some people keep their budget on their refrigerator as a constant reminder. But remember that it is then also visible to anyone who comes into your kitchen, and I like to keep those things private. My phone is PIN protected.

The goal is for you to keep it real: if there are additional expenses, make sure you add them to the list. If you aren't going to be honest about what you spend, you're wasting your time by creating a budget.

Once you have established your budget, it's a really good idea to try and save a little from each paycheck for your emergency fund. Even if you save $15 a week, that's $60 a month. That's more than $700 a year that you wouldn't have had for a rainy day. As we all know, unexpected things always seem to pop up, such as a flat tire or fees for your children's extracurricular activities. As your child grows, so does your child's wardrobe and shoe size. These expenses can really add up too.

Special Considerations

Health Insurance

Health insurance deserves special attention. You may have been using your former partner's employer-provided coverage. Many insurance plans allow you to enroll only during certain periods, but major life changes, such as divorce, allow you to continue lost coverage (COBRA [Consolidated Omnibus Budget Reconciliation Act] of 1986]), as long as you enroll within 60 days of that change. Make sure you understand your options, and talk with the human resources manager at whatever business provides your enrollment.

Will or Living Trust

Do you have a last will and testament, a living will, or a life insurance policy? It's likely that your former partner is the beneficiary and key decision-maker in each of these documents. Many states do not allow you to disinherit a spouse until the divorce is final, but look at these documents and consider any changes you can make regarding decisions about your health and estate. If you have any joint credit cards or other debts, see what you can do to remove yourself from the accounts before the separation or divorce. Your ability to take your name off a credit account depends on whether you are an *authorized user* (yes) or a *co-borrower* (no). Regardless, the lower your balances are at the time of the separation, the simpler your financial life will be.

Additional Concerns

Consider any major purchases you were planning to make or expensive assets you were hoping to sell before starting legal proceedings. Courts often restrict divorcing couples from making major financial changes until assets have been divided, so if you need to, for instance, replace your car or sell the boat, get it out of the way now. Also, if you were considering hiding some of your assets, just don't; that's not legal, and it sets a poor tone for everything to come. It can also cost you dearly in penalties and fines.

Take a moment to think hard about your home, especially in light of the budgeting you're doing. It's natural to become attached to a place and to all the memories it holds for you and your children. You may try to keep it as part of the separation or divorce settlement, but are you in a position to pay the mortgage, utilities, and property taxes, as well as to keep up with repairs? How old is the roof? The water heaters? Do you have a home warranty, and what does it cover? Is value stored in the home that might help you with your new life, were the home to be sold? This may be one of the most emotional decisions you make, and involving someone such as a professional financial adviser, who can approach it as a business decision, may help you prevent a costly mistake.

Moving out of your home can also have dramatic consequences down the road, especially in a divorce. Laws vary from state to state; where I live, in North Carolina, for example, once a party moves out of the home, the party may not return to it until divorce proceedings are finalized. Leaving the home may also affect future decisions about child custody, so be sure to check your own state's laws before you make any decisions or changes.

There are other considerations as well. To use North Carolina as an example again, the state requires that couples be legally separated for 365 days before they can file for divorce. If they are living together in the same home, the state does not recognize that a separation has occurred, no matter what other measures the parties take to avoid interacting. While you may feel that you simply cannot stay another day, consult an attorney if at all possible before you move out. The exception, of course, is if you or your child is being abused. In that case, your safety is most important, and you can address all other decisions once you're secure.

Retirement

While many couples consider a shared home to be their greatest asset, they often overlook retirement accounts, whose values may well exceed that of the home, after the remaining mortgage debt has been subtracted from a realistic sale price. Be sure that you have records for any 401(k) plans, IRAs, or other retirement savings that either of you owns. If you helped your partner or spouse build a business or obtain a valuable degree, the value of these contributions will also be counted, so keep them in mind.

Family Heirlooms

If you brought a family heirloom, such as artwork, jewelry, or antique furniture, to the marriage, note it, as you can likely plan on keeping it. You are also probably entitled to keep any gifts that were given solely to you. Special consideration is often given to the division of wedding or engagement rings. You most often keep the ring you wore, and it is up to you to do as you see fit once the divorce is final. Most common, mothers save their rings to pass on to their children born of the union or, on occasion, construct other jewelry and hand it down to their children. It is really a private matter that should be decided between the parties.

School and Child Care Considerations

If you haven't already, keep a diary of your and your partner's involvement in child care. Who, for example, gets the kids to soccer drills, piano practice, and school? Do you both attend concerts and games? Do you volunteer at school? Attend parent-teacher conferences? Doctors' appointments? Be sure to have copies of your child's class schedules and teachers' contact information, and inform the school if you anticipate a move or change in circumstances.

> **❝** *My children's mother and I share equal custody of our children.*
> *We split the week and alternate holidays. This means the children*
> *do homework at both our homes. Their mother NEVER tells me*
> *anything, from when there is a test to when there is a special*
> *report due. It's very frustrating, and my children are failing!* **❞**

It would be nice if all parents compared notes, but at the beginning of the divorce process, most are so angry or frustrated that they look for ways not to talk with each other. Of course, this isn't right, but it honestly takes a while to calm down and realize that it's your responsibility to co-parent *with* the other parent. While you are making the adjustment, remember that each school, and this means elementary, middle, and high schools, has an online portal that offers *both* parents a record of all completed assignments and upcoming projects. Usually, a school calendar is listed that tells parents about back to school night, Parent-Teacher Association meetings, and parent-teacher conferences. Rather than fight with your now co-parent, contact your child's teacher through email. Each year, explain that your child now lives in 2 homes, offer the parenting plan schedule, and request that 2 of everything be sent home. Explain that you are very interested in your child's progress and you are available to discuss ways to help your child at any time. And two wrongs don't make a right. If you find out something that your co-parent doesn't know, set the stage for positive co-parenting in the future by filling that person in. Remember, the goal is your child's success.

Other Things You May Need

If police reports or incidents call into question your partner's fitness to safely care for the children, you should have those on file as well. Although you may not be able to get copies of actual records if child protective services was called to intervene, you could request the name and contact number of the child protective services worker who did the investigation and offer that information to the court. If mental health is a concern, a release of confidential information form will have to be signed by the party with the diagnosis, but this will enable a judge or court-appointed mediator to talk with the professional treating the parent to ascertain whether the mental health concern will interfere with the ability to keep the child safe. If custody or visitation is contested in legal proceedings, the more objective information you have, the better.

Building a Support Team

A support team consists of the people you compile to support you legally, emotionally, and psychologically as you move through the breaking-up process. How extensive this team is likely depends on how much you can afford. Of course, your support team will likely begin with your closest friends and most supportive family members. You will face intense waves of fear, anger, and frustration, and you're going to want sympathetic ears to listen, hands to hold, and shoulders to hug.

Your support team could also include a mental health professional—a licensed therapist, psychologist, or counselor who can help you wrap your head around what's happening and find the most positive ways to think about the process. Last, but certainly not least, you may choose to be represented in court by an attorney.

The People Who Can Help With the Stress of Separation or Divorce

Once you realize that you can use some help coping with the stress of separation and divorce, your next step is to find a professional who can meet your needs. The array of choices can be confusing, so here's a guide to help understand who can do what. You might check with friends, your insurance company, or your child's pediatrician for assistance finding the right person for you. Regardless of whom you choose, check to see what training professionals have had, whether they're licensed to practice in their field, and what sort of clinical or academic experience they've developed.

- **Clinical social workers.** Social workers have completed a master's degree in social work, and many go on to receive specific training in counseling and therapy. Certifications include licensed independent clinical social worker (LICSW), licensed clinical social worker (LCSW), and Academy of Certified Social Workers (ACSW).

- **Counselors, clinicians, and therapists.** These titles all refer to professionals who have completed master's-degree level training in a mental health field. They generally also meet strict licensing requirements to practice. Examples include licensed professional counselor (LPC), licensed marriage and family therapist (LMFT), and licensed clinical alcohol and drug abuse counselor (LCADAC). Members of these professions can help with emotional problems through counseling and talk therapy.

- **Divorce coach.** A divorce coach supports clients by helping them create a solution-focused action plan for living happily after a breakup. The plan often includes things such as developing effective ways to communicate with a former spouse, designing a healthy co-parenting strategy, and forming a more positive mind-set that will help the clients stay centered and hasten their ability to successfully move forward.

- **Pastoral counselors.** Pastoral counselors are clergy members who have completed training in clinical pastoral education. They may diagnose and provide counseling. Pastoral counselors are members of the American Association of Pastoral Counselors and can have equivalents to a doctorate in counseling.

- **Psychiatrist.** A psychiatrist is a doctor of medicine (MD) who attended medical school and then completed at least a 4-year residency in psychiatry. Some may have completed additional fellowship training in child and adolescent psychiatry, addiction medicine, or neuropsychiatry, among other choices. Psychiatrists can prescribe medications, and, today, many psychiatrists focus more on the diagnosis and treatment of mental illness than on counseling and talk therapy. If you think you may need medication for anxiety, depression, or bipolar disorder, a psychiatrist should be able to help.

- **Psychologist.** A psychologist has a doctor of philosophy (PhD) or doctor of psychology degree (PsyD). Psychologists may lead individual or group therapy sessions, but their advanced degree offers training specifically in testing, diagnosing, and managing mental health problems. Psychologists can prescribe medications but not in all 50 states. Currently, psychologists may prescribe medications in Iowa, Idaho, Illinois, New Mexico, and Louisiana—as well as in the US Public Health Service, the Indian Health Service, the US military, and Guam.

Hiring an attorney can take a lot of stress out of the process, but there are also stressful aspects of working with an attorney that are discussed later, in the Retaining an Attorney section of this chapter. Finally, if you are in the financial position to consider one, a financial planner to help you make wise decisions with your money in a time of stressful distraction will round out the team.

Why Do I Need a Therapist? I Can Just Talk With My Friend

Quite frankly, a therapist can feel like a luxury—the cost may be of concern, and some cultures still find therapy to be self-indulgent gobbledygook, but there's good reason to seek therapy when you are facing trauma. A therapist is trained to listen and offer direction, whereas a friend, who, at times, may feel more comforting than a therapist, may be afraid of hurting your feelings and also identifies with your point of view, which could keep you stuck and unable to rise above the breakup. I call it a "closed conversation." Friends love you. They were there when your partner or spouse walked out—or when you did. They were there when you fought. They understand your pain firsthand, and a friend can easily take your side and not tell you when you're stuck or thinking incorrectly. Friends are great support, but a therapist can remain objective.

What to Look for in a Therapist

Therapy is not magic. The person you choose to lead you through coping with your breakup is not a magician. Therapists are human and have good days and bad days, just like everyone else. A marriage and family therapist may be either married and happily adjusted or facing very similar issues to what led you to your breakup. If this is the case, it will be difficult for the therapist to remain objective. Do your research. Friends and family may make suggestions, but you may not connect in the same manner as they did. To find the right therapist for you, consider the following points:

- ▶ First, consider whether you feel more comfortable with a male or female therapist.
- ▶ Next, do you feel comfortable with your choice as an individual?
  - Do you find yourself feeling judged when you confide your true feelings during the session?
  - Do you feel as if the therapist is truly listening to you?
  - Does the therapist offer feedback to what you say?
  - Does the therapist allow you to figure out things for yourself or just tell you what to do?
  - Does the therapist confront you when your reasoning is questionable?
  - Does the therapist close the wound created by exploring an issue at the end of each session, or are you allowed to leave the office hurting or confused?
  - Does the therapist give you homework at the end of each session to help keep your mind moving toward resolution until your next scheduled appointment?

How Can a Divorce Coach Help Me?

As you can tell from this chapter, separation and divorce are major undertakings that require time, organization, and tremendous emotional investment. It can be helpful to have one person who can help you keep it all straight and also give you a sense of perspective. Divorce coaches do this all day, every day, and know the ropes. They keep you focused and are your personal cheerleader, if you find yourself distracted by the stress of it all. Divorce coaches may be members of any of the professions mentioned earlier in this section—lawyers, certified financial planners, or mental health professionals—but they are all experienced in helping people get through this struggle as well as possible.

Hiring a coach may sound like one more indulgent expense at a time that you're trying to save money, but one thing coaches can do is streamline your conversations with your attorney and help you organize your goals and documents. Because divorce coaches generally charge less per hour than lawyers, this service alone can save you money over time. Coaches can also help you build a rational approach, rather than an emotional approach, to the process of separation, saving you anger, anxiety, and time. Finally, a coach can help you organize your financial and child custody issues with the other party in a way that might keep both of you out of a more contentious process.

Focusing on the best interests of the children, parenting lessons for both parties can help improve long-term outcomes. If you are worried that your partner parents differently than you, working with a parenting coach can help both of you ensure that your children's lives include the support and the structure they'll need to thrive, especially as they face one of the hardest challenges in their lives.

Retaining an Attorney

If you decide to retain a lawyer, the lawyer might be regarded as the team captain. Locating one you feel comfortable with and can trust may seem like the hardest step. You might already know an attorney, or you may have friends who can make a recommendation. Ask your child's pediatrician for a recommendation. The internet, of course, can supply names, as well as help you check qualifications, and even online reviews. Start with your state bar association. Here you can see when attorneys were admitted to practice law, where they went to undergraduate and law schools, and whether they have ever been disciplined, for any reason. It's a good idea to look for a lawyer who attended an accredited law school and who has been in practice for at least 5 years. Plan on interviewing at least 3 attorneys before finalizing your decision. You're about to spend a lot of money and a lot of time, and you deserve to work with someone whose approach and experience fits your needs, someone who is going to listen to you and answer any questions you have along the way. You may be tempted to run out and find the meanest or most expensive attorney you can, imagining that this person will land you the "best deal" or be the "best lawyer." The best lawyer, however, is going to be the one whose temperament, experience, and approach are best matched to the goals you created and wrote down at the beginning of this process. Consider the following process instead.

When You Meet With a Prospective Attorney About Separation or Divorce, You Should Have Some Questions Ready to Ask

Question. How many family law matters have you handled?

Answer. If the answer is less than 50, you may want to look elsewhere.

Question. What is your hourly rate?

Answer. Be sure to ask about the hourly rates for paralegals and secretaries as well. Will you be charged for emails and telephone calls; is there a minimum fee for each? What if you call but don't get to speak with the attorney? Ensure that you'll receive a bill itemized by the work done, the person who did it, and the amount charged. You should also expect to pay for direct costs, such as filing fees, express mail, and photocopying, so those fees should also be laid out.

Question. How does the retainer work?

Answer. In many cases, you'll be asked to pay a fee up front, known as the retainer, from which costs will be subtracted as they occur. An *evergreen* retainer will always need to keep a certain balance. For example, if the retainer is $5,000 and the first month's costs are $3,000, you may be expected to add back $3,000 to keep the retainer balance at $5,000. This information will be key to your budgeting process.

Question. Will you have a clear written agreement with the attorney to lay out how the relationship will work?

Answer. This should be a routine part of any legal arrangement. What will the attorney do for you exactly, and what are your financial obligations to the firm?

Question. Ask about your attorney's malpractice insurance.

Answer. Lawyers, like doctors, can commit malpractice, and they, too, should always be insured to protect your interests.

Question. Ask your potential new attorney whether you can expect a response to calls and emails within 24 hours on business days.

Answer. It's likely that at some point, you'll have pressing questions that you need answered quickly, and you need to know what to expect.

Question. It's important to assess how comfortable you feel with this possible attorney.

Answer. You're likely to be divulging very personal information about yourself and your former partner, and if you feel any hesitation in trusting your lawyer, you might need to find someone else to represent you.

Once you have an attorney to work with, you'll need to invest in building a strong, productive working relationship. Start by sharing your goals for the separation or divorce, even if they're not necessarily reasonable or achievable.

What are your goals for financial security? How much time do you think your ex should spend with the children? Depending on your circumstances, these desires may be completely reasonable or utterly ridiculous. Your lawyer's job is to look at the facts of the case and honestly assess what you might expect. To make that judgement, your attorney is going to need all the facts from you, including ones that may potentially put you in a bad light. The following tips can serve as a guide.

Tips on Sharing With Your Attorney What Led to Separation or Divorce

Do

1. Consider writing out a timeline of the relationship along with key points you want to make before you meet with your attorney. Remember, you'll be paying by the minute, so the more organized you are, the better. It may be faster for your lawyer to read through this narrative than for you to try to recount it.

2. If you have ever been arrested, for any reason, disclose it now, no matter how long ago it occurred. The arrest may have no bearing on your case, but that's for your attorney to decide.

3. If you have ever been accused of substance use, let your lawyer know, especially if you have gotten into trouble for it at work or with the law.

4. Share your résumé or curriculum vitae with your lawyer, including a complete history of jobs you've held and why you left them. It should also include your complete educational background.

5. If you have had romantic relationships outside the one you are now leaving, let your lawyer know with whom and when they started.

6. Tell your attorney how you discipline the children and whether you ever hit them, including spanking.

7. Let your attorney know whether you were abused as a child and, if so, how and when.

8. If you are currently living with someone other than your spouse or another partner, make sure your attorney knows, including whether that person has ever been arrested, for any reason, or has had a substance use issue; what sort of employment that person has; and who pays for your current residence. If that person is also providing child care for you, your lawyer is likely to want even more detailed information. The person you're living with should expect to be investigated by attorneys on both sides of the case.

9. If you work outside the home, share your work schedule with your lawyer, including a realistic assessment of holidays, weekends, and nights you may be asked to cover.

10. Bring 3 years' worth of the financial records discussed earlier, in the Dividing the Assets section of this chapter, ideally organized by type and date. Remember, you'll be paying for every minute that your lawyer or your lawyer's paralegal spends organizing your files.

Don't

Don't bring anyone else with you to meet with your attorney. Conversations you have with your lawyer are private and confidential (attorney-client privilege). Conversations you have with other people, including friends and family members, enjoy no such privilege and can become part of your case, even if the conversation occurred in front of your lawyer. In fact, having a guest in the room can turn your lawyer into a witness in the case and force you to find (and pay) yet another attorney.

Other Potential Members of the Team: A Mediator

A mediator may be employed during breakup proceedings to help with communication breakdowns, the distribution of property, and designing your child custody parenting plan. It's a less formal approach than hiring an attorney, but a mediator can also work with an attorney to help the process move along more smoothly. A mediator does not file paperwork but concentrates more on improving the parties' communication so that they can come to agreement about things that must be decided before the breakup or divorce can be finalized. That agreement would then be added to the divorce paperwork as part of the final divorce decree. A mediator's educational background may vary from business to law to possibly psychology. Some attorneys specialize in mediation as well as some therapists.

You might even learn some tips that help you as you strive to create the best possible new life for yourself and your children.

CHILD CUSTODY OR DIVORCE MEDIATION

Whether the parties agree to mediation voluntarily or are court ordered to attend, the primary goal of divorce or child custody mediation is to reduce acrimony between the divorcing parties, thereby creating an environment through which the parties can together make an agreement in the best interest of their children.

Almost every state requires mediation of child custody disputes, although individual state law determines exactly how mediation is performed in that state. Today, mediation, either voluntary or court mandated, is the principle form of conflict resolution used by divorcing couples.

ADVANTAGES TO A MEDIATED DIVORCE

Mediation is a forum for conflict resolution in which a neutral professional with a background in a subject such as psychology, social work, or law facilitates positive interaction between parties to promote a fair settlement for their dispute. Mediation is well suited for divorce or custody disagreements, because, when approached properly, it reduces hostility between parents for a faster solution to their child custody or divorce dispute. Many divorcing couples find mediation helps them avoid the expense and emotional upheaval associated with a litigated divorce.

WHEN MEDIATION MAY NOT WORK

Mediation does not work for everyone—however, that says more about the people than the process itself. While most parties find mediation to be a good alternative to traditional litigation, it may not be as effective when one party fears the other, as in child custody cases with domestic violence overtones or when there is so much animosity between the parties that they are unable to discuss a solution rationally. In addition, like many professionals, mediators have specialties—some are well versed in child custody disputes, whereas others may be more proficient in financial matters. A mediator's orientation will supply clues to the mediator's strengths—a psychologist might be better prepared to mediate child custody cases; an attorney, financial affairs.

THE DIVORCE MEDIATION PROCESS

In many states, divorce cases are referred for mediation by the court or they end up in mediation because of the parties' written prenuptial agreement stating they will go to mediation before filing for divorce. If the court refers a case for mediation, it notifies the parties that mediation is required. In most states, the parties then have an opportunity to object to mediation if there is a reasonable basis—say, domestic violence in the home. In California, for example, if there is a domestic violence background, the survivor cannot decline mediation if the judge decides it is necessary; however, the protected party (as in the case of a *restraining order* or an *order of protection,* depending on the state you reside in) may ask for separate mediations, enabling the parties to discuss their preferences with the mediator individually.

MEDIATION PROCEDURE

Both parties are present. The mediator compiles contact information and explains the approach unique to the state in which the mediation will take place. As a retired court-appointed mediator in the state of California, I started with the *moving party,* or the parent whose idea it was to come to court. These parents explained their desires, while the other parents just listened. I encouraged the other parents to take notes so that they would not interrupt when they disagreed and could easily refer to topics of agreement or disagreement when it was their turn to speak. Perhaps the most trying task of a mediator is to keep the parents focused on their children and away from their hot buttons. Once an agreement is made, the parents sign a stipulation agreement and that becomes the court order.

Importantly, mediators do not determine who is right or wrong. Instead, they help facilitate an agreement between the parties on their own.

FINDING A MEDIATOR

Once the decision to mediate is made, it is necessary to find a mediator, and you will need to decide exactly what issues you want to mediate. Property division? Child custody? If a mediator is court appointed, the mediator is either employed directly by the court or contracted in private practice. That means offices of mediators may be at the courthouse or you will be required to go to their private office. Court-appointed mediators can help you only with decisions regarding child custody, and the service is offered as part of the divorce proceeding. A mediator in private practice can help you with both child custody agreements and personal property division but will charge accordingly. Many counties have community-based mediation centers. The fees charged vary mediator to mediator and case to case.

And a Financial Planner Rounds Out the Team

Another professional you may want to consider for your support team is a financial planner, if you are in the financial bracket to merit one. While paying someone to help you save money may seem like a horrible way to actually save money, a certified financial planner is likely to find savings and to offer budgeting tips that more than pay for those services. Find out whether your bank or insurance company offers free financial planning support. You might also want to go a step further and check with the Institute for Divorce Financial Analysts (https://institutedfa.com) to locate a planner with specific training in separation and divorce issues. Once you have a truly realistic budget, you will be in a better place to plan for your next steps.

What Is a Collaborative Divorce?

Collaborative divorce is a kinder and gentler approach to the legalities of a breakup than the conventional "duke it out in court" philosophy. *Collaborative law* refers to the process of removing disputes from the "win or lose" approach to divorce to a "problem-solve and compromise" approach, using mediation and open discussion in negotiation.

In a collaborative divorce, both parties hire attorneys and all 4 work together to solve the disputes, rather than cultivate the aggressive court-based approach often adopted by divorcing parents. If the attorneys have difficulty resolving issues, a mediator may then be brought in to help guide the parties to agreement.

It's often standard procedure for all parties to sign a *no court* agreement that directs both the parents' attorneys to withdraw from the case if it cannot be solved without court litigation. The final agreement is then filed with the court in the form of a stipulation, or uncontested agreement between the parties.

Perhaps the most positive aspect of a collaborative divorce is that it sets the stage for parents to work together after their divorce is final. Being that they approached the most difficult aspect of their divorce calmly and with problem-solving, they continue to problem-solve, using the same peaceful tactics, in their efforts to co-parent after the breakup.

Filing for the Divorce

Here are a few approaches to filing for a divorce.

1. Using an attorney to file your papers and advise you

2. Using a paralegal who has been extensively trained in filing procedures but does not have a license to practice law and, therefore, should not offer legal advice

3. Doing everything yourself

One, if you can afford an attorney, hire one. Your attorney will take care of filing all the paperwork and give you the appropriate legal advice as you progress through your divorce. It is always helpful to have an expert to help you handle legal matters, as separation and especially divorce are subject to laws that vary widely from one state to the next. But to get through this ordeal with the best possible outcome, you'll want a deeper bench. You'll also want to give serious thought to how much of a fight you want this process to be. Every dollar and every minute that you commit to a legal battle is a resource you could have saved for some higher priority, such as your children. Do you really want to be paying money toward attorney fees, or would you rather put your hard-earned money toward a new home, now that you will be moving out?

Two, hiring a paralegal is a good alternative if you do not want to handle the filing paperwork. A paralegal charges far less than an attorney and usually knows the ins and outs of the courthouse filing procedure as well as an attorney, but they do not have a license to practice law and should not offer legal advice. If your divorce is uncontested or simple in property division, consider hiring a paralegal.

Three, do everything yourself. This is a good alternative if you don't own property or it is an extremely amicable split. Online services provide step-by-step templates that walk you through the legal aspects of filing for divorce at your kitchen table for a tiny fraction of what it would cost to consult a lawyer. This option might be practical when both parties feel extremely amicable and agree on most or all aspects of what their lives should look like moving forward. Can you sit down for hours with your former partner or spouse and, without becoming too upset or having one party dominate the conversation, hash through issues involving the division of assets, spousal or child support, and child custody? If so, this option may be fast and economical, but when children are involved, these subjects can become complicated and emotional very quickly.

Also, self-help clinics in each courthouse around the country employ know-ledgeable people who can help you fill out the paperwork and direct you to the proper filing procedure. Many self-help clinics employ attorneys, but the nature of the clinic does not allow it to offer legal advice, only advice about filling out the paperwork and proper service.

If your former partner or spouse has already retained a lawyer, you may want to seriously consider working with one as well; however, it is not imperative. Involving attorneys does not mean that proceedings have to become adversarial, but you don't want them to become one-sided either. Chances are that your lawyer is familiar with the other party's counsel, either directly or by reputation, and can help you anticipate how things are likely to proceed.

How Do I Tell My Partner I Want to Separate or Divorce?

Be Certain

The first step in announcing the permanent separation of your marriage or part-nership is being certain that this is what you want to do. Have you tried every-thing you can to make the relationship work? Is it clear that no viable alternatives are left? Is your partner violent or having problems that endanger the safety and well-being of you and your child? (See the "What if I'm Worried My Partner Will Become Violent?" sidebar below.) Once you head down this path, it's difficult to change your mind.

What if I'm Worried My Partner Will Become Violent?

Unfortunately, intimate partner violence is one of the common causes of separation and divorce. If your partner has a history of violence or anger management issues, here are some steps you can take to safeguard yourself when you inform your partner that you're leaving.

- If you think it's safe, ask someone else to be present with you during the conversation.

- If you think the situation is unsafe, move out along with your children, and deliver the news by phone from a safe location.

- If there is documented proof of past domestic violence, you may want to consider obtaining a restraining order from the court in advance of the announcement (depending on the state you live in, this might also be referred to as an *order of protection*).

- Violent partners are most likely to act out in the first 24 hours after they learn of a separation, so ensure that you and your children are in a safe place for at least that long.

- Consider asking local law enforcement to drive by your location periodically for the first day.

What's Your Action Plan?

If you are clear in your intentions, be ready to say so firmly and to repeat yourself often. In some cases, both partners in a relationship find themselves ready to end it, but more often, one partner is much less prepared than the other to call it quits. Be ready to hear a flurry of reasons that the relationship needs to continue, and prepare to calmly repeat that you are ready to move on. If what you want is a trial separation (a period of time that partners legally spend apart without dissolving their marriage), offer that, but if that's not really what you want, don't suggest it as a compromise.

Everything goes better with practice, so take some time to rehearse what you want to say. That does not mean rehearsing every complaint you've ever had about the relationship or counting the number of ways your partner has let you down; you've probably rehearsed those things plenty. Instead, practice the calm, kind, firm language we discuss later in this section. If you have a friend or family member willing to role-play with you, you may be even better prepared for the difficult moment ahead.

In planning the conversation, consider how surprised your partner will be. Perhaps you've been in couples' therapy for months, and it's clear to both of you that you're not getting any closer to a solution. Or perhaps your partner lives in a state of denial and is happily going on, as though everything is fine. Knowing your partner's mind-set will give you a sense of how this next step is likely to proceed.

Give some thought to the place and time you're going to have this conversation. A private location, such as a room in your home, is often the best place, but there are exceptions. If you've already been in couples' therapy, consider asking whether your therapist might be willing to mediate the conversation, especially if you are worried about your partner's reaction. Do not choose a public place, such as a restaurant, as emotions are guaranteed to run high, and your partner is going to need some space to express strong feelings freely. Turn off mobile devices to prevent interruptions, and have the conversation when your children are not in the home.

What Is a Restraining Order or an Order of Protection?

A restraining order or an order of protection is a court order prohibiting a person from coming near you, your home, your work, your school, or other locations as listed on the order.

For the Record

The 2 types of domestic violence restraining orders are

1. A restraining order issued by family court
2. A restraining order issued by criminal court

A family court restraining order is issued in response to domestic violence but is separate from a criminal case. If the domestic violence was so severe that the perpetrator was charged and sent to jail, criminal court issues a separate restraining order from that court, protecting the survivor, and a criminal protective order trumps anything issued by family court.

If the children were witness to the violence, they may also be listed as protected parties, and if that is the case, the court has deemed that it is in the children's best interest not to see the perpetrator. No visitation will be ordered until the restraining order listing the children is lifted or is adjusted to remove the children.

When a Restraining Order May Complicate Matters

Technically, a restraining order will stop someone from coming near, and if perpetrators violate the restraining order, they will go to jail, but if they are imbalanced, it may exacerbate violence, and the people getting the restraining order must be cognizant of that and put in the proper checks and balances to keep themselves and their children safe. Also, restraining orders prevent co-parents from speaking with each other. In an emergency, say, little Jason fell off his bike and is in the intensive care unit, you cannot call, text, or even email the other parent to notify; you must employ the help of a third party. Many parents who have faced domestic violence get a restraining order but have it adjusted to include "peaceful contact regarding the children." Translated, this means a restraining order is in place, but the parents may talk, text, or email to notify each other of emergencies and can be in each other's presence to exchange the children, but they may speak only about the children, no small talk or a discussion about possible reconciliation. In these cases, it's best to communicate in writing—text or email—so that both parties have proof of what was said. Anything written down in text, in email, or on social media is admissible as evidence, if you must return to court.

Timing can also be important. If you have an option, try not to add this news to another highly stressful event, such as the diagnosis of a serious illness, the loss of a loved one, or a major financial setback. Sometimes, of course, you have no choice, but in general, we do better when we address one big challenge at a time.

Once you have a decision, a place, and a time, be prepared with what you are and are not going to say. This is a conversation about you: your feelings, your needs, and your plans. For that reason, you'll want to use the word *I*, as in "I've been thinking about this for a long time, and I think it's time that we end this relationship. I really don't see any other way forward." Use the word *you* to project sympathy: "I can see this is very hard on you, and I'm sure you have a lot of questions, but I know that you are strong, and in the long run, I suspect that you will be happier too."

It's always possible that your partner will respond with relief, but the response is far more likely to involve anger, sadness, and fear. Your partner may lash out with a history of everything you've ever done wrong, a list of all your perceived faults, and dire wishes for your future. It's going to be hard, but this is not the time to be defensive or to try to answer every accusation. This conversation is not about blame, and any attempt to arrive at a shared understanding of how you got to this place is almost certain to fail.

Instead, acknowledge your partner's feeling, and keep bringing the conversation back to the future: "Of course, you're upset and angry right now; I see that. But I really feel that we need to end this relationship." Your goal is not only to be calm, kind, and direct but also firm. Speaking of kindness, you may respond to your partner's emotions with an instinct to offer a hug, a kiss, or some other physical sign of affection. Doing so at this moment can send your partner mixed messages about how you're feeling, so consider leaving it at a firm hand-holding.

Your partner's next response is likely to be a grasp for answers about what the future holds: "What about the house? Child custody? Alimony and support payments?" The only answers you have right now should be who is going where immediately after this conversation. Have you made plans to leave with the children and stay somewhere? Are you asking your partner to pack some things and move out now? You should have an answer to that question but defer all the others to the process that's now starting, with a reassurance that you're committed to a fair outcome for both of you and for the children.

The one other question both of you will need to answer now is how and when to tell the children. (For further guidance on that, see Chapter 4, Helping Our Children Cope.) Talk about putting the children first and how establishing a civil co-parent relationship from the start will help lay a firm groundwork for your children to cope with this development. If you hope to be able to enjoy your children's achievements and celebrations together in the future, mention that. At the end of the conversation, thank your partner for listening.

There is one more detail. If you're filing for divorce, your partner must be served a summons. If you are representing yourself, you cannot serve the other party; it must be done by another third party. Some people ask friends or relatives to do it, and others contact a process server (someone who specializes in serving summons) or the police or sheriff's department in their county. If you have questions about how to properly serve your partner, the self-help clinic at the courthouse is an excellent place to start. If you are represented by an attorney, the attorney will take care of serving your former spouse for you. As you can imagine, summonses are among the least welcome surprises anyone can receive.

You can take a moment to talk about how and where your former spouse would like to be served that summons or whether a lawyer can accept it on your spouse's behalf.

Finally, make an effort to forgive. Forgive yourself and forgive your partner. Making a life with another person is a really, really hard thing to do, and sometimes it just doesn't work. Take a deep breath and start the rest of your life.

Tips for Presenting Your Separation or Divorce Action Plan

- Be confident that a separation or divorce is what you want to do.
- Determine ahead of time exactly how you want to proceed with the separation or divorce.
- Practice what you are going to say.
- Choose an appropriate time and place to have the conversation, preferably not in public and not when your children are around.
- Focus on "I" statements for what you want to see and "you" statement to express sympathy.
- Acknowledge your partner's emotions, but avoid intimate gestures.
- Focus on the future, not on the past.
- Provide concrete answers about your plans, but don't conjecture about the future.
- Focus on how you can work together as co-parents to ensure your children's well-being.
- Discuss how and when to tell the children together.
- Practice forgiveness, with your partner and yourself.

3

What Do Children Need to Be Healthy?

Ask any child development expert, and they will tell you that children do not develop in a straight line. There are no average children. There are no standard children.

CASSI CLAUSEN

Over and over again, we advise parents to do whatever is "best for the kids." The concept is simple: if both parties focus just on the children's needs, rather than the parties' pettier concerns, everything becomes a matter of problem-solving in the best interest of the children. Why, however, should 2 people who had a difficult time agreeing when they were together find it easy to concur on what's best for their children now that they have separated?

Each parent is likely to have a unique set of values and a specific perspective on the children's personalities. Complicating matters further, children are likely to behave differently in each home, naturally responding to cues from the adults around them. For that reason, I think it helps to review some of the basic principles of child well-being and consider these principles when disagreements arise, as they most definitely will.

How Can We Rank People's Universal Needs?

Maslow's Theory of Human Motivation

As long as there have been humans, people have wondered why we do the things we do. The most successful attempt to answer this question came from psychologist Abraham Maslow, PhD, in 1943, when people all over the world were coping with the traumas and deprivations of World War II. Maslow's theory of human motivation has since become so ingrained into our understanding of behavior that it seems almost too obvious to be worth discussing, but at the time, it was revolutionary (Figure 3.1).

Maslow suggested that people face a "hierarchy of needs," a ranking of the resources that we must have to live and thrive. The base of this list is formed by physiological needs—things such as air, water, food, sleep, clothing, and shelter— without which we die. We might add medical and dental care and basic hygiene to that list. When we think about cases of child neglect, it is the failure of care-givers to provide these most basic elements of physical care that most often results in a child being placed into protective custody.

We'd like to imagine that no parent would ever fail to provide a child any of the base needs, but separation and divorce can put tremendous financial strain onto parents, resulting in homelessness, food insecurity, and inadequate medical and dental care. According to the US Department of Agriculture, 1 in 5 children in 2015 experienced periodic hunger caused by lack of food. On any given night in 2017, about 60,000 families with children were homeless in the United States, according to the Annual Homeless Assessment Report to Congress, Part 1. Fear of these sorts of consequences drives some parents to remain in abusive relation-ships, even when they know they should leave. If you're afraid that you won't be able to provide your child food or shelter, your child's health care professional should be able to refer you to a social worker who can help you make the most of resources in your community.

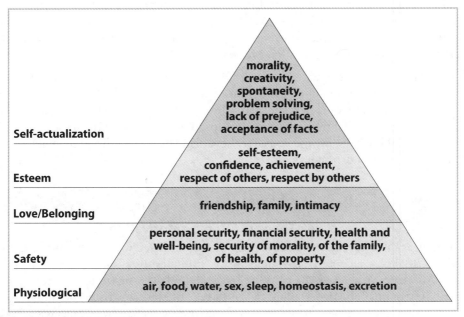

Figure 3.1. Maslow's Hierarchy of Needs

After physiological needs, Maslow ranked safety needs, such as personal security, financial security, and health and well-being, next in priority. For these needs to be met, children would have homes and we would think here about not just providing kids enough food but including fresh fruits and vegetables instead of packaged or fast foods. Kids don't just need a bed to sleep in and a roof over their heads; ideally, they'd get 8 to 16 hours of quality sleep daily, depending on their ages. Their neighborhoods would offer opportunities to play outdoors without risk of violence. Their homes would be free of pests and pollutants, such as lead and diesel exhaust, and they'd be able to rely on adequate light, clean running water, and heat and air conditioning when needed. In times of financial uncertainty, any of these necessities can become scarce, but a variety of public and private programs are designed to address these needs.

Maslow identified the next tier of needs as including "social belonging," including family, friendship, and intimacy. Children have a need to feel that they belong and a need to feel that they are loved. A child will love both parents, and in most cases, children do better when they have regular contact with parents and siblings. There are exceptions: when a parent has committed abuse or neglect; has a history of violence, severe mental illness, or drug use; or refuses to have contact with the child, the risks of contact with that parent outweigh the benefits. But in the absence of such extenuating circumstances, children benefit from being around their family members.

A child's friendships may be more difficult to maintain in the setting of separation and divorce, but they remain important. As a rule, the younger the child, the easier it is to make new friendships. Newborns, infants, and toddlers have little regard for individuals outside their own families. Preschoolers can move from one relationship to another relatively easily as well. In elementary school, bonds of friendship are longer-lasting, although they may be tested and broken by various circumstances. By middle school and high school, kids and teens find it increasingly challenging to move from one school, team, or group of peers to another. As you consider your children's best interests, this need for close friendships can weigh heavily in decisions regarding how much time they spend at each home.

The highest tiers in Maslow's hierarchy include esteem—the respect of others as well as self-respect—and self-actualization, the process of achieving one's full potential in life. Certainly, these goals are harder to measure, but they also reflect the dreams and wishes we all have for our children. Schools, teams, sports and clubs, bands, and faith-based groups can all play a role in helping ensure that children reach these milestones. In the setting of separation and divorce, individual and group counseling and therapy can be important additions. These considerations matter deeply when you are thinking about where your children will spend the most time going forward; they may also affect the amounts of any support payments from one parent to the other.

In the rest of this chapter, we dive deeper into ways that you can ensure all the hierarchy of needs are met as you navigate separation or divorce.

The Need for Shelter

Few needs are more basic than safe and stable housing. Hopefully, you have already sketched out a budget for the coming year, and if you have, it's likely that housing is your No. 1 expense. If you have not made that budget yet, now is the time. You may have to look at some creative solutions to ensure that you and your child have a home that will serve your needs.

If you already know that your income will not support a home of your own, you might consider talking with friends and relatives who might make space for you, at least until your life feels more stable. If those options don't seem realistic, you can start at USA.gov "Find Affordable Rental Housing" (www.usa.gov/finding-home) or you can call a housing counselor from an agency sponsored by the US Department of Housing and Urban Development at 800/569-4287 to explore a variety of programs that might help you.

The government subsidizes rent in many areas for families who meet income and family size guidelines. These rentals are owned by private parties who may have other requirements—regarding pets and smoking, for example. The USA.gov web page can help you locate rentals in your community.

Your local public housing agency should be able to offer a couple of other options. Section 8, or housing choice vouchers, pays part or all of your rent directly to a landlord. Finally, public housing offers shelter to families who have few other options. While public housing may not be ideal, the actual settings offered vary widely from one community to the next, and you might be pleasantly surprised. Either option requires that you apply at your local public housing office. Unfortunately, these programs can have waiting lists. The best thing you can do in that case is to put your name onto the list and check back daily for any progress.

Wherever you live, you will want to craft a personal space for your child to call her own. It may be an entire room, a space shared with siblings, or a corner in a shared room. If she is old enough, give her some choice about what she would like there: special toys, a blanket, or pictures can give her a sense of ownership and control at a moment that may feel out of control indeed. If your child is splitting time between 2 homes, do as much as you can to ensure that she doesn't have to live out of a suitcase. Have a toothbrush, a pillow, a blanket, clothing, books, and toys at each home so that she rarely has to travel back and forth to pick up forgotten items. Help teach your child how to organize school and after-school activity supplies in the same way, and take a moment for a folder and backpack check during the school year to prevent Sunday night panics.

The Need for Food and Water

Food insecurity remains heartbreakingly common in the United States today, and any event, such as a separation or divorce, that causes a financial strain can be the difference between reliably affording food and having to stretch. Families facing food insecurity can turn to public options and private options for help when they need it. To locate a food bank near you, call your local Department of Social Services or go to Feeding America "Find Your Local Food Bank" (www.feedingamerica.org/find-your-local-foodbank).

You may be surprised to learn that you qualify for the federal Supplemental Nutrition Assistance Program (SNAP), formerly called "food stamps." Applications go through local offices, but you can find your closest office at "SNAP State Directory of Resources" (www.fns.usda.gov/snap/state-directory). If your family qualifies for SNAP, your school-aged children also automatically receive free or reduced-price school meals, which typically include both breakfast and lunch. Increasingly, school districts are continuing to provide meal assistance to children outside the traditional school year, recognizing that the need does not disappear just because classes are not in session. Even if you don't qualify for SNAP, your children may be able to enjoy free and reduced-price school meals. You can find out how to apply with your local school district at the US Department of Agriculture Food and Nutrition website (www.fns.usda.gov/school-meals/applying-free-and-reduced-price-school-meals).

Depending on what the stores in your area offer, budget and transportation constraints can make it difficult to find fresh fruits and vegetables. If you have any choice at all, however, try to avoid packaged, processed, and fast foods in favor of fresh foods that you prepare yourself. If you have access to any space you can garden, you might find that growing even a few fresh vegetables or fruits enhances your family's diet, and gardening gives kids an educational opportunity and a sense of accomplishment.

When it comes to what to drink, once your child is older than 1 year, water is always the best option. Plain water is not only generally the least expensive beverage available but also the best for dental health. We recommend 2 servings a day of dairy products, such as 16 fl oz (473 mL) of cow's milk. But no child needs juice, soda pop, sweet tea, flavored water, or any other beverage. Many parents worry that their children won't drink enough plain water to stay healthy, but we can't allow ourselves to go thirsty for long. If flavored beverages are not available, children will happily drink water before they will allow themselves to become dehydrated. If you like, a little ice or a squeeze of lemon or lime can add flavor, but children are resilient, and even if they start by throwing a fit, they will learn to enjoy water.

Clothing Needs

I still remember the moment that my middle son first expressed an opinion about fashion. He was 4 years old, and I was dressing him for preschool in adorable brown, short overalls that made him look like an advertisement for Gap. Frustrated, he tugged at the straps and cried, "My friends are not wearing these!" It was true, and the sentence has become a staple of family lore, shouted in our best approximation of a 4-year-old's voice. Peer pressure had arrived.

Ideally, if splitting time between 2 homes, your child won't need to pack a huge suitcase for the transitions. That means keeping a reasonable supply of basics at both houses. Special items, such as winter coats or an especially fashionable shirt, may need to go back and forth, but, overall, your child's clothing needs will increase, even double, depending on the custody arrangement. The financial stresses of separation and divorce can make this change particularly unwelcome.

Fortunately, we live in an age with more clothing options than ever before. A variety of clothing retailers specialize in inexpensive versions of popular designs. Resale and thrift stores have proliferated, and online platforms, such as eBay and Craigslist, make it easier to find specific items at reduced prices. Especially as your child grows older (and more opinionated about fashion), it's OK to have a frank discussion about your budget. If a single item is a must-have for this school year, talk about the cost, and let your child help brainstorm about the trade-offs that may be necessary to afford it. You may be surprised with your child's creativity in finding a solution or in understanding why now just isn't the right time to make such a purchase.

Safety Needs

A comprehensive guide to child safety by age could easily occupy the rest of *Co-parenting Through Separation and Divorce*. Instead, we focus on the most critical issues, likely to affect each home. When you're budgeting for separation and divorce, you may need to account for the following safety items and precautions.

Newborns and Infants

▶ Sleep surface. A safe sleep surface is critical. Babies should sleep in their own bassinette or crib, ideally in the parent's room, for at least the first 6 months after birth. Cribs with drop-side rails or those manufactured before 2011 are unsafe and should be replaced. To prevent sudden infant death syndrome (SIDS), newborns and infants must sleep on their backs until they can roll over themselves. They should not sleep with heavy blankets, stuffed animals, or crib bumpers. No one should ever smoke indoors, as tobacco smoke exposure poses an increased risk of SIDS. Caregivers must be especially careful not to fall asleep with a newborn or an infant in a chair or sofa, when suffocation risk is higher.

▶ Car safety seat. You must use an appropriate infant car safety seat, mounted in the back seat of the car and rear facing, for all car trips, no matter how short. People may not realize that car safety seats expire, but each infant car safety seat should have an expiration date printed on it, so check that, especially if you're not buying a new one. If your car was manufactured after 2002, you should be able to attach the seat securely using the LATCH (lower anchors and tethers for children) system (see your car owner's manual for details).

▶ Bathing. If you have moved, check the temperature setting on your new home's water heater. It should be no higher than 120°F (48.9°C) to prevent unintentional scald injuries (check the home owner's manual or consult a plumber if the marking is not obvious). Even if you're using an infant tub with a strap, always keep one hand on your baby at all times during bathing.

▶ Changing surfaces. You may appreciate having a changing table at diaper time, but the floor or a bed works just as well. Again, even if you're using a changing table with a safety strap, never leave a baby alone on an elevated surface. Babies wriggle and squirm, and unintentional falls are common, whether from changing tables, beds, or sofas.

▶ Home safety. If you've moved, ensure that your new home has working smoke detectors and carbon monoxide detectors.

▶ Thermometer. For infants younger than 3 months, a fever should always prompt a medical visit; newborns younger than 4 weeks should be seen immediately. The best way to check a baby's temperature is with an inexpensive digital rectal thermometer; a reading of 100.4°F (38°C) or above indicates a fever.

▶ No infant walkers. Here is some good news: the one thing you don't need to buy for any home is an infant walker with wheels. While exercise saucers can be safe and entertaining, walkers that roll put babies at increased risk for falls, burns, and injuries from pulling over heavy objects.

▶ Gun violence. The safest home for any child is one without a firearm, but if you keep a gun in the home, safe storage is critical to prevent unintentional injuries. Weapons should be locked up and unloaded, and ammunition should be locked up in a separate location. If you're planning to move in with a friend or family member, take a moment to ask about whether weapons are in the home and how they are stored.

▶ Animals. There are all sorts of reasons to keep animal companions, but be aware that no matter how gentle they seem with a baby, animals are still prone to respond by biting or scratching when they're startled, and babies tend to jump, grab, and bite without warning. Make sure that your baby is never left unattended with a pet.

Children

▶ Children still need a safe sleep environment once they transition to a bed. Bunk beds pose a risk of falls, and some may collapse if they're not well manufactured or installed. If space is a concern, look for a trundle bed or even an air mattress or a futon instead. Also, avoid placing beds by unsecured windows, especially if those windows are above the ground floor level.

▶ Once children outgrow their infant car safety seats, they should transition to a reversible or rear-facing toddler car safety seat. They should continue to face backward until they reach the maximum height and weight marked on the seat, usually well after their second birthday. Children are much safer in this position in a crash, even if they can't fully extend their legs; it's the head and the spine that need protection.

▶ Toddlers are increasingly curious and increasingly skilled, which makes them prone to injuries such as falls and poisonings. Keep all household chemicals and medications secured out of children's reach, and avoid buying laundry detergent pods, which seem especially dangerous to young children. Button batteries and rare earth magnets are also especially dangerous to young children. If your child will be spending time at another house after the separation, ensure that both homes are equipped with similar safeguards. Make sure to have the Poison Control Center phone number (800/222-1222) handy at all times. Remember that alcohol can be a potent poison, so ensure that drinks aren't left at a level that children can reach.

▶ Use sturdy stair gates until children are adept at walking up and down stairs without help, usually around age 2 years.

▶ Continue to monitor children around pets until children are old enough to behave predictably, usually around age 5 years. Most bites come not from strange animals but from trusted family pets. Teach children never to touch a dog's face or to try to kiss a dog. Children can learn to stand still, "like a tree," if a dog is jumping or excited and to curl up, "like a rock," if a dog knocks them over.

▶ Swimming pools can be tremendously entertaining, but they also pose a risk of drowning, especially for young children. No child, even one who swims well, should be in a pool without direct adult supervision, and young children should always remain within arm's length of an attentive adult, even when wearing a flotation device. Swimming pools should be behind a fence at least 4 ft (122 cm) high with a gate that a child cannot unlatch. Remember that babies and toddlers can drown in a bathtub, a bucket of water, and even an open toilet when unsupervised, so never leave them unguarded in such situations, even for a moment.

▶ If you've moved, make sure your new home has working smoke detectors and carbon monoxide detectors. Once your child is old enough, you can talk about fire safety: how you will escape from the home in case of a fire; how to stop, drop, and roll; and how to avoid hazards such as stoves, lighters, and candles. If you have a fireplace in your home, avoid using it until your child is old enough to understand not to touch the enclosure.

▶ Check any window coverings for cords that can pose a strangulation risk, especially closed loops from old blinds, and cut or secure the cords so that they're out of reach.

▶ As your child learns to ride a tricycle or bicycle, get your child in the habit of using a helmet every single time. The same rule should apply to anything with wheels, including scooters, skateboards, and roller skates. Set a good example yourself!

▶ The safest home for a child remains one without a gun. If you keep a firearm, ensure that it is locked up and unloaded with the ammunition locked up separately and that any firearms at other homes the child may visit are stored similarly. If you have a teenager, remember that the availability of a firearm is a major risk for suicide death.

The Need for Sleep and Enough Rest

Sleep may not seem as important as food, water, and shelter, but adequate sleep is critical to children's health, both physical and mental. Under-slept children are more likely to become ill, to have emotional outbursts, and to underperform in school. Over the long term, sleep deprivation is linked to a higher risk of accidents, injuries, high blood pressure, weight issues, diabetes, and depression, including suicidal thoughts and self-harm.

Divorce and separation can pose a number of challenges to healthy childhood sleep, from increased stress and anxiety to disrupted schedules to breakdowns in discipline. Because good sleep depends so much on consistency, this is an important topic to address as you craft a new life for your children.

Many adults underestimate how much sleep children need at night. Unlike grown-ups, under-slept children are more likely to act hyper than they are to look sleepy, giving the impression that they're just poorly behaved, when, in fact, they're exhausted. While individuals vary in how much sleep they need, almost all children fall into the following ranges by age. The values include both nighttime sleep and naps.

- Infants (4–12 months): 12 to 16 hours
- Toddlers (1–2 years): 11 to 14 hours
- Preschoolers (3–5 years): 10 to 13 hours
- School-aged children (6–12 years): 9 to 12 hours
- Teenagers (13–18 years): 8 to 10 hours

Children thrive on consistency, especially when it comes to sleep. It's tempting to allow children to stay up late on weekends, but if you've ever had to adjust to jet lag or even just to the "spring forward" change of daylight savings time, you can grasp how much of an adjustment a bedtime change of just 1 hour can be! If you, in any way, can keep your children's bedtimes similar between the homes where they stay, everyone's life is likely to be easier.

Bedtime rituals are also helpful. They don't always have to be the same between homes, but the most calming routines often involve a bath, quiet play, and a bedtime story or reading period. Make it a rule to avoid screens at bedtime, because the electronic screens emit blue-enriched light, which has been proven to disrupt sleep quality and duration, with measurable effects on mood and academic performance. Try to move video games, mobile device use, and watching shows and movies earlier into the evening, with screens ideally turned off at least 1 hour before bedtime.

Divorce and separation naturally cause stress that can make it harder for children (and their parents) to get to sleep. It may be tempting to bring newborns or infants into the bed with you during this time, but co-sleeping with a parent increases the risk for SIDS and should be avoided through the baby's first year after birth.

Toddlers, preschoolers, and even older children may respond to stress by trying to get up repeatedly or by trying to sleep in your bed. While this habit isn't dangerous following the first year after birth, be aware that our brains use cues to tell us it's time to sleep, called *sleep associations*. Typical sleep associations might include a special blanket or plush animal, the sound of a fan, or just a pillow. If any of your children's sleep association becomes you, however, they may find it very difficult to fall asleep when you're not with them. You yourself may even find sleeping alone difficult at first and see co-sleeping as a win-win situation, but remember that once it starts, it can be a very difficult habit for your child to stop.

In the midst of all the changes with a divorce or separation, children will naturally try to determine what the new rules are. The only way for them to find the real limits is to push them and see what happens. A child may get out of bed repeatedly, asking for a sip of water, a trip to the bathroom, or one more story. When this happens, place a cup by the bedside, make sure she has used the bathroom right before bed, and then calmly direct her back to bed each time she gets up, explaining that her needs have been met and now it's time to sleep. Especially the first night, you may be doing this for hours, but if you're consistent, over time she'll almost certainly get the hang of staying in bed. If sleep problems persist, talk with your child's pediatrician.

A variety of techniques can help children with sleep problems related to anxiety. One technique that can help even very young children is to focus on one part of the body at a time. Tell your child in a soft, slow voice that you're going to put her to sleep in steps, starting with putting her toes to sleep, then her feet, and then her ankles, until you reach her head. You may end up repeating this process a few times, but it can help. Older children can focus on counting backward from 100, one number for each breath they take. Consistency is an important way to show your child that things are going to be OK.

Medical Needs

Among the many aspects of life that divorce and separation can disrupt is medical and dental care. Will your child be able to keep her doctor? Her dentist? Whose health insurance will cover her? If you both have insurance, will your child be doubly covered? Who will take her to her medical and dental visits, and who will have the right to make medical decisions for her? Let's look at some questions that you can answer to help ensure that your children's health care remains stable at a time when it's especially important.

What Is the Custody and Visitation Arrangement?

It's always easier to get to a doctor or dentist who is close to home. *Home,* however, may now have a different meaning. If one parent is more likely than another to arrange and attend medical visits, it's wise to look for professionals who will be convenient to that home. Sometimes the parents live far apart, so your child may need a set of professionals in each location. If this is the case, make arrangements ahead of time to allow professionals in each place to share records by signing a release of medical information form at both offices. Make it clear at each visit that you would like the records sent to the other office so that everyone can stay on the same page. Electronic health records are making sharing easier in some cases, but many offices still rely on photocopiers, mail, or fax machines to transmit information, so you may need to check back to make sure it was sent.

The most important medical information, however, is usually in the hands of the person caring for the child. A diagnosis as simple as sinusitis, for example, often hinges on whether a child has had cold symptoms for 3 days or 10 days. It's tragically common in my practice that a parent tells me, "I just picked her up from (the other parent's), and I have no idea when she got sick or what has been going on." This is another situation when I remind parents to put the child's needs over their own difficulties. Ensure that "handoffs" include an exchange of basic information about your child's health, such as appetite, sleep, and signs of illness—for example, fever, cough, or stomachaches.

Ideally, each home would have an adequate supply of any medications your child needs. Insurance companies, however, tend to frown on paying for duplicate supplies. Ask your pharmacist whether medications can be packaged in separate bottles with a supply appropriate for the time your child will spend at each home. If you have concerns about your child receiving appropriate care in the other home, a pharmacy refill record or a pill count at transitions can be reassuring (or not).

Who Has Medical Power of Attorney?

Power of attorney laws vary by state, so be sure to discuss this issue in detail with a lawyer. This conversation is especially important when parents have substantial differences of opinion regarding medical care. In my own practice, I've met couples with one who understands that vaccines are safe and effective in preventing deadly childhood diseases and the other who has a different belief system. One may be opposed to all psychiatric medications or, in extreme cases, distrust medical care altogether. A parent can always petition family court for help in finalizing the decision. If the parents anticipate that they may disagree about medical care, medical care arrangements should be spelled out clearly in the separation agreement and the divorce and custody decree.

In cases of shared custody, both parents have the right to bring the child to the doctor, consent for medical treatments, and access all medical records. If you have a custody arrangement, it may spell out exactly how each parent involves the other in medical decision-making, such as whether routine appointments must be scheduled at times that both parents can be present.

The exception occurs when the court issues a judgement terminating parental rights for one parent. Without this determination, no doctor's office can deny the noncustodial parent's right to obtain medical records and participate in a child's medical care. If this is your situation, be sure to provide the doctor's office with a copy of the termination of parental rights document to place into your child's chart, and ask that they put some sort of alert in the record regarding how to handle inquiries from the noncustodial parent. Electronic health records all provide for on-screen alert; paper records may use a literal red flag.

You may find that you're relying heavily on family members or friends to help with medical care for your child. Many doctors' offices can supply you with a medical consent form that will enable these helpers to bring your child to the doctor easily, but it will not allow them to consent for nonemergency procedures, such as elective surgeries or even vaccines. Will you be able to answer the phone and provide information and consent for treatments? If not, you can ask a lawyer to draw up a medical power of attorney for that person as well, so long as you feel comfortable with that person making decisions for your child.

Does Your Child Have Any Chronic or Special Health Care Needs?

While divorce and separation already complicate parenthood, for parents of children who have special needs, the complexity grows. For example, asthma affects 1 in 13 children, and many of those affected require both daily controller medications and as-needed rescue medications to remain active and out of the hospital. Other common conditions, such as attention-deficit/hyperactivity disorder (1 child in 9) and epilepsy (1 in 100), often require daily medications and frequent medical visits to manage successfully. Children with conditions such as cerebral palsy (1 in 500) and autism spectrum disorder (1 in 59) often benefit from physical therapy, occupational therapy, speech therapy, and adaptive equipment, all of which require a parent to coordinate and participate in care. Needs such as these can be challenging to manage in a 2-parent household and overwhelming for single parents.

As part of the divorce or separation process, ask your child's health care professionals to specify the sorts of therapy likely to be needed. You should include medications, therapy visits, laboratory and imaging studies, and medical appointments in the list. For conditions such as asthma, food allergies, and epilepsy, every household where the child spends time should have a copy of the emergency care plan and adequate supplies of all rescue medications. Both homes should have whatever adaptive equipment the child requires, such as bathtub railings or a wheelchair ramp. Relatives, friends, and new romantic partners who will be caring for the child should also be trained in those needs and in responding to any emergencies that might occur. Talk with your co-parent about any concerns you have with the environment at the other home—for example, indoor smoking that can trigger an asthma attack or a sporadic sleep schedule that can increase the risk of seizures. If things are this severe and your co-parent does not take your concern seriously, agencies can help. Document the situation, and a call to child protective services will prompt an investigation. Hopefully, it will never get to that point. Your ultimate goal is to ensure that both you and your child's other parent remain equally committed to your child's well-being during this disruptive process.

Financial Security Needs

All the needs listed so far depend, in large part, on financial security. Some of the ways are obvious: food, housing, and medical care all bear direct costs. Finances, however, can affect other needs more subtly. Finances, or the lack thereof, can affect kids' abilities to participate in sports and school activities, which can affect their self-esteem. Or take sleep, for example. I remember evaluating one child in my office whose behavior and school performance were being affected, and everyone thought he had attention-deficit/hyperactivity disorder. As it turned out, he was merely sleep-deprived. He and his mother had moved into a 1-bedroom apartment with his grandmother, and she stayed up until the early morning hours watching TV. Nowhere in the home could he escape the light and noise from the TV, and he was on the verge of being expelled from school as a result.

Hopefully, both parents want their children to have healthy food, safe housing, medical care, and the ability to pursue whatever interests help them fulfill their potential. It's more common than not for separating and divorcing parents to have huge fights over money, but if both parents are putting the child first, child support payments become more about math than about emotions.

Social Belonging Needs

Family separation is among the most stressful events a child can face, and nothing protects us from the effects of stress better than human connection. Study after study shows that the stronger and more numerous our bonds to the people around us, the better we do. We talked in Chapter 2, How Do I Begin?, about building your support team for this process, but your children need their support team just as much, if not more. So who is on that team?

Building Your Child's Support Team

It starts, of course, with both parents. As we progress through this book, we examine cases when one parent is so impaired that contact is not healthy, such as when a parent has been physically or psychologically abusive or violent. Short of these extreme cases, however, children will still love, need, and benefit from both their parents. In the heat of a divorce or separation, you may feel so negatively about your ex that you can't imagine how that person can be good for anyone, especially your child. But your child will find things to love about each parent, and the goal is to keep both parents as involved as possible (how that is done will occupy much of the rest of this book).

Extended Family Support

Family, however, doesn't stop with parents. Many evolutionary biologists think that the reason humans live so long after their reproductive years is that their love and wisdom serve to protect their children and grandchildren for decades. My own birth father ended up being so impaired by mental illness that he stopped being a positive force in my life, but his mother, "Granny," was present for many of the happiest moments of my childhood and did more than almost anyone else to preserve my mental health. Making time for grandparents and "bonusgrandparents" is among the best steps you can take to help your child through this process, and it may even give you some time for badly needed self-care.

Siblings are another source of love and belonging, even if they can also be a source of annoyance and competition. During my separation and divorce, I could see how my 3 kids looked out for each other and cared for each other. There are still stories they won't share with either me or their mom, but when I imagine these stories, I smile. They are the only 3 people in the world who know what it's like to grow up in these 2 households, and they have a unique perspective on the challenges of coping with each parent in their lives. As your process continues, stepsiblings (or, better, "bonussiblings") may enter the picture as well. In Chapter 11, The Making of a Family, we discuss these relationships in depth, but for now, just know that bonussiblings can also help your child thrive.

Stepparents (or "bonusparents") are another source of love, support, and inspiration for your child. Bonusparents don't enter the family with the same automatic acceptance that birth parents have, and we spend much of this book talking about how to build healthy relationships in your newly reformed family, but hopefully, a "bonusparent" will add some perspectives and strengths that complement both the birth parents'.

Friends

A child's social supports extend far beyond the family. Most of us can still remember our best childhood friends in tremendous detail, and I bet you can recall a moment that you might not have been able to get through without your best friend's help. Friends become a constant at a time when your child needs something stable. The separation or divorce may involve a move, which can make it harder to maintain friendships, but, thankfully, today's children have a powerful tool at their disposal in the form of social media. From simple video chats to shared projects created together, from thousands of miles away, moving no longer means losing touch with friends. It goes without saying, however, your children's social media interactions can be a huge indicator to what they are thinking and how they are feeling. This means it is imperative that both parents monitor their children's use of social media when their children are in their home and compare notes, if necessary, in order to keep their children safe. Even having a conversation with your children to coach them on how to talk with their friends about their parents' divorce will help them overcome any awkwardness they may be feeling.

Others on the Team

Beyond these circles lie other caring adults: teachers, coaches, counselors, faith leaders, and neighbors—in the life of every successful child, we can find at least one safe, stable, loving adult who cares. Do what you can to help your child nurture these relationships as well. Sometimes a child's day turns around just with a smile from a cafeteria worker or a school custodian. Even casual relationships, when they are supportive, protect us from feeling alone.

Consistency Is Key

School

If I were to ask you anytime to tell me about yourself, I bet that 90% of the time, you'd mention your job. You might also mention your hobbies, athletic pursuits, and faith community. A kid's job is to learn, so when we think about social belonging, we have to think about school. If your child can stay in the same school throughout the separation and divorce, it may provide a source of social stability as other elements of your child's life are shifting. Even then, however, it's important to let school staff, including teachers and counselors, know what's going on. Chances are good that your child may be unusually withdrawn or perhaps easily angered. When the people who deal with children every day understand what these children are dealing with, they have an opportunity to be more supportive and tolerant.

If your child has to change schools, take that opportunity to talk with teachers and counselors as well. This change is likely to be stressful for a while, and your child will need all the help one can get. If you are able, look for ways that you can become involved in the new school, perhaps helping as a Parent-Teacher Association member or an athletic booster, so that you can better understand your child's new environment.

Other Ways to Find Social Belonging

School, however, is only one place a child might find social belonging, and for many children, it's not even the most important. Sports teams, faith communities, the arts (eg, music, dance, visual arts), and clubs or hobbies all help a child build an identity, find friends, and earn a sense of accomplishment. This doesn't mean that you have to frantically schedule every second of a child's day; free play is critical to healthy development. But if your child expresses interest in an activity and there's some way you can help in pursuing it, go for it!

Building Self-esteem

Self-esteem serves as a pillar of mental health, but our understanding of how to help a child build strong self-esteem has evolved over the decades. From the time I was a child in the 1970s until I had my own children in the 1990s, we thought it was a simple process: tell children they're great as often as you can or at least every time they accomplish something. "Look how smart you are!" "Look how fast you are!" and other similar exclamations rolled off our tongues.

Then we discovered a problem with this sort of praise: everyone eventually finds individual limits. Smart kids fail tests, fast kids lose races, and still others stop achieving as expected. When kids equate their excellence with things coming easily for them and then things inevitably grow harder, they assume they're no longer excellent at whatever they're trying, and their self-esteem collapses. This realization has led to a huge change in the way we advise parents to build self-esteem. We now recommend praising a child's effort more than the outcome, even when the outcome is great. "You're so smart!" becomes "You studied really hard for that test!" The idea is to grant children a "growth mindset," the concept that you can get better at anything when you apply yourself. After all, if you tell children they're good at math and bad at basketball, why would they work hard to improve at either one?

If children are to build strong self-esteem, they'll need strong role models: their parents. Depending on what is happening with your separation or divorce, you may not feel like modeling self-esteem at this moment. You may feel, as I did, like a total failure. But for that very reason, now is the perfect time to list your strengths. Look at your own talents, consider the things you've worked hard to master, and share with your child what makes you most proud. Let children know that they can be proud of completely different things, but these are the things that help you walk tall.

Then comes the harder part: helping them find self-esteem in your co-parent. You may be distracted by all the faults that led your ex to become your ex. It may be hard to remember what about that person attracted you in the first place. But your judgement can't be that bad; things about that person must have drawn you into the relationship. Remember that children know they have traits from you and from their other parent. So if your ex is good with tools, or funny, or artistic, or athletic, or whatever, feel free to say that too. "You are good in math, just like your mother," is a great self-esteem builder, possibly for both of you.

Self-actualization Needs

This academic-sounding term *self-actualization* breaks down into a simple and universal idea that may be the most widely shared goal of parents worldwide: we want our children to be able to grow into the best possible versions of themselves. There are as many different versions of success as there are children, but we all hope to see our kids flourish as they grow. Toward that goal, it helps to have a sense of what children's developmental tasks are at every age and how we can help them achieve those goals.

Newborn Period and Infancy

The first year after birth involves the most dramatic transformations imaginable at every level. A newborn with little functional mobility or vision will end the year understanding and using some words, going where she wants on her own, and exploring the world eagerly with all her senses. Through all this change, her primary job will be building strong emotional attachments to the people in her life who love her the most.

Initially, your new baby will know you by sound, smell, and touch. Newborns can smell their mothers' breast milk and will squirm themselves into position to breastfeed immediately after birth. Maximizing skin-to-skin time ("kangaroo care") during the newborn period helps reinforce these sensations and has been shown to help newborns regulate their temperature, heart rate, and breathing. Feedings reinforce security for newborns and infants; learn hunger and satiety cues and respond to the signs that baby is hungry and to the signs that baby is full. Hold your baby whenever you feel the urge, and know that you cannot spoil a baby by too much holding.

Early infancy is a vulnerable time for many parents in the best of circumstances. Up to 1 in 5 mothers experiences significant postpartum depression, symptoms that go beyond the baby blues to affect daily function. Fathers are not immune to postpartum depression either, with up to 1 in 4 experiencing symptoms. Divorce and separation can compound the stress and worsen matters as well. The American Academy of Pediatrics recommends that pediatricians screen mothers for depression at every health supervision visit between birth and age 6 months, and doctors now suggest screening fathers as well. But you don't have to wait for a screening examination to seek help. If you are feeling unusually sad or tired, and especially if you are thinking about harming yourself or your baby, call your doctor now for help.

Newborns and infants learn emotional security and attachment from the continual back-and-forth interactions they have with their caregivers, most often their parents. With every smile, coo, and squint, they are watching and listening to your response and learning how to manage their own feelings in the process. When you are depressed or anxious, your own interactions with your newborn or infant are muted, so taking care of your own emotional needs at this time can be critical for your child's healthy development.

Try to make ample room for play. It's never too early to sing to your baby, read to her, play with her hands and feet, and nuzzle her. No matter how stressed you are, these special moments will bring both of you happiness, as well as the emotional connection she needs to develop and grow.

Toddler Years

The second and third years after birth remain a period of dramatic growth and development. Your child's concept of the world expands rapidly as she transitions from barely walking to running full speed, becomes skilled at manipulating the objects that surround her, learns that other people have thoughts and feelings like her own, and develops an ability to fully express her ideas. She is also spending this time exploring the limits of her behavior, which means that discipline can be challenging, to say the least.

Because your child has all these developmental skills to master, it's easy to imagine that you need a whole host of specialized toys to help with the job. Nothing could be further from the truth. Children are programmed to find the things they need to learn and grow. Pots and pans, cardboard boxes, and the tubes inside rolls of paper towels—these are toys for the ages. The things you buy should have many purposes and foster imagination. Dolls and stuffed animals, books, balls, blocks, and toy cars and trucks—just a handful of each will be more than enough to propel your child's imagination and development.

Activity is critical to development as well. No need to enroll your toddler in an organized sports program. Toddlers will be thrilled to run in the yard, chase birds from the sidewalk, and swing on the swing set. If you take some time to be active with toddlers, they will follow your example *and* you'll probably feel better too!

Preschool Years

I don't believe that there is such a thing as a "best" part of childhood, but ages 4 and 5 years are awfully fun! Children this age are learning huge concepts about rules, gender, reality compared with make-believe, and how people get along with each other successfully. They are able to communicate clearly and extensively and to express ideas about the future and the past. They are learning to count, to draw, and even, in some cases, to start reading. They can hop, skip, climb, swing, and somersault.

Supporting these skills requires no special equipment or training, just a safe and loving environment. Access to the outdoors as well as to books and drawing materials, combined with your attention, will give children everything they need to master age-appropriate skills. They should have time to play with other children as well as the space to solve problems on their own with only enough parental help to keep everyone safe. Feelings will be hurt, knees will be scraped, and you will be there to dry the tears and send them back out to do and learn more.

Your job with separation and divorce at this time is largely to support and communicate. Is there a chance at transition time to share what your child has learned since the last visit with the other parent? Does your child have any new interests? New friends? One advantage of having 2 environments is that there will inevitably be different things to learn and do at each home and different ways that each parent encourages exploration and development.

School Age

From kindergarten to high school, your child and then teen will learn more and more outside the home but will still need a strong home base and plenty of support from you. The changes you see now will be gradual but constant.

Counting gives way to adding and subtracting, which yields to multiplication and eventually the basics of algebra and geometry. Children go from decoding simple words to writing research papers and from running across the yard to scoring goals. Mainly what they need from you is support, encouragement, and involvement.

Divorce and separation can pose challenges that you'll need to address. Will your child stay at the school she knows, or will she need to enroll somewhere new? Can both parents get her to practices, games, and lessons to support her interests? Will you both attend performances, meet with teachers, and cheer on the sidelines at games? Do support payments account for the equipment and classes she needs to succeed? As your child's needs and interests evolve, you may need to readdress aspects of your custody agreement from time to time. Children at this age are increasingly able to express their own wishes about where and how they spend their time, and while you don't necessarily have to grant their every request, you should be prepared to take their feelings into account as your arrangement evolves.

Teen Years

In some ways, your child's transition during this period is almost as dramatic as what occurs during the first year after birth. She begins this phase still largely dependent on you for clothing, food, transportation, and emotional support. The end goal is that, while maintaining a close and loving relationship, she learns to take care of all these things on her own. Getting there involves a lot of pushing and pulling on both your parts, and it rarely occurs in a straight line. Instead, expect that both of you will overreact to some situations and underreact to others as you struggle to maintain your footing on shifting emotional ground.

As your child forges her own identity, she will naturally reflect on how the experience of separation and divorce has affected her outlook. You're likely to have some painful conversations around this topic, especially around your role in the separation. As parents, we recoil at the idea that our actions may have made our children unhappy, and it's tempting to dredge up the old injuries that led to the separation in the first place and to explain how the other parent is more at fault.

When this temptation arises, take a breath and instead remember that your child also loves her other parent and that she may look within herself for whatever faults you are about to highlight, wondering whether you think the same of her. Remember, too, that she is getting old enough to make her own judgements about other people's strengths and flaws, especially those of her parents. Whatever you have noticed about your ex, she probably has noticed as well. You have every reason to be generous, or at least neutral, in your assessments and instead let her come to her own conclusions.

4

Helping Our Children Cope

The way we talk to our children becomes their inner voice.

PEGGY O'MARA

How Do We Tell the Kids?

Once you decide to actually call it quits, the big question is "How do we tell the kids?" We all want to soften the blow, making it as easy as possible on them, but the truth is, it won't be easy, and it will hurt.

For some children, the news won't be a surprise. They have been witnesses to the fallout—the fighting and insults, the possible domestic violence, and the addiction issues—and for them, the message "We are getting a divorce" may be a relief. But for others, those too young to understand or those who simply had no clue, it will be a surprise, and how they are told will set the stage for how well they adjust once the final decision has been made.

On the next few pages, you will find some suggestions for how to approach the kids—how to read their stress level, what to say, and how to take care of them once you move on. We start with examining what your child is most likely feeling, depending on your child's age, and move into what specifically you can do to help your child. The goal is to take a proactive approach, rather than a reactive approach; anticipate the problems; and have a solution ready.

Age Matters: Understanding Child Development

You've probably heard "When speaking with children, use age-appropriate language," but, in practical terms, what does that mean? It simply means "Play to your audience." Use words, phrases, and concepts children will understand at their age.

For example, we all know you can't talk with a toddler in the same manner you can talk with an adolescent, or a teenager. Why? Because toddlers simply won't understand. Infants who cannot talk rely on their parents to anticipate their needs and respond appropriately. But this observation is also true for older children, and sometimes, overexplaining things is just as bad as not explaining them at all. For some, it may be even worse. Too much information confuses some children and can easily frustrate toddlers or preschoolers. Those 2- or 3-year-old tantrums can be rooted in a lot of things, from exhaustion to frustration with not understanding what's going on around them.

It's important to remember that your child's age and stage have general developmental and behavioral characteristics, but your child is not a textbook and may not react in a textbook manner. Siblings may not even respond alike. One child may take disappointment in stride, while the other is devastated. Sometimes, kids feel embarrassed or frightened asking questions, and your approach will have to again be adjusted. One-on-one conversations are often the answer; however, when siblings are close, they may want the comfort of their sister or brother when things get serious. You know your child best. Adjust your approach with your child's temperament in mind, but, on average, the information in this chapter is designed to help you pass on and discuss difficult information each step of the way.

Setting the Stage

66 *We were fighting a lot, and when it came to making up, the sex was great and we weren't that careful. In the back of my mind, I thought a baby might help. I was wrong. As the baby got older, the fights got worse, and by the time we decided to break up, my child was a mess.* **99**

When you can see your child is stressed-out, sometimes the best thing to do is just hold your child in your arms and gently whisper, "I'm here." For younger children, you may choose to rock them for a while and then ask, "Feel better?" The reaction will most likely be "Yes." And you can then add, "Me too. Sometimes we just need to take a minute to relax and take deep breaths." Bonding at the time of crisis offers a special kind of security to both parent and child, and it offers the child a soft place to fall when things start to feel overwhelming. You build a bond with your child during these times, and hopefully, your child will choose to come to you when things get overwhelming.

The difficult part as a parent can be when you are feeling angry, hurt, or filled with anxiety in response to your breakup: How do you set the stage for your child so that your child will not be affected by your negative emotions?

Start by taking care of yourself—take note of your attitude, go to counseling if necessary, exercise, meditate, call a friend, and do whatever else you have to do, even though at times, you may just want to get into bed and pull the covers over your head—and that's when you say, "No, my kids are watching and I have to set the example." (For more information on your personal journey, see Chapter 5, Facing the Transition: Moving From We to Me). Concentrate on the effect your breakup has on them. Use your child's well-being as the criteria for your decisions and you will handle the situation correctly every time.

Reading Our Children

Reading Your Babies Aged 0 to 3 Months

Most would think that good communication depends on words. How many times have you heard "Just talk to me!" But words are not the only tool in the communication toolbox, particularly if a child is too young to speak. Both your actions and reactions set the stage for your child's emotional well-being—and if your babies are too young to understand your words, they depend on your vibe, or what they feel from you.

From birth, newborns model their emotional responses on their parents', particularly their mother's. While in the womb, fetuses can hear their mother's voice, feeling her reactions to stress firsthand—her heart speed up when she is elated, angry, or upset. Once born, newborns emulate their caregivers' reactions and look to them to set the stage for the proper response to a given situation. This is reinforced by recent studies that verify when parents are anxious and then come into contact with their child, their child becomes anxious as well.

Communication Toolbox to Help Us Better Communicate With Our Children During Separation or Divorce

- **Patience.** Set the stage for each conversation by mentally counting to 10 before you speak. It doesn't matter if you are already calm—make it a ritual so that when you are under stress, you are sure to count to 10 first.
- **Empathy.** Put yourself into your child's shoes. You will respond appropriately if you feel what your child is feeling.
- **Ask questions.** Talking issues out is important. Ask your child open-ended questions that require more than a yes-or-no answer. Instead of "How was your day at school?" try "What was the best thing that happened today?" or "Tell me one good thing and one bad thing about your day...."
- **Active listening.** To prove to your child that you are listening and that you understand, paraphrase what was said: "It sounds like you're really upset your mom didn't pick you up."
- **Reframe.** Present negative observations as positive. A "quiet" child becomes "thoughtful" or an "impulsive" child becomes "spontaneous."
- **Humor.** Using gentle humor often helps you address even the most sensitive issues and keeps things lighthearted and in the proper perspective.

SIGNS OF STRESS IN INFANTS

66*My child is only 3 months old. She's too young to be stressed.***99**

Not true. Just because your infant can't tell you how she feels doesn't mean she doesn't feel.

If parents are at odds—yelling, screaming, threatening each other, or even not talking and just avoiding each other—children can feel the tension from these situations. Some children will respond by becoming anxious and fussy themselves.

Of course, crying indicates stress, but it indicates a lot of things in newborns and infants, from being overtired to simply having a dirty diaper. There are also other signs to look for—difficulty sleeping, for example—but this one can be tricky. Newborns and infants often don't sleep through the night, so look for difficulties when babies are going down for a nap. A baby's appetite is often affected when the baby is stressed. You may find your baby rejects food or sometimes can eat too much. Spitting up or gagging may be reactions to stressful situations.

Other things to look for may not be as obvious. When a baby is lying quietly and then arches his back, stretches his arms or legs out straight, holds that position for a second or two, relaxes, and then does it again, it could be a reaction to stress and attempt for the baby to self-soothe. (If this behavior is repeated or comes with shaking, however, it could also be seizures, so check with your baby's pediatrician.) Splaying their fingers or toes is also a subtle indicator of stress in newborns and infants, as well as hiccupping, yawning, or sneezing.

We all know that each time your child yawns or hiccups, it is not necessarily an indicator that he is in distress, but it could indicate that he is getting too much stimuli, and something should be changed to keep his distress from increasing.

CHECK YOURSELF

Loud voices do not set the stage for a calm environment, so if you and your child's other parent are working on that breakup and your arguing escalates to screaming or domestic violence, even if you think your newborn or infant won't get it, he will respond to all the negative stimuli in the home. Don't disregard your child's reaction to stress because you think *he is* too young. Just because you can't see it doesn't mean your child isn't feeling it.

Coping Mechanisms of Babies Aged 0 to 3 Months

Here are some other clues that indicate your baby may be responding to stress and attempting to self-soothe.

- Grasping a blanket or his own hands
- Excessive sucking on his fingers
- Dozing off to a light sleep

Problem is, it's quite common to see all these things, even if things are just fine. The key is to watch whether behaviors become excessive or *if there is a change in behavior.*

If you suspect your newborn or infant is reacting to the stress in the home, knowing what keeps you calm is the best way to keep a baby calm. Talking softly in a reassuring manner, humming, or cooing quickly calms a child. Try decreasing the noise level or the light in the room, and simply hold the baby close to your body and rock. Newborns and very young infants respond well to swaddling to reduce their stress.

As you and your baby get to know each other, it will be easier to read his cues and anticipate what he is "saying" to you when his needs have or have not been met.

Parenting tip. Rocking a baby not only calms the child but calms the parent as well. While rocking is known to promote sleep in children, research suggests that the swaying motion when a parent is rocking a child also has a calming effect on the parent. When a parent is calm, it allows the parent to react more effectively to a crying child, thereby reducing the possibility of an aggressive response toward an agitated newborn or infant.

Reading Your Toddlers and Preschoolers, Aged 1 to 5 Years

SIGNS OF STRESS IN TODDLERS AND PRESCHOOLERS

Change, again, is the key word. Signs of distress in toddlers and preschoolers include fear, acting out, anger, or emotional instability, which, in practical terms, looks like clinginess, protesting, crabbiness, and being anxious. If your toddler previously slept through the night but now frets before going to sleep or has started to wake up with nightmares, again, that can indicate stress. If a preschooler has been potty-trained and then starts to wet the bed again, that change is a common reaction to stress and a strong indicator that something needs to be addressed. Toddlers or preschoolers often throw tantrums when they are frustrated or don't get their way, but if that behavior increases or the child seems overly sensitive to normal requests, stress from your breakup could be at the root of it.

WHAT TO DO

When we are stressed or keyed up, we *react* to negative stimuli. So do children, and they become anxious when they are unsure of what to expect. Even if they can't talk yet, they can still read discord around the house and perceive, for instance, that Mom is upset and Dad is angry, and then they may wonder, *"Who is going to take care of me?"*

Consistency in approach is key. Consistency is more than just soothing. Consistent routines, such as regular bedtime, feeding, and playtime, and visiting consistent and familiar people can be comforting to your kids. For your children, knowing that they can reach out to you for comfort is comforting in itself. Figure out what calms them, whether it's rocking or reading a story, and use that method each time your child needs comfort. As your child gets older, the method may have to be adjusted, but stay alert and make those adjustments when needed.

WAYS TO SOOTHE TODDLERS

▶ Keep the feeling in the home as relaxed as possible. Monitor outside stimulus, such as TV or movies.

▶ Stay organized and plan ahead.

▶ Establish a dependable schedule for naps, meals, and bedtimes.

▶ Offer nutritious meals and find outlets for exercise.

▶ Try not to get flustered when things don't as planned.

▶ Set aside plenty of time for hugs, kisses, and cuddling.

Finally, if behavior really changes—you notice your child pulling or chewing on his hair, picking at his nails until they bleed, incessantly rocking, or displaying nervous ticks or agitation—this is a strong indicator that your child has been severely affected by the stress in his life, and you must get proactive. Don't be afraid to seek guidance from a professional who can offer specific tools to help your child cope with the stress he is experiencing. Talk with your pediatrician about your observations. Your pediatrician might recommend seeing a developmental and behavioral pediatrician or a child psychologist.

SEPARATION ANXIETY

Separation anxiety is a normal stage of development for infants and toddlers. Young children often experience a period of separation anxiety when a parent returns to work or even leaves them home to go shopping. As a result, we see separation anxiety as early as 6 months to around 3 years of age.

When parents divorce and a child's normal routine is upset, separation anxiety can be particularly troublesome. The child becomes needy, becomes fearful, and cries when separated from the primary caregiver. Children don't understand that Mommy or Daddy or other caregivers will eventually return, and they begin to panic. At this age, it's not uncommon for a child to cry when you leave the room. Most children outgrow separation anxiety on their own when they realize that a caregiver will return, but it may be more challenging when the parents do not live together and are not on the same page when their child responds anxiously in going between parents' homes.

Remember, stress may cause a child who seemed to be adjusting well to regress, so if you are fighting with your child's other parent in front of your child, expect him to react to the chaos. Don't be surprised if you must explain things you thought you explained before. We often think young children understand something because they say they do—but they don't—and then we must calmly explain the concept again. Things such as time and how long a parent will be away are difficult concepts for a toddler or preschooler to understand.

Example of Separation Anxiety During Separation or Divorce and Ways to Respond

Question. My ex and I have been divorced now for 18 months. I know all research points to kids doing better when both parents are active in their lives, but I'm afraid MY kids are having separation anxiety. Whenever it's time to change houses, all hell breaks loose. And, to make matters worse, I think I go into mourning the day before they are scheduled to leave. What can I do to help my family…and me…adjust to our new life?

Answer. Unfortunately, the separation anxiety you speak of is not exclusive to kids who go back and forth between parents after divorce. Even children who live with both parents go through a certain amount of separation anxiety when they face a new situation. For example, it's natural for children to become anxious before their first day of school or in anticipating having to go to child care when, say, their mother works outside the home. It's not uncommon for caring parents to experience the same feelings when they anticipate their children leaving. It simply takes some getting used to the changes. However, here are some dos and don'ts to help make the transition from house to house easier on everyone.

Make sure to

- Keep your goodbyes short and sweet. In doing so, you are sending the message that you have confidence in your child's abilities to cope.
- Develop loving goodbye routines or comforting rituals. A secret handshake or a simple thumbs-up every day before you leave each other is a great way to quietly say, "I love you, always."
- Send clear messages. Your child needs to know that you see his time with his other parent as a positive experience—and when you see your child adjusting well, no backtracking with a parting such as "But Mommy (or Daddy) will miss you." That will not make your children feel more secure. It gives them anxiety, thinking that they are creating your unhappiness, and makes their transitions back and forth more difficult.
- Not bargain or bribe your child to behave if your child balks at going to Mom's or Dad's or other caregivers'. It undermines your ex's parenting skills, which will ultimately interfere with your child's adjustment after the divorce. In other words, don't say things such as "Be a good girl and go to Daddy's (or Mommy's) without crying and you and I will go to a movie when you get home." Going to see the other parent is not something your children must endure—they just have to adjust now that their parents are divorced—and if you present it negatively, you are doing your child a huge disservice. You may not care for your ex, but it undermines your children's trust and security when you teach them to do the same.
- Not tell your children that you will come get them if they are unhappy at their other parent's home. Part of adjusting to co-parenting after divorce is learning to trust your ex's parenting skills. The goal is for your children to trust and feel secure with both parents. If your children are upset when they are with the other parent, allow the other parent to be a parent and comfort the children. A truly loving parent always helps one's children feel loved and secure. Your children deserve 2 loving parents.
- Not discuss problems with the other parent when you are dropping off or picking up the kids. Better to keep that time upbeat and positive. Save serious conversations and questions for a private phone call.

> ### Example of Separation Anxiety During Separation
> ### or Divorce and Ways to Respond (continued)
>
> - Not be surprised if your child again becomes anxious about leaving you after a holiday or a bout with an illness. Illness and holiday celebrations make us all feel a little vulnerable. Consistency is the key to coping with a setback. Remember: separation anxiety means that you and your child have a strong and loving bond. Don't turn that bond into a disability. Reinforce the love of both parents and your child will grow to be a loving and secure human, even if you parents no longer live under the same roof. And, to ensure that you don't "go into mourning" each time your child leaves, have a plan for your time alone. Meet friends, work out, play tennis, go shopping, or have alone time with your new significant other. Use the time *living* your new life, not mourning your old life. Then when your child returns, you *both* have something new to share.

ADJUST YOUR APPROACH AS YOUR TODDLER GROWS OLDER

When children become verbal, that's when simple declarative statements will guide them to a more peaceful place. Make sure you explain your comings and goings before you leave. Things such as "Mommy (or Daddy) is leaving now, but I will be back" set the stage. Use time frames that your toddler might understand. When my daughter was young, she loved a TV show that was a half hour long—and she knew how to count to 10 at 2 years old. So, if I was leaving for an hour, I would explain it to her by saying, "I will only be gone for 2 PAW Patrols." Use any activity you can equate to a time frame your child will understand. She understood exactly what I meant and began to use other favorite TV shows or activities to measure time.

If you are going to be gone for days—for example, you share custody and the child goes back and forth between homes—a simple calendar can be helpful. Even if a child cannot read numbers, you can use the child's favorite color to mark off the days and explain exactly when you will be back.

Be aware that saying something such as "We'll see each other in 2 days" can be confusing to a young child who is not sure how long a day truly is. Try explaining, "When it is light and the sun is out, that's a day. When it is dark and the moon is out, that's a night." And then use those explanations to explain how long it will be until you see each other—or he sees the other parent. I caught myself saying, "I will see you in 2 suns and 2 moons." My daughter knew exactly what I meant.

THE SPECIFICS: TELLING TODDLERS AND PRESCHOOLERS ABOUT THE BREAKUP

Although we don't think toddlers understand what is happening when their parents choose to split, they understand fighting, they understand arguments, and they understand when something is not right with their parents. What you will hear if your toddler can speak are simple questions, such as "Where is

Daddy (or Mommy)?" Be succinct in your answers and explain exactly what the child can expect: "Daddy has a new home. He is at work and he will pick you up tonight after work." Reinforce both parents' love for the child: "We both love you very much."

Co-parenting tip: Possibly the most important tip I can offer? When speaking with your child about your separation, declare your love for your child, not your dislike of the other parent. *Never* blame or bad-mouth the other parent, no matter what.

Your goal is to help your child feel safe and secure in possibly the most chaotic time of your child's life. Children inherently understand their DNA. They know they are half Mommy and half Daddy. Bad-mouth the other parent and children will personalize it. They will either push it down and develop anxiety, and, as a result, get very clingy to the parent who is being bad-mouthed, or reject you for talking badly about their beloved parent. When you are bad-mouthing their mommy or daddy, you are bad-mouthing half of them. It changes who they are. It's a lose-lose proposition.

Reading Your School-aged Children, Aged 5 to 9 Years

Because school-aged children can tell you how they feel, parents often take them at their word, but the common parental query "Are you OK?" may not be enough. Your child may tell you he is fine because at this age he can't put his finger on exactly how he feels. School teachers have confided that moodiness and lack of concentration in students of this age can be caused by something as simple as not having breakfast in the morning. But ask a child of 7 or 8 if he is hungry and he may not make the correlation. Loss of appetite is a common childhood symptom of coping with stress.

Here are other things to look for in this age-group.

▶ Sleep disorders (nightmares or an inability to fall asleep or stay asleep)
▶ Avoidance
▶ Crying
▶ Disorganization and inability to concentrate
▶ Refusing to go to school or refusing to participate in activities they used to enjoy
▶ Headaches or stomachaches and other physical ailments

Co-parenting tip. Parents must make a special effort to read their children's concerns. If you start to hear "I don't feel good," more than usual, your child is probably reacting to the stress in his life.

My own "bonusdaughter," Melanie, constantly complained of stomachaches after her parents' divorce. These complaints continued for years, and her parents had her at the doctor's office on a regular basis. When all the test results kept coming back negative, it was obvious the problem was caused by the anxiety created by her parents' breakup and, sometime later, the changes that came when my daughter and I were added to their family. Plus, it seems stress can be contagious in a way, and although the kids got along well on its face, my own daughter started to have nightmares—something that may have been developmental but that she had not faced prior to the combining of families.

CHANGE IN BOWEL HABITS

A change in bowel movement is often a strong indicator that a child may be overwhelmed by the stress in the child's life. *Encopresis* is soiling in inappropriate places by children who are past the age of toilet training. As a practical explanation, children hold their poop for so long it leaks into their underwear. Because all children are potty-trained at their own rate, medical professionals don't consider soiling to be a medical condition until the child is at least 4 years old.

Although encopresis is sometimes caused by a physical abnormality, there seems to be a psychological component as well. In most cases, it starts with chronic constipation. Over time, the child becomes unwilling to pass bowel movements, and holding it in becomes a habit. Eventually, the colon becomes so stretched out that the child no longer senses the need to pass stool. At first, only small amounts of stool leak out, producing streaks, and parents may assume their child isn't wiping properly. Unfortunately, if this condition is not dealt with properly, over time it will worsen.

For children with this diagnosis, the psychological component seems to be in response to an inability to control what is happening around them. Their parents are going through a difficult and stressful time. As a result, their children don't feel safe and are unsure of what is going to happen to them. They can become riddled with anxiety or possibly defiant, and the way they attempt to control their environment is they hold their stool. No matter the reason this is happening, you should never punish a child for this. It is not the child's fault.

There is a strong, unique odor to encopresis soiling. As a result, older children often hide the evidence in unconventional places. Finding soiled underwear under old clothes in the closet, under the bed, or in the garbage is often the parent's first clue that there is a problem.

What to Do

Professionals believe the best treatment of encopresis is a combination of medical treatment and individual therapy. Begin with a visit to the child's pediatrician to make sure a medical condition isn't causing the problem. Ask your pediatrician for a referral to a therapist who specializes in treating children. Together, the professionals will design a joint treatment plan and work together to help the child figure out the root cause and overcome the soiling.

When at home, there are some things you can do—and these are ***great suggestions for all families going through a breakup, not just families dealing with encopresis.***

▶ **Get organized!** In the world of your child going back and forth between homes, this may mean make sure your child knows where his backpack is before school, not running around to find shoes at the last minute. Eliminate inquiries such as "Where are your shoes! Did you leave them at Dad's?" You're the parent. Your young child looks to you to keep him organized. Get organized together by taking time to show your child how to follow a checklist of having his shoes, homework, and lunch in his backpack. If you don't, anxiety sets in.

▶ **Establish regular bathroom habits at the same time each day.** A suggestion? Look for a regular time during the day when you know your child is relaxed. In other words, don't make the time he's supposed to sit in the bathroom right before you must rush out to school, because that will just increase your child's anxiety if he is pressured to be on time for school. You may have to alter your daily routine—wake up a little earlier or change the time you go into work—but establishing a regular bathroom schedule is critical, particularly for school-aged children. We all naturally go to the bathroom after we eat, so have your child sit on the toilet for at least 5 minutes after every meal. Make that time enjoyable by letting him bring books, toys, or games in with him.

▶ **Design a reward system.** Offer positive reinforcement for the child's active participation. Younger children respond well to sticker charts, while older kids respond positively to earning extra privileges, such as special outings with friends or additional video game time. Try to stay away from food as a reward. Food rewards set the stage for the child to look for special treats to lift one's spirits. This could lead to obesity later in life. When your child has an accident, it can be stressful, but make sure to respond positively. Let your child know that accidents are OK and children just have to keep trying and doing their best.

IF IT WALKS LIKE A DUCK, AND QUACKS LIKE A DUCK, IS IT ALWAYS A DUCK?

66 *My son's father and I decided to separate about 8 months ago, and it has taken a while for us all to get adjusted. One thing I have noticed is that my son is very unorganized around the house, and his teachers are telling me that he can't concentrate at school. After school, I have a difficult time getting him to settle down to do his homework. He's also very forgetful and doesn't seem to hear me when I tell him to do something. He has trouble sleeping, and now he can't find his shoes when it's time to go to school! I think he may have ADHD [attention-deficit/hyperactivity disorder], and I'm considering putting him on medication.* 99

When Attention-Deficit/Hyperactivity Disorder Is Suspected

The child in the scenario could very well have attention-deficit/hyperactivity disorder (ADHD), but the symptoms described are also symptoms of childhood depression or even post-traumatic stress disorder, which is not just an anxiety disorder of war veterans but a very real diagnosis for children traumatized by their parent's breakup.

An inability to concentrate, trouble sleeping, disorganization, and moodiness are symptoms of all 3 diagnoses, and because the symptoms are all so similar, it is sometimes difficult to zero in on what's really wrong. Depending on how traumatic things were leading up to the parental breakup, it could be all 3! All children do not react the same. If you are going through a breakup and you notice these changes in your child, he could be reacting to the changes and stresses associated with the divorce, and medicating him may temporarily mask the true problem, but it could also complicate the situation. Now the child is attempting to deal with the stresses brought on by his parents' behavior, plus trying to cope with the changes in taking medication that he really doesn't need.

Attention-deficit/hyperactivity disorder is usually the first diagnosis that comes to mind, and there is a logical reason. Teachers start to pinpoint ADHD at around ages 5 to 9 years, beginning at school age, when children are first asked to follow a regimented school schedule, follow directions, keep their hands to themselves, and follow other rules. If they don't adhere, a red flag goes up. Parents don't realize how their aggressive behavior toward each other affects the child emotionally and how those emotional responses translate into everyday trials. Instead, parents look for a physical ailment as a reason behind the child's lack of concentration and disorganization. Physical is tangible. "It must be ADHD, a brain dysfunction, or something wrong with the child. It can't be something I am doing."

But it very well may be something you're doing. Children respond to and model their parents' behavior. If the parents are distracted, angry, and disorganized, don't be surprised if the children act in a similar manner.

This is when parents say, "I don't know why they are acting this way; we never fight in front of the children!" However, the kids overhear them talking with each other on the phone. They listen to what is said to friends and other family members. No, the parents may not fight in front of the children, but the children know all the same, and that uncertainty and pain translates to a lack of concentration and disorganization and an inability to sleep. That's why depression or post-traumatic stress disorder may be at the root of the behaviors, not ADHD.

How Do We Diagnose Attention-Deficit/Hyperactivity Disorder?

For many reasons, a child may not pay attention as well as others, so diagnosing attention-deficit/hyperactivity disorder (ADHD) requires thoroughly exploring all the possibilities. The symptoms that characterize ADHD—inattention, hyperactivity, and impulsivity—occur in most children from time to time. However, ADHD can't be determined by a simple blood test, or laboratory test.

Classically, a child with ADHD will show symptoms before the age of 12 years. Symptoms should be present in more than one place, such as at home and at school. So having observations from parents, family members, your child's teacher, and other school professionals helps provide critical feedback. Sometimes these people will be asked to interview or to fill out a questionnaire specifically designed to evaluate behaviors seen in children and adolescents with ADHD. Symptoms that occur only in one environment suggest a problem with the environment. Most important, symptoms should not arise from some other cause. Among the most common other causes are poor sleep, anxiety, depression, and stress. We also consider problems as simple as hearing loss and near-sightedness and as complex as learning disorders, such as dyslexia. So you can see how a diagnosis can be even more challenging when other problems exist.

As a pediatrician, when I see a child for attention concerns, I quickly ask about sleep. Separation and divorce can disrupt a child's schedule, and if that disruption leads to poor sleep, this is the first problem to address. Some ADHD diagnostic tools, such as the Vanderbilt Assessment Scales, include questions about anxiety, but if anxiety seems to be playing a role, I'll add a questionnaire such as the Screen for Child Anxiety Related Emotional Disorders form, designed to screen for childhood anxiety. The Patient Health Questionnaire-9 is a similar questionnaire that your child's pediatrician might use to look for depression. If you have any questions or concerns regarding your child's behavior, make sure to discuss them with your child's pediatrician.

During the examination, I always ask my patients about stress too. A child who is being bullied is going to have a hard time paying attention in school. Likewise, a child who is under stress from a separation or divorce is likely to be distracted. That doesn't mean that these children don't also have ADHD, but if nothing is done to address the stress, treating ADHD alone is unlikely to help.

How Can We Help Our Children?

Truth is, disorganization is the natural order of things at the beginning of a breakup. There's moving to consider and, with that, a change in schools, homes, teachers, and friends. A child may simply not be used to the new lifestyle—shoes are kept in different places or they may be left at the other parent's home. New partners enter the mix, and there's an additional home to get used to—so the children are going back and forth not only, say, between Mom and Dad's home but possibly between the homes of their parents' new partners as well. Is it any wonder that homework may be affected, or they can't find their shoes before they leave for school?

Ways to Help Your Child Stay Focused and Organized During Separation or Divorce

Look for ways to help your child stay focused and organized during separation or divorce by doing your best to eliminate any guesswork your child may have to cope with now that you and your partner or spouse are no longer together.

For example,

- Get the child's backpack ready and by the door so that he can just grab it when it's time for school or time to go to the other parent's home.
- Establish an after-school schedule for resting, homework, bathing, and going to sleep at a reasonable time.
- Your child will adjust more easily to the back and forth between homes if both parents coordinate efforts and offer similar schedules.
- Be available to comfort your child when he has meltdowns. Hugs and cuddles work wonders. Implement calming rituals so that your child learns to depend on a proven way to calm down.

A **calming ritual** is a type of ceremony or behavior consisting of specific actions performed in a specific order.

A calming ritual is a behavior you can teach your children that will help them calm down if they are upset or having trouble coping at the moment. Counting before you lose your temper, saying a prayer before bed (or anytime, for that matter), and even singing the "Star-Spangled Banner" before a baseball game are all good examples of rituals that calm or reinforce unity. These are the types of things you can explore and develop with your children to help them stay calm when things seem at their worst.

Cognitive behavioral therapy is a technique that therapists use to help their patients combat anxiety. Basically, it's a method to actively change your thoughts from ones that cause anxiety or agitation and pain to ones that bring on happiness or relaxation. For kids, I often liken it to changing the channel on the TV from a program they don't like to a program that makes them happy. A simple reminder such as "OK, honey, time to change the channel" may be enough to help your child go from ruminating about the changes faced to acceptance. Figure out together what the happy thought is first, then put it into practice—that's part of the ritual.

Deep breathing is an easy calming ritual your child can take anywhere. Figure out a way for it to be fun.

For example, my watch has an app that can read my pulse and reminds me to relax and take long, relaxing breaths for 1 minute. The watch vibrates to signal when it is time to breathe. This serves 2 purposes, and I have been known to take off my watch and put it onto the wrist of a child to teach him this method to calm himself down. The child is amused by the vibration as it prompts him to take the next breath, but it also gets his mind off the problem that is upsetting him as he waits for the vibration to signal that it's time to breathe.

Keeping a journal or blog. Although physically writing in a journal used to be a tried-and-true way to help someone work through crisis—and it is still a great tool—now having your own blog is easy and literally at your fingertips. The blog can be kept private or published and should be monitored by an adult.

Listening to music or dancing. Even the youngest children can listen to songs that distract them and change their mood. A very good adult friend who has a very stressful job just downloaded "Baby Shark" because it makes him laugh. It's the same principle. Find songs that amuse your child or get your child moving. Exercise gets those endorphins moving, and that's when moods change to the positive.

THE SPECIFICS: TELLING SCHOOL-AGED CHILDREN ABOUT THE BREAKUP

When children hit school age, you can be more specific about your decision to separate or divorce. If you can, it's best to be with the other parent when you talk with your child. Again, simple declarative statements are best—for example, "Mommy and Daddy have decided to not live together, but we both love you and will always be here if you need us." This approach works well with older children as well. Ask whether they have some questions and answer them to the best of your ability.

Other professionals suggest an explanation such as "Daddy and Mommy no longer love each other, but we will always love you." It has been my experience that this approach is not comforting to a child.

First, a child reasons, "If you fell out of love with Mommy or Daddy, you might fall out of love with me." It does not make children feel safe and secure to fear that your love for them may change.

Second, it's not uncommon down the road for parents to tell a child, for instance, "I'll always love your Mommy (or Daddy); we just can't live together." Think that one through as well. The word *love* means longevity to a child. They wonder, *"If you love Mommy, why aren't you together?"* or, *"You say you love me. Will we not be able to live together again sometime soon?"*

Co-parenting tip. My suggestion, if you must reinforce your affection for your child's other parent, is to use the term *care about,* rather than *love.* "I will always care about your dad…" calms children. Then they know their parents don't hate each other—and that's what they want to hear.

Talking With Older Children, Aged 9 to 11 Years

Again, if you can, be together when you tell the children of your plans to separate. If you can't be together when you break the news, discuss how it will be presented before telling the children and stick to your agreement. It goes without saying that divorce is confusing for kids. If one parent is telling them one thing, and the other parent is telling them another, they will undoubtedly be confused.

For the sake of the children,

▶ Agree on the approach.
▶ Stick to the facts.
▶ Stick to your agreement.

As children get older, their biggest concern is "How will this breakup affect me? How will my life change?" They want to know things such as "Will I have to move?" "Will I have to leave my friends?" "Will I have to change schools?" "Will I have to share a room?" or "May I take my dog?" The questions that they want answered are not necessarily about the breakup, although that is important information, but, more important, about how their life will change because of this breakup.

Anticipate their questions and have the answers in place before you sit down with them. Explain when they will be with each parent and any other changes they should expect. Do not leave them floundering or guessing what will happen to them. They will fill in the blanks with made-up answers based on their limited experience while being on this earth. If you find you don't have the answers, be honest, but give the impression that you know where to find the answers and you will go to that source immediately and report back.

Lying to the Children About the Breakup

There's a fine line between offering appropriate information and offering inappropriate information about the breakup to your children. The easiest way to know whether the information is important is to ask yourself, "How will knowing this specific information help my children feel safe and secure? Is it developmentally appropriate to their age? Will their knowing 'the truth' at their age calm them? Will it help them understand how their life will change? How will offering this information affect them?"

Eleven-year-old Vanessa came home after school to her mother cutting up her father's clothes and throwing them in the middle of the living room. Under the guise that her child needed to know "the truth," Mother blurted out, "I'm sorry, honey, but your father has left us for another woman. He doesn't want us anymore. He loves her and has gone to live with her. I don't know if we will ever see him again. 99

Of course, the child in the scenario was devastated, and offering information that specific, in that manner, did not help her feel safe and secure when her life seemed to be falling apart. Undermining the other parent, no matter what that parent has done (short of specifically abusing the child in some way), will not help your child cope with the breakup of the family. It's the parents' job to offer comfort to the child, not be at the root of the child's emotional mayhem.

Parents say,

66 *Are you saying I should lie to my child? I think she needs to know what kind of a father she has!* 99

From an emotional standpoint, your child continues to need both parents after the breakup—especially after the breakup! Undermining your child's relationship with the other parent because you have been hurt is not in your child's best interest. Offer only information that will help your child understand what to expect before, during, and after the separation. More information can be offered as the dust settles and as you can see how that additional information is developmentally appropriate for your child and will help your child understand and eventually heal.

Co-parenting tip. Never put a child in the position to find out "the truth" from friends or acquaintances without being prepared. If you can see that your child may find something out that may need to be clarified—for example, neighborhood gossip, an unexpected post on social media—it's best to openly discuss the situation by using age-appropriate language and put your heads together to develop the proper response.

66 *So, you're telling me I should lie to my child!* 99

Truth is, parents tell stories to their children all the time. When children ask tough questions, parents don't necessarily lie, but sometimes they are vague in their answers. You have to remember to respond with developmentally appropriate answers, with the goal of helping the child to feel more secure. "Even though Mommy and Daddy care about each other, too often we were making each other unhappy. We will be better parents for you when we are happy and live separately. And being a good Mommy and Daddy to you is the most important thing for both of us right now."

Take the ever so popular question: Where do babies come from? Most parents don't specifically describe the details of how a baby is created when their 4-year-old asks. Most parents share age-appropriate information that answers the question at that time it is being asked and address the question again as the child gets older and asks more questions. Approach talking about the reasons behind your breakup in exactly the same manner.

Bottom line: although it's important to be honest, it may not be important to be literal. It depends on the age of the child and the information requested. You can say, "Mommy is living in an apartment for a while and you can talk with her anytime you want." You don't have to add "with her boyfriend who she obviously cares about more than us."

Reading Our Middle Schoolers

Middle school is a trying time for children, even if they live in a calm, well-balanced 2-parent home. It is a time when their bodies are changing, they begin to view things sexually, and they are developing a more sophisticated sense of reasoning. They are beginning to understand adult foibles—so if the family broke up because of an affair, domestic violence, mental illness, or addiction issues, they may understand it intellectually, but emotionally, they are still not equipped to cope without direction.

Spotting stress in this age-group is particularly important because this is the age when children start to look outside themselves for solutions to make them feel better when they feel bad. Their friends become really important to them and they can stop sharing information with their parents. Drugs, alcohol, sex, or even suicide is first addressed at this age. Many parents can't believe their middle schooler would look to these solutions—"MY baby drinking?"—but they do. Alcohol is easily accessible at the home of working parents, and this is also the age when parents feel the child is old enough to be left by himself or with other children his same age. On the contrary, the older the child, the more he may need adult supervision and direction, especially if the child is facing a stressful, traumatic event, such as his parent's breakup.

Spotting Stress in Middle Schoolers

Raging hormones are often blamed for preadolescent and adolescent anxieties. Recently, however, scientists are realizing that important changes occur in the brain during the preteen and teen years, and that is what contributes to the moodiness parents see. It is also what may make the preadolescent or adolescent have problems coping with stress. Stress increases feelings of irritability and anger, which can increase the likelihood of emotional outbursts and withdrawing socially. So something traumatic happens in a middle schooler's life and one minute, they can cope; the next, they fall apart. Because the human brain doesn't fully develop until the mid-20s, the only predictable piece is that a middle schooler, or even a teen, is hardwired for emotional instability…

...and then the middle schooler's parents decide to get a divorce.

Common reactions to stress are experienced by middle schoolers and teens—physical ailments, displays of distress, moodiness, hopelessness, changes in appetite or sleep patterns, lost interest in something previously enjoyed, and lack of focus—but sometimes, parents are so wrapped up in their own breakup drama, they miss the cues, and their reactions exacerbate the problems, rather than defuse.

For example, "ongoing complaints of headaches and stomachaches" are often the physical manifestation of stress and anxiety. Instead of sitting down and exploring what could be going on with a middle schooler, a busy parent may suggest, "Take some Tylenol." End of story.

Displays of distress translates to what may seem like an overreaction to when things don't go the child's way. Being snappy is one thing, but if snappiness progresses to screaming in response to being asked to do normal chores or duties, it's a signal your child is in distress. In response, an exasperated parent might protest right back: "Why are you being so crabby?" But it's a rhetorical question. The child doesn't perceive the parent is asking what is wrong but sees it as a way to find fault or label the child negatively. And, at face value, the child doesn't really know the answer. These children's lives have just been turned upside down, and nothing was solved by their parent's approach.

Lost interest in something previously enjoyed translates into your child suddenly refusing to go to school or possibly sports practice. When prompted that it's time to leave, the child makes excuses or out-and-out says, "I don't want to go." The parent then demands the child's attendance. Instead of recognizing this as a symptom of stress, the parent tries to cut through the perceived power struggle and yells, "You're going! No arguing!" Again, no solution was found, and the discord continues.

Lack of focus translates into not listening in class or not completing homework. Ironically, a note home alerting the parent that assignments are not being completed might be the first clue that the parent has about child distress. Rather than search for the reasons behind the behavior, the parent restricts the child from things that bring him joy—and, again, as a result, the child continues to be in distress without tools to relieve the pressure.

This is when parents must stand back and realize that they are not the only ones facing the disruption of a breakup. They are not the only ones facing big changes, coupled with feelings of rejection, anger, or betrayal. But unlike their children, they have the life experience to know they need help. The parents can make the choice to be proactive, meditate, or go to counseling, whereas a child must look to the parents for guidance, parents who, in the midst of their own pain, may not have the ability to connect all the dots for their child.

Ways to Help Your Middle Schoolers Deal With Their Emotions

▶ **Give your middle schooler permission to be upset or angry.** When children act out, parents often tell their kids, "Don't be angry," or, "Don't be upset." However, if at any other time anger or disappointment are justified, it's when your parents break up. Telling children not to react in a justified manner discounts their feelings and only adds to their frustration. Let them know that anger or sorrow in response to the breakup is normal, but some ways to cope are better than others.

▶ **Demonstrate patience and coping skills firsthand.** Now is the time middle schoolers are learning to properly respond to frustration, anger, resentment, love, envy, and jealousy—all the emotions that trouble us all—and they are taking their cues from you. If you are reacting in anger to something relating to the breakup—say, their other parent has lied to you—and you're throwing a tantrum—screaming, yelling, and threating to hurt someone or breaking things—don't be surprised if they (or a child of any age) react just like you are.

This is your opportunity to model positive ways to deal with stress or disappointment. Let them see you take a breath when angry or meditate or go for a run. Show them how to talk about their anger in a constructive way, without sitting in blame or fault, but constructively dealing with one's own feelings. This can be trying because frustrated adults don't necessarily respond properly, but knowing that your child is watching may be an incentive to set the stage more constructively.

Try something such as "I'm really frustrated right now, and I think I'll go for a run. When I get home, if you would like to talk about it, I'll be here to answer any of your questions, and we can look for solutions together."

▶ **Reinforce it's not their fault.** You might imagine that at this age, your child would have a clear sense that he is not the reason for his parents' breakup, but when faced with tragedy, we all wonder whether there was anything we could have done differently, even when that question makes little sense. Preadolescent and adolescent brains are still maturing, and any people who have ever been preadolescents or adolescents might remember that their thoughts can be ruled by their emotions.

▶ **Recognize that they are likely to turn to friends for support.** Experts agree that peers influence a middle schooler's behavior more than parents, but those experts are also quick to point out that in times of crisis, if the proper groundwork has been laid, preadolescents and adolescents look to their parents for counsel and direction. Therefore, don't take it personally when your middle schooler looks to friends for solace and advice—it's natural and normal at this age, but be available to discuss all concerns.

▶ **Don't take it for granted that everything is OK because they are not talking.** Middle school is the age that children begin to experiment with drugs, alcohol, and sex. All 3 things are forms of self-medication, and if children are in an emotional whirlwind, they are candidates for experimentation. If you are drinking too much to cope, don't be surprised if your kids look for the same answer.

Talking With Your Middle Schoolers About the Breakup

Children of middle school age will tell you they want to know everything and act as if they deserve to know and are old enough to understand, but volunteer too much information and you will undermine their personal security; plus, their relationship with you or their other parent may be affected if you assign your personal sense of fault and blame to any explanation. Middle school children may not be able to separate their actions from their parents' actions and, once again, blame themselves for things that are out of their control.

With that in mind, when talking with middle schoolers about a potential break-up, focus on what is known. Will these children live with one parent and visit the other, or will they go back and forth between homes regularly? Will they share a room? Will their pets go back and forth with them? How will their friends know where they are? Will they have to change schools? Will they continue to participate in their extracurricular activities in the same manner as before? Who will take them to practices and games? All these questions are important to children this age. Know the answers before you speak with them.

Reading Our Teens

From Boss to Mentor

Much of what was discussed earlier, in the Reading Our Middle Schoolers section, about spotting stress pertains to teenagers as well. The biggest difference from successfully dealing with a middle schooler to successfully dealing with a teen is simply *approach*. Brain development continues, and the ability to read and deal with stressful situations continues to be a challenge.

Parents are used to being the boss, telling their children what to do and how it will be. This works because preadolescents are just learning to form opinions and still depend on their parents for their daily needs, but striving for independence and forming their own opinions is the natural order of things for teens. One of the greatest obstacles a parent must face when raising a teen is finding a way to stay connected at a time when the teen is naturally pulling away. Add that parents often rely on their own memories of their teen years to empathize with what their teen is going through, and parents could easily alienate their teen during a conversation, rather than bring their teen closer.

❝ *My parents broke up when I was a teenager, and I remember how it was....* **❞**

Most parents truly believe they are well-informed and know exactly how their teen must feel, but studies show they may not. A Northwestern Medicine study likens memory to a game of telephone and showed that memories tend to distort over time. Each time you recall a memory, the brain adds facts that may not have been available at the time the memory was formed but are available now, so the recalled memory shifts. "I remember how it was…" may not be true at all. You may have added your perceptions based on your adult experience, and those perceptions may not pertain to your child.

Plus, you must consider, from the impact of social media to texting as the primary mode of communication, things are not the same for your teen as they were when you were a teenager. If you find yourself saying, "I remember when I was your age…," as the introduction to understanding how teens must feel about the breakup, rethink your approach. You may not, and your teen may turn off when hearing those words.

There's more. Teens can be naturally narcissistic in their outlook and believe their feelings are unique. Knowing that fact, ironically, empathizing with "knowing how they feel," can actually be misunderstood and translate to diminishing their feelings, especially if you come off old-fashioned. A teen will be far more open to your direction if you approach a conversation as a mentor, available for consultation, rather than as a boss. Listening and really hearing your teen's concerns about your breakup is more important than attempting to empathize with your teen's plight.

In other words, ask how teens feel; don't tell them how it was—and then listen to what they tell you.

Questions Your Teens Might Ask

All that said, there are some common questions teens ask once they learn that their parents intend to break up. It starts and ends with how all the changes specifically affect *them*. Know the answers *before* you start the conversation.

Again, if at all possible, both parents should be present when telling the kids about their upcoming separation or divorce. If that's impossible, the parent present must talk from personal point of view only. That parent should not speak for the other parent or speculate the reasons behind the other parent's actions. Let other parents speak for themselves when they have their conversation with their children.

WHY IS THIS HAPPENING?

It's imperative to be honest, but the details behind why your marriage fell apart, regardless of whose fault it was, are really better left private, particularly if cheating was involved. Even though your teen may demand to know the truth, some details are simply not the teen's business and, if known, will increase teen anxiety and impair teen ability to cope. There is still the risk of older teens blaming themselves for the demise of the family but also feeling obliged to take sides, so whatever information is offered must be true but fair and not undermine their other parent. Concentrate on what you know to be true—that maintaining adult relationships can be a challenge, but the love the parents share for their children and teens remains constant and will never change.

DO I HAVE TO MOVE?

If teens have to move, be honest. Explain where they will live and why the move is necessary. Answer their top questions, such as "Will I have a room?" "Who will take me to school?" and "When will I see my other parent?"

WITH WHOM WILL I LIVE? DO I HAVE A CHOICE?

Although a collaborative approach seems to work best with teens, one of my favorite reminders to divorcing parents is "A voice is not a choice." Teens want their opinions heard and seriously considered, but you are still the parent and the final decision where your teen will live lies with you parents.

> 66 *My husband and I have just told our 15-year-old son that we are getting a divorce. He screamed at the top of his lungs, 'I'm going to live with Dad!' I'm heartbroken. We were together when we broke the news, and I thought we did everything right, but I still lost.* 99

It has been my experience that when a child reaches anywhere from 13 to 15 years old, the child, now a teen, tends to gravitate to the like-gendered parent. It often hurts the other parent, feeling as if one has "lost" the battle and not understanding why the teen made such a choice. The parent agonizes about what could have been done differently, considering bribing the teen with puppies or video games, but the truth is, it's nothing personal. It's simply biology. Teen sons gravitate to Dad. They can talk about the game, changing bodies, and "guy stuff." The same is true for girls of this age and their mothers.

But just because teens say they want to live with a particular parent does not mean it is best for their emotional development. Children and teens need both parents—each offering something unique. Taking their teen's wishes into consideration, the parents may want to present a parenting plan that allows their teen more time with the like-gendered parent but also supplies adequate time to maintain a loving relationship with the other parent.

At What Age Can a Child Legally Choose?

> 66 *My child is old enough to know his own mind and choose which parent he wants to live with.* 99

"At what age can a child legally choose?" is a question I am often asked when mediating parents who wish to separate. They are usually locked in a battle of wills and have forgotten what their primary concern should be—offering their children a soft place to fall in the midst of the chaos of divorce. The correct answer to what age can my child legally choose is "It varies from state to state." In California, where I practice, the answer is that a teen may ask to be heard by a mediator or judge at the age of 14 years. Notice that the law does not state the teen can choose at 14. And the law goes on to require that the *teen* requests to be heard—not the parents. It goes on to specifically say that a mediator or judge will take the teen's opinion into account when deciding on a parenting plan; however, the professionals working with the teen take this responsibility very seriously. Teens of 14 may choose a parent who they believe to be "cool." This might be the parent who lets them stay out until 10 o'clock on a school night or use drugs or alcohol or who doesn't care whether they do their homework regularly. So because a child can be heard doesn't necessarily mean the professional will accept the child's recommendation as the perfect answer. Professionals listen to the child's concerns, but lots of things are considered before a final decision is made.

More important, my answer to this question usually begins with "If you have backed your child into a corner and are asking him which parent he wants to live with, your family has much bigger problems than can be decided by a judge." Asking a child to choose is rooted in a parent's selfishness, insecurity, and desire to "win." Children deserve both their parents—not one or the other—and should *never* have to choose which parent they prefer. If you are suggesting they do so, you have done your child a disservice.

Where Do We Go From Here?

Remember that just because you told your child once, no matter your child's age, about your decision to separate or divorce, you are far from done. Children will need to hear things over and over again as it makes sense to them. "Why are you breaking up? Where am I going to live? What could you have done differently? What is going to change?" You may get tired of repeating yourself and feel tempted to yell, "The same thing I said last time!" Don't. Your breakup is a huge event for your children to process. As they grow and develop, they will need to process it in new and different ways. Your patience now may be among the most helpful things you have to offer your children. Be kind. Be patient. Be present. This was your idea, not theirs.

5

Facing the Transition: Moving From We to Me

Some people believe holding on and hanging in there are signs of great strength. However, there are times when it takes much more strength to know when to let go and then do it.

ANN LANDERS

Separation and divorce usually involve some balance of relief and fear. The act of finally ending a relationship usually follows months to years of pain and stress, and being able to move on with life may feel like that moment when you realize you were trying to drive with the parking brake partly engaged. On the other hand, even the most dysfunctional relationship comes with a sense of familiarity. We like knowing what to expect, even when it's unpleasant, and separation and divorce disrupt our lives massively. They threaten our very identities. At the time of my separation, my entire sense of self was wrapped up in the words *husband, father,* and *family.* Who was I if I was not someone's spouse? How did I reply when someone asked where my kids were or how they were doing? "With their mom" and "Quite poorly" were the honest answers, but then who has time to address the inevitable follow-up questions?

Transitioning From Living Together to Living Apart

As a couple, you build. You establish a home, intertwine your finances, have children together, and weave a shared reality that comes to define your life. Now it seems as if a storm has come through and torn down everything you made. You will rebuild. What you make now will reflect you and your children, your dreams and your needs. It will be a work in progress, and it will not be perfect, but it will be yours.

During this period, I sought out therapy. I remember asking my therapist, "I know that eventually I'm going to feel better, so can we just get to that part?" He shook his head. "No," he said, "you're right, you will feel better, but the only way to get there is to be here first." It was frustrating, but he was very, very right.

Mental Separation: You're Not a Couple Anymore

On our first date, my ex-husband looked into my eyes— I could see he was thinking about something. As I watched the mental wheels turning, I thought he was going to say something romantic. What I got was "So what kind of music do you like?"

I laughed, "If I answer correctly, do I get the big prize?"

"Well, sorta," he answered. He would listen only to country music, and, evidently, that was a bone of contention during his first marriage.

When we got a divorce, I realized that I had listened to only country music for 23 years. I liked country, but it's only a sampling of what I like and what's on my current playlist. I have more diverse tastes, always have, but, evidently, I forgot, and, slowly, my preferences became what my husband liked. That took a while to settle in—to realize what I had done without really knowing it. The transition from married to single was far more difficult than I had realized—and I'm a therapist.

Sleeping alone was not the problem, although in talking with thousands of couples facing a breakup over the years, that is one of the things most noted in the transition. For me, it was just getting used to the fact I was no longer a married person— after 23 years, everything was in reference to my husband, all my memories, all my stories, and if I did not refer to him in my conversation, I found I had very little to pass on. My friends would comment, "You must really miss Larry. That's all you talk about." I did miss him. I didn't miss his cheating, but I missed our life together, and almost all my adult history was intertwined with him, so if I talked about the kids, he was there. If I talked about the dog that was allergic to absolutely everything, he was holding him down as I gave him the shots. If I talked about my mother's passing or the financial hardships that followed or moving 8 times in 9 years because he was a building contractor—there were just no single memories, and that gave the wrong impression. It looked as if I was stuck—and, in a way, I was, but I was also moving on, creating new memories and a new life. It just took a while.

How Long Does It Take?

Professionals say it takes at least 2 years to successfully move on. I have found that it is directly proportionate to the trauma one has faced. If it is an amicable divorce, the transitionary period from together to apart seems shorter. If one is traumatized by an affair, or the death of a child or anything, actually, the time it takes to feel whole and think single after a breakup takes longer.

Many just want to move on, but the danger of moving on too quickly is that it will eventually catch up with you. If you have intertwined your families—your new spouse's children with yours—and there is another breakup, you will set your children reeling through yet another divorce. That's why it's best to give yourself time to breathe, to reflect, and to realize who you are now. There's really no hurry, even though, in the midst of it all, you may want to find that new normal as quickly as possible.

Tips for the Transition (For the Parent)

Remember Who You Are

Like me, lots of people lose themselves in their marriage. Although I always worked, my identity so completely merged into being a wife and mother that even my work centered around my family. As I became more known as an expert on combining households and founded a nonprofit organization, Bonusfamilies, that offered parents help in navigating the trials of family blending, once I was divorced, my personal life was affected, and so was my work. I feared that because I was divorced, people would no longer see my advice as credible. My identity as part of a couple disappeared, and I wasn't sure who I was as an individual anymore either.

This is a common dilemma for many people who choose to break up. Figuring out who you are as a single person, transitioning from we to me and finding that new normal—while the kids look on—is not for the faint of heart.

And…it takes time. It takes self-exploration, a lot of soul-searching; it may take therapy, but if you want to offer your children, and possibly a new partner in the future, a whole person, you have to find yourself again. You must be true to yourself to be truly happy.

How Do You Do That?

Once you separate, you often hear that you need to revisit the things you loved to do before your relationship—remind yourself of and relish the person you used to be. This time around, I wasn't sure I was that person anymore. I suppose aspects of the old me were still there, but I felt as if my most current life experiences were the most relevant to my personal growth and the most helpful to others. I just had to learn to approach life from my own point of view. Because I was a mother, my primary priority was always the best interest of the children, but my children were all adults by this time. Add "empty nester" to "divorced woman," and we were looking at an identity crisis in the first degree.

But this was not my first rodeo. I had been divorced before this marriage at a completely different time in my life. Then I was a divorced parent of a very young child, and, like so many in that position, I worked outside the home Monday through Friday, 8:00 am to 5:00 pm, but I rarely got home before 6:00 pm. I had always been the primary breadwinner, and now that I was getting a divorce and going from a 2-income home to a 1-income home, I had to work even harder. My life consisted of getting myself ready for work, getting my daughter ready for child care, coming home, feeding her, bathing her, reading her a bedtime story, and then, both of us exhausted, collapsing into bed. It was true, her father saw her every other weekend like clockwork, but there was one big difference between then and now—I simply didn't have the time for an identity crisis. I was living on overdrive. My daughter's welfare and co-parenting with someone with whom I did not get along were my 2 primary concerns. I appeared centered but driven. People would always ask me how I did it. I had all those balls up in the air. I was anything but centered.

Creating a New Normal

On examination, something that has registered very strongly is that recovery from a breakup, both then and now, is not that different emotionally. There are different concerns for each stage of your life, but, in each, you still have to start over. You still have to create a new normal.

When I was moving from a 2-parent home to a 1-parent home, my first step to create that new normal was learning to ask for help. That was not easy for me. As a young mother, I felt as if everything was on my shoulders, but I simply couldn't do it all myself and I knew it. I relied heavily on my mother for a caring ear and to help with my daughter when I couldn't get home in time. The child care I used charged a dollar a minute if I was late! The ability to call my mom and say, "Please go pick up Anee, because I'm stuck in traffic," took the weight off my shoulders, but many do not have the luxury of having extended family nearby. If we got along better, my daughter's father would have been a likely candidate to ask for help, but we were struggling to co-parent and he lived in a different city that was 50 miles away.

Other Places to Look for Help During Separation or Divorce

- **Join a divorce support group in your community.** I know I am a mental health professional, but I have to admit, joining a support group is not something I often do. Intellectually, I know that any recovery process will be more successful by surrounding yourself with people you can talk with when things get tough, but I wasn't a joiner by nature. However, my friend found a support group listed in her son's school newsletter and dared me to go. Hearing their stories and offering mine helped normalize the experience and realize firsthand that everyone, including professionals, struggles to get on the other side of a breakup. I got to know the members of the group and traded for help. I didn't have a lot of time during the week, but I did on the weekends, particularly on the weekends my daughter was with her dad. On those nights, I made dinners for the week and froze them—I learned to make 2 lasagnas and trade for babysitting or simply for dinners when we were all too tired to cook after a long day. The barter system among friends is a necessary evil when times are hard and funds are scarce.

- **Check out online forums.** I was not into online dating at the time, but I was into going back to school and taking online classes to further my education. I met some wonderful people interested in the same things in which I was, and they did not live too far away to meet for a drink when I had some downtime. They became an excellent resource for everything from confidant to babysitter, to supportive study partner.

- **Get creative.** Some of the people I met along the way were in the same boat as me— working, sleep-deprived, and trying to figure out their lives, but they had extended family willing to help their friends. Your new friends may not have the time to fill in when you need help, but their grandmothers might. My best friend's grandmother knew my children since birth and became an irreplaceable resource for help. Forming a support system is all about networking—and giving more than you take.

Second, I needed to weed through my old friends who did not want to hang around with a single woman, and I needed to find the friends who didn't mind me being a third wheel.

Unfortunately, most breakups involve some level of rejection, but it's not just from a former partner. It could be friends, relatives who believe they know the true story, church groups, the Parent-Teacher Association, or anyone who feels compelled to take sides, gossip, or judge your actions or the actions of your ex. Even though most know better, very few put their best foot forward during a breakup. I have found that a necessary part of transitioning from married to single is developing a strong personal sense of self coupled with a very thick skin.

> **❝** *My husband and I live in a very small town. We are motorcycle enthusiasts, and we each have a bike of our own. When we were married, we rode with a group of husbands and wives every weekend. My ex and I decided to break up, and I just found out that the wives don't want me riding alone with their husbands. For some reason, the guys don't care if my ex rides alone, but the women care if I do.* **❞**

Or…

> 66 *My now ex-husband and I were best friends with his boss and her husband. They were our go-to couple when we went on an excursion, wine tasting or just hanging out. Now that we have separated, his boss announced it had been fun, but her allegiance is to my ex— and, besides, they work together. His boss was my best friend.* 99

Or…

> 66 *I'm not choosing sides. You were both my friend when you were together, and you will both remain my friend now that you are apart….* 99

It's not uncommon for friends to feel as if they must take sides when couples part ways, especially if they stood on the sidelines and watched while a sordid scenario played out. Perhaps one of the divorcing partners cheated and the other was devastated, or the other was a lifelong friend and it was not comfortable to maintain the friendship with both sides. You find either allegiance or distrust at the root of a requirement to choose. One of the most common breakup questions I receive from readers is "Whose side should I be on?"

Unfortunately, there is no right answer. Each situation is its own story, but it is possible to take a stand and not take sides. Often that stance infuriates one side or the other, and your choice is removed from the table—but more often than not, you will be respected for remaining neutral, and both sides will be grateful for your friendship once the dust settles.

Juggling then becomes the order of the day….

> 66 *I'm throwing a surprise 40th birthday for my husband this year. Our best friends just got a divorce, and I am struggling with who to invite. We met them as a couple 10 years ago. If I invite one, the other will be hurt. Both are our friends….* 99

And both can remain your friends. Rather than struggle with a decision based on something *they* chose to do, let them make this decision as well. Invite them both, informing them that they both have been invited, and let *them* decide who should attend. Clarify that if they both attend, they are expected to be respectful of each other in your home.

Third, professionals caution parents about involving their children in their dating lives. You often hear "Don't introduce the kids until you know it will be a serious relationship." The thought behind this is that serious relationships last longer than casual dates. Your children need consistency, and if they get attached to a "friend" who quickly moves on, each time they will feel as if they are facing yet another divorce. The emotional upheaval can be devastating.

The psychological complications of introducing multiple partners to your children have been documented in countless studies. It has been found that as a result of multiple breakups of their parents, children may have difficulty forming long-lasting relationships, and, as children mature, they learn to withhold affection for fear that the person they love will eventually leave.

Here is the rub: while you may be attempting to move on, your children may still be in mourning and need your calm understanding to help them through the breakup. This is an important distinction. Just because you are ready to move on does not mean your children are ready.

Coping With Grief of Separation or Divorce

We go through different stages of coping when dealing with any tragedy. The renowned expert on death and dying, Elisabeth Kübler-Ross, MD, designed a model in her book *On Death and Dying* to help those dealing with grief better frame and identify what they may be feeling. I include this model in just about every book I write about coping with a breakup because it is so relevant to working through the pain. It consists of 5 stages—similar models have added a stage here and there, and I have adjusted those stages to conform to the needs of those going through a breakup, but I add something different here—noting how your children may feel as they pass through the stages of grief along with you. It's important to note, however, that not everyone goes through each stage in the order listed, and sometimes, in the course of healing, we revisit or skip a stage. Everyone experiences grief in a unique fashion, but most face these stages at some point during their journey, parents and children alike.

❶ Denial

Parent: This stage is filled with disbelief. Your partner wants to leave or has just left, but you think your partner's mind will change: "This can't really be happening. He'll come to his senses and come home."

Child: Disbelief is also at the forefront. The child is shocked by the news but trusts the parent to reconsider. Trust is an important component here. A breakup shatters a child's trust in a parent or in what the child thought was the security of their union.

❷ Anger—For Example, Resentment

Parent: You are angry about the situation, about the pain you feel, and about the pain the kids feel. It's difficult to control your emotions, particularly in relationship to your ex, because you are so furious. Blame and fault also play a big part in this stage: "It's his fault! Look what he has done!"

Child: Anger is a very common emotion that exemplifies anger, of course, but for children, anger also masks their sadness. Children may lash out as the reality of the breakup registers. At this stage, it would not be uncommon for them to blame a parent or possibly try to take the blame themselves.

Coping With Grief of Separation or Divorce *(continued)*

③ **Bargaining**

Parent: You try to negotiate to change the final outcome. For example, "I'll change if you don't leave," or, "If you come back, I'll do this…."

Child: The inner blame game continues: "Maybe Dad or Mom left because of something I did. I'll be a better kid if you come home."

④ **Depression**

Parent: You begin to realize that things will not change. The breakup is permanent, with no reconciliation. You may have mood swings, feel down, not want to go to work or get out of bed, or find that your memory is waning, that nothing seems right. Because it has been some time since your initial breakup, friends or family, or even your kids, may ask, "What's wrong?" and not connect that your depression is a result of your divorce. You may not connect the dots either and wonder, *"What's wrong with me?"*

Child: You will see the same reasoning in children; however, it translates into losing interest in extracurricular activities they once loved or refusing to go to school. Homework is affected, with lots of crying and distancing themselves. Children notoriously cannot connect the dots as to why they feel sad or angry or down, so simply asking, "What's wrong?" may get you a blank stare or a shrug. Plus, time moves slower for a child; a week feels like a month to children, so they may get impatient with their parents' struggle to get on the other side of the breakup and lash out, clam up, or cry for what seems like no reason.

⑤ **Acceptance**

Parents: Although you haven't forgotten what happened, you are able to forgive and move forward. You realize you must let go of the negative thoughts and emotions you equate with your ex, and you are ready to co-parent with that person in the best interest of the children you share.

Child: Acceptance, as a concept, can be fleeting for children. The finality of their parents' divorce is a difficult pill to swallow. Most children, no matter their age, fantasize about their parents getting back together. At one point, they may appear to accept the reality of the situation, but something may come up, a milestone, an old memory, or an upcoming holiday, and they revert to one of the previous steps, most commonly step 2, "Anger—For Example, Resentment," or step 4, "Depression."

Just remember, it's healthy for a child to see a parent navigate pain and grief in a productive manner. If you take a proactive approach to the grieving process you must go through after a breakup, you are offering your children a guide to dealing with their own personal traumas both now and in the future. If you trip a little along the way, it's fine. The key is to have a plan to pick yourself up again and let your children know it and see you trying firsthand.

Co-parenting tip. Finally, the greatest gift you can offer your child at the juncture of creating a new normal is your patience.

Understand that this breakup is the parents' choice, and, because of that, it may take your children longer to accept the inevitable. A parent can move on from an ex, but children cannot move on from their parent. They struggle with their allegiances because they love both parents. If a child knows that one parent, in particular, caused the breakup, the child will struggle with the love for that parent as opposed to with the disappointment in that parent.

The Practical Side of Grief

Unfortunately, many panic when facing trauma and don't give themselves time to grieve. They begin a campaign to get over it, thinking that's the way to move on. Some people are lucky enough to afford a therapist. Others will find comfort in talking with friends, family, or spiritual advisers. Look and see if there is a support group in your area you can attend. It will all help, of course, but grieving the loss of your relationship is a necessary part of the process. It sets the course for the next stage of your life—and you will find that if you do not sufficiently grieve, it will be difficult to move forward.

To drive this observation home, on a personal note, my mother died quite tragically when I was in my early 40s, and I was having trouble moving through the grieving process. I thought I should be adjusting quicker, and the physical symptoms I was facing—stomach problems and an inability to sleep—prompted me to go to a doctor. He very wisely asked whether I had faced anything "out of the ordinary for me" in the past few months, and when I explained that I had, he prescribed medication. But the medication made me feel flat and really didn't help with the emotional loss, which was at the root of the physical problems. At my next appointment, my doctor and I decided the medication was not for me and I would fare better in talk therapy. For me, that's when the grieving process began.

❝I went to therapy. It doesn't work.**❞**

Therapy works, but it's not an instant fix, and it works only if you are invested and have patience with the process—and you feel comfortable to tell the truth. It will take a while to feel better. If you find a therapist you trust, enlist the therapist's help to not only deal with your feelings regarding your breakup but also design a "survival plan" for the future.

Dealing With the Aftermath: What Is Your Personal "Survival Plan"?

When addressing any challenge, I am of the mind that we need a goal for our end result and a plan to reach that goal, something to hold in our mind to remind us of who we want to be after the dust settles and how we want to get there. Without a plan and a goal, we flounder. Depending on time to heal the wound is fine, but there is no construct to the process. You are at the mercy of time, dodging the emotional bullets thrown at you as your recover without shelter from the pain of the breakup process. Even if the goal is merely "I don't want to hurt anymore," what is the plan to no longer feel that way? It usually begins with finding proactive ways to cope with stress that *really* work for you—and that may take some soul-searching and experimentation.

Coping With Stress

Meditation

❝ *I remember a time when I was in college, driving somewhere with my family. They were driving me nuts. Rather than lose my temper, I closed my eyes and began to meditate in the back seat. They all laughed hysterically, especially my dad, trying to goad me into an argument. It didn't work. I had a tool to stay calm.* **❞**

Numerous studies have documented the benefits of meditation, from real medical proof of how it can reduce stress and anxiety to improving sleep, improving memory, and making you a kinder, gentler person. But the true beauty of meditation as a calming tool is that it is available to you at just about any time, and you can meditate just about anywhere. When you meditate, you are taking an active role in your own mental health.

❝ *I've tried meditation. I can't sit still that long and think about nothing.* **❞**

To meditate properly, you have to sit quietly, but there's more to it than "thinking about nothing." The problem is that it is so easy, some people simply miss the benefits. With quite a few different approaches to mediation, you may have to experiment a little to find the approach that works best for you. Each is designed for a different purpose. Here are just a few.

▶ **Focused attention meditation, or mantra meditation,** asks you to clear your mind of thoughts and distractions by concentrating on an object or a mandala or possibly using a calming sound, or *mantra*, such as "Om" or humming.

▶ **Open-monitoring meditation, also known as awareness meditation,** again, uses breathing as a center, but it also suggests a widened observation of the environment around you. You allow thoughts to comfortably pass through your mind, bringing your attention back to your breath as a way to calm and center yourself.

While you are doing all this breathing and relaxing without really trying, your heart is slowing, you are reducing your blood pressure, and the production of cortisol, the drug produced by your body during stress, is reduced.

► For those who have trouble calming themselves, there's **guided meditation.** Here a calming voice guides you through the meditation process. A guided meditation starts by suggesting you gently relax each muscle, beginning at your head and ending at your toes. At that point, there may be a suggestion to visualize a warm light or follow a story, creating a peaceful distraction from the day. Many use guided meditations as a way to calm their mind and fall asleep. Countless guided meditations are available for free online. Listen to a few, and find the style and voice that you find soothing.

► **Loving-kindness meditation.** This type of meditation has its origin in ancient Buddhist teachings but has been adjusted to Western culture sensibilities as a way to center one's self and strengthen feelings of kindness and connection. Very recent clinical studies document that loving-kindness meditation improves one's overall sense of well-being and increases one's ability to feel empathy and compassion, something that could be very useful to battling exes, who are searching for common ground to aid them in problem-solving.

How Do You Meditate?

It may help if you find a teacher to guide you through the meditation process the first few times, but, for informational purposes only, meditation is most often done sitting up straight in a comfortable chair. Some ancient practices suggest you sit on a comfortable pillow with your legs crossed, but because the premise is to relax, just sit somewhere comfortably. I wouldn't suggest that you lie down, because you may fall asleep. If that's your goal, lying down is just fine.

Here is where the different approaches to meditation come into play. All are methods to quiet your mind and start by simply closing your eyes and mentally following the rhythm of your breathing. But, at this point, some methods introduce sounds or chants (mantras) to maintain focus. Loving-kindness mediation is more visual in its method and suggests you imagine people who love you standing at your right and then at your left. That is why I suggest you do some research into the type of meditation you want to practice. The methodologies are all slightly different, but the end goal is the same: quieting your mind and relaxing.

How Long Should You Meditate?

It is suggested that beginning meditators start slow, meditating for 3 to 5 minutes at first and progressing to longer sessions as they become more proficient in the practice. Loving-kindness meditation suggests meditating for 15 minutes each time, while the transcendental meditation techniques suggest meditating for 20 minutes twice a day, but don't let that overwhelm you. Meditation should be a calming practice, with added benefits when performed regularly. That means meditate for as long as you feel comfortable.

Exercise

Physical activity helps the production of endorphins produced in the brain, and when endorphins are present, you just feel better. Walking at a quick pace, running, swimming, playing tennis, or playing any quick-paced sporting activity increases the heart rate, produces those endorphins, and helps you forget about the stresses of the day.

Like meditation, exercise can help calm you and keep you centered, but it also improves your sleep, helps fight depression, and reduces anxiety. It starts with a few simple steps—literally. Try easy things, such as a walk around the block after work or on the weekends. If you aren't exercising because the kids are home, get everyone walking. Build up your fitness level gradually.

Any form of exercise can help improve your health and reduce the stress in your life. For most healthy adults, the US Department of Health and Human Services recommends at least 150 minutes a week of moderate aerobic activity, such as that walk around the block, or 75 minutes a week of vigorous aerobic activity, say, you progress to jogging around the block. You can also combine moderate activity and vigorous activity, and don't forget to incorporate light weights to keep the bones strong.

Sound like too much? Don't get overwhelmed. The goal is to reduce stress, and any form of exercise is beneficial. Experiment and do what you love. After trying all sorts of exercise methods, I found I love to walk outside, but I will avoid exercising if I have to walk inside on an elliptical or treadmill. I do not like gyms, but I love yoga classes. I love to dance, so in a pinch, I have been known to put on music I like and dance my heart out—alone—with weights in both hands. After a half hour of that, I am exhausted and nothing seems to bother me— even a surly ex with no tact or timing.

The key is to set aside the time and do it. Again, like with meditation, start out slow. That 75-minute vigorous exercise suggestion breaks down to about 10 minutes a day.

Alcohol and Drugs: How Much Is Too Much?

Alcohol use and drug use begin as diversions from "the problem," but, if you are not careful, they can become the problem. Drinking is legal and marijuana is legal in some states; therefore, partaking in these diversions becomes a problem only when it is excessive. If you are going to use alcohol, it's your job as parents to demonstrate firsthand how to partake responsibly. Basically, that means having a glass of wine with dinner is fine. Drinking 4 glasses of wine until you fall off your chair is not.

During child custody interviews, children have often told me that their parent's alcohol or drug use scares them, but parents who use drugs or alcohol to excess don't necessarily believe that their children are fazed by their behavior. But they are, and it's not for the reason you think. If a parent is impaired, the child agonizes, "If something happens (such as a fire, or an accident, or their parents' divorce), who will take care of me?" Because a child's world revolves around only the child, the child feels alone, frightened, and unsafe when a parent is under the influence. But, mostly, kids have told me it's the unpredictability of what their parent might do. Children of parents who use alcohol to excess have said that they are always waiting for the other shoe to drop. That fight-or-flight reaction kicks in, the natural reaction when someone has anxiety—and that keeps that person on alert, never able to fully relax.

Most parenting plans offer parents enough downtime to party or date when their kids are not around. If you find it difficult not to drink when your children are present, that indicates a problem.

The use of alcohol influences your ability to communicate with your child's other parent. Alcohol exacerbates emotions, both positive and negative. If you are happy, alcohol increases that happy emotion. If you are angry, vengeful, or frustrated, alcohol also increases those emotions. That means if there are unresolved issues between co-parents, being under the influence of alcohol will not help solve the problems; odds are it will only make things worse. If you feel as if you are drinking more than you should, reach out to someone for help.

When Domestic Violence Is Part of a Custody Case

Almost all the domestic violence I have seen when working on custody cases involves alcohol or drugs. When people are drunk or high, they simply do not have the ability to stand back, analyze a situation, and use their best judgment to solve a problem. And, as previously mentioned, alcohol intensifies emotions. Things may spiral out of control, and this can easily begin what is known as the "cycle of abuse." Because friends understand your pain firsthand, a friend may easily take your side and not tell you when you're thinking incorrectly. No new insight, and the conversation is closed—hence, "closed conversation." Friends are great support, but a therapist will remain objective.

Understanding the "Cycle of Abuse"

US government statistics suggest 95% of domestic violence cases involve women survivors of male partners. Research studies also tell us that many violent relationships follow a common pattern. This pattern or cycle is referred to as the "cycle of abuse" and was first popularized in the 1970s by an American psychologist, Lenore Edna Walker. The cycle of abuse has 4 basic phases. Other, more recent, models break the cycles down further, but, for reason of explanation, the following phases mark the cycle of abuse as it pertains to intimate partner (domestic) violence:

1. **Tension-building phase.** Survivors of domestic violence describe this phase as if they are walking on eggshells or constantly waiting for the other shoe to drop. Tension builds over issues everyone faces, such as financial concerns, disciplining the children, or job woes. Verbal abuse starts, and the survivor attempts to dodge a bullet by pleasing the perpetrator or avoiding the perpetrator when that person is home. Tension eventually reaches the boiling point and physical abuse begins.

2. **Acute battering phase.** The physical violence is usually triggered by an external event or by a whim of the perpetrator, not the behavior of the survivor. The attack is unpredictable, and the intensity of abuse may accelerate with time.

3. **Reconciliation, or honeymoon phase.** This phase begins with the perpetrator's embarrassment and remorse. The remorse seems genuine, with a promise that the abuse will never happen again, followed by, for instance, kind, loving behavior and presents. The survivor, craving love and acceptance, is swayed by the perpetrator's loving behavior and ultimately forgives that person.

4. **Calm phase.** The last phase is often thought of as an extension of the stage 3 honeymoon phase. During the calm phase, the relationship seems peaceful. The perpetrator may agree to go to counseling and attempt to create a "normal" life with the survivor. The perpetrator's apologies and requests for forgiveness become less sincere, and the frequency usually depends on the fear that the partner may leave the relationship or of police intervention. However, the tensions experienced in the stage 1 tension-building phase eventually return and the cycle starts over again.

"Why Did You Stay?"

Those who have not experienced or worked with people who have experienced domestic violence can't understand why anyone would stay with someone who seems to maliciously hurt them. The first thing out of their mouth when they hear the stories or see the bruises is "Why did you stay?" There are quite a few reasons; fear is usually at the heart of it, but you also have to remember that survivors of domestic violence have often been brainwashed to believe that they are worthless and would never survive without the perpetrator in their lives. The intimidation factor is overwhelming and takes over reasoning. Survivors are usually threatened that there will be consequences if they tell anyone or report the abuse to the authorities. They are simply afraid for their lives or possibly afraid that the perpetrator will retaliate against the children if they talk. That is why if you notice that someone may be a survivor of domestic violence, reach out. These people may not be able to help themselves. You may have to be their voice.

What Abuse Means in a Custody Dispute

If domestic violence has occurred in the home, custody may have to be adjusted to protect the survivors, which may include the mother, most often, but also the children—and if there is a concern for the children's safety, a call to child protective services (CPS) is a must. It will then open a referral and start an investigation.

My experience is in California, and I have found that some things are a little different from state to state, but, for all intents and purposes, this California model will give you an idea of what happens when a referral is made to an agency that protects the welfare of your children.

Here are the 4 official responses to a CPS investigation.

1. "Evaluated out," which means the reported problem did not rise to the level of the need for an investigation. For example, one parent spanked the child and the other doesn't believe in spanking as a form of discipline. The parent upset about the spanking reports physical abuse to CPS. Unless there are bruises, that is a parenting concern and CPS will not get involved.

2. "Unfounded," which means there was an investigation and the allegations were found to be untrue.

3. "Inconclusive," which means the incident may have happened but there were conflicting stories between parent and child or other family members or witnesses, and CPS could not pin down exactly what happened.

4. "Substantiated," which means there was an investigation, the allegations were proven to be true, and there will be consequences. Child protective services will most likely impose a family safety plan, which offers the family specific services supplied to the community to help them overcome the trauma associated with surviving domestic violence. Depending on the severity of the finding, this could include anything from free counseling services to police involvement and the requirement that the perpetrator leave the home. Or, if that person stays, the children may be removed from the home and placed with a relative or into foster care.

The reason this information is important in a custody dispute is that a judge must have proof to make a finding and therefore have reason to change custody. In a domestic violence case, this can be pictures of bruises or other injuries or possibly the damage done to the home during the incident, doctor's records, and hospital bills, but most of all, it is police reports. Many survivors of domestic violence are too afraid to go to the authorities, but without a report verifying an incident, the courts will have a difficult time adjusting custody. *Report domestic violence!*

The Effects of Domestic Violence on Our Children

The Domestic Abuse Round Table, a community-based nonprofit organization in Massachusetts, quotes that 3 to 4 million children and teens between the ages of 3 years and 17 years are at risk of exposure to intimate partner violence each year. Other studies quote even higher statistics. These statistics are not limited to the actual survivor of the abuse but also include witnessing or hearing threats of violence. Parents often do not take responsibility for their actions seriously, believing that yelling or arguing is no big deal and, when the fighting stops, their children will be just fine. This is untrue. There may be no visible scars, but children who have witnessed violence or abuse are in constant fear and agonize when something else will happen. They fight anxiety and constant humiliation and are often threatened with additional violence if they talk about the incident. Afraid someone will find out and they will be faced with retaliation for telling, children may feel isolated, may feel unable to have friends to their home, and, as a result, may have difficulty learning to interact with peers. They can be starved for real attention and affection, creating a skewed idea of what love actually looks like and therefore reenacting violent behavior in their own adult relationships.

Worrisome Signs to Look for in Your Children

Children often manifest conflicted responses to witnessing or surviving violence; on the one hand, they are concerned for their safety and the safety of their loved ones, but they may also be frustrated with the same loved ones— both the perpetrator for the violent behavior and the survivor for being unable to stop that person.

Be on the lookout for the same warning signs of childhood emotional distress mentioned in Chapter 3, What Do Children Need to Be Healthy?—concerns of headaches or stomachaches, bedwetting, nervousness, inability to concentrate, and disorganization but also flashbacks of the traumatic incident, intrusive thoughts, or an increased startle reflex when the child is unexpectedly surprised. Your child may act out, react violently toward siblings or peers, withdraw, or, to prevent another incident, be eager to please. Disorganization and an inability to concentrate may affect schoolwork. Watch for signs of depression and possibly self-injuring in older children and teens.

Co-parenting tip. Children may overhear their parents arguing, hear their own names, and assume they are the cause of the argument. This can lead to feelings of guilt, self-criticism, and unworthiness. Anticipate problems such as this, and have loving advice ready to sooth the feelings of unworthiness and blame: "Honey, do not blame yourself. This was not your fault."

The concern is that children who are raised in abusive homes learn that violence and intimidation are effective ways to resolve conflicts and will reproduce those behaviors as they get older. Statistics show that children from violent homes have higher risks of substance use, such as alcohol or drug use; post-traumatic stress disorder; and juvenile delinquency. Studies also continue to reinforce that witnessing domestic violence is the single best predictor of juvenile delinquency and adult criminality.

Unfortunately, the father as the perpetrator and the mother as the survivor is not just a stereotype. Ninety-five percent of all domestic violence reported lists the male (boy or man) as the perpetrator and the female (girl or woman) as the survivor. It has been said over and over that children who have witnessed parental domestic violence, now referred to as *intimate partner violence,* are more likely to recreate that same behavior in their own adult relationships. This is not just an idle statistic. I have seen it firsthand in my own practice. I have asked countless couples who struggle with domestic violence whether they ever witnessed their parents in violent arguments or fights. Everyone said yes. The boys reported they saw their fathers as the perpetrator and ultimately became a perpetrator as an adult. The girls reported that they used threats and arguments in a relationship and saw the behavior as normal. Therefore, the cycle of violence is just perpetuated generation to generation.

How to Help Your Child Who Has Post-traumatic Stress Disorder

- Empathize with your child's plight.
- If your child is comfortable with physical touch, give lots of hugs to help to keep your child calm.
- Encourage your child to talk with you.
- Listen to your child without judgment.
- Reassure your family that you'll do everything you can to keep them and their loved ones safe.
- Let your child know she will not get into trouble for anything she tells you.
- Always answer your child's questions honestly.
- Protect your child from additional information that will further traumatize your child.
- Avoid discussing worst-case or negative what-if scenarios.
- Limit excessive replays of the traumatic event.
- Limit violent movies, video games, or TV programs.
- Try and stick to your family's daily routine as much as possible.

> **How to Get Help for Domestic Violence**
> - Call the National Domestic Violence Hotline (800/799–7233).
> - Call your local police or sheriff's department (911).
> - Report any concerns to the child protective services in your county.
> - Find a therapist who specializes in coping with domestic violence or post-traumatic stress disorder.
> - Look for community-based organizations that offer free services or services offered on a sliding scale in your area.

Survival Plan

Are You Really a Single Parent?

As a child custody mediator, I hear a classic line during mediation: "Now that I am a single parent...." And I always bristle a little when I hear it. Single parents are parents who do not share their children's time with another parent *at all.* The other parent does not participate in the child's life, and the mother or father or other caregivers are solely responsible for all the decisions associated with that child. Many parents who are no longer together call themselves or express concern about being "single parents." Rarely are they. They are just bad co-parents. Yes, *bad co-parents*! All parents who share their children have help—*each other*! But because few relish confrontation, or arguments, or accusations, or gaslighting, they don't want to ask. You have an ally in all this. There is someone who loves your child as much as you do—your child's other parent. Because of that, you are single, yes, but you are not a single parent unless you don't share custody; then you are doing it by yourself. You are a parent—and so is your ex. That makes you co-parents. You can do it right—in the best interest of your child—or do it wrong, in the best interest of *you.*

Setting Appropriate Boundaries as You Transition From Parent to Co-parent

It's a difficult time right after the breakup, when the family moves from doing things as a 2-parent family to Mom and Dad or other caregivers doing things separately with the children. It's a time when clear boundaries are necessary, but families who are attempting to "do things right" often confuse their children—and themselves—with fuzzy personal boundaries.

> 66 *The transition right after our split was a hard one to maneuver. I wasn't always mad at him, so there were times I simply didn't know how to act. He missed the kids and would just show up Saturday mornings and ask if we could all go out for breakfast. I wasn't sure how to respond. The kids would get excited and want to go, and if I said no, I looked like the bad guy.*99

There are a few red flags in the scenario, so let's take a look at them, one by one.

First, a divorced parent should never show up at the other parent's home unannounced. Too many things could be interrupted that may get in the way of future co-parenting, particularly if the parent has already begun to date. During the transition, parents who are estranged often continue to think of each other as, for example, "my wife" or "my husband" and believe it is appropriate to just show up. It is not. An agreement must be made for what is appropriate, and there should always be a phone call or a text asking permission to come over.

That said, something such as breakfast together is great in concept, but, in reality, remaining enmeshed in each other's daily lives can be confusing for the parents and the children. The children get excited when their parents get along, and they get frustrated when one parent appears to be trying to put everything behind oneself, while the other drags one's feet. "Let's go, Mom! Can't you see Dad is trying to be nice?" puts a lot of pressure on Mom who appears to be committed to the breakup. If she agrees to go to breakfast, it will give their children a false sense of hope that reconciliation is possible.

Ironically, an activity such as going to breakfast each Saturday is often offered in the guise of weaning the children from living in a 2-parent home to living in a 1-parent home, when, in actuality, it's the parents who are having trouble with the transition and the blurred boundaries confuse everyone.

This all means that if you choose to do something such as Saturday morning breakfast with your children and their other parent, make sure enough time has elapsed that your children are not confused by all the togetherness.

Who Moves Out?

"Who moves out?" is a big question—and it could determine all sorts of things after the breakup, from who gets primary use of the home to who is responsible for rent or house payments. As in all things breakup, using the children's best interest to finalize the decision will easily give you the right answer.

To keep your children's lives on track with as little disruption from their daily routine as possible, ask yourself,

- "Where will the children feel the most comfortable?"
- "Have they always lived in this home?"
- "Do they attend school from this home?"
- "Are their friends nearby?"
- "Do their extracurricular activities originate near this home?"
- "Does everyone have to move, or can the children stay in the home they are used to?"

In the name of consistency, is it possible that one parent continues to live with the children, while the other moves out? "Bird's nest custody," or, simply, "nesting," is a living situation whereby the children stay in the family home and the parents take turns going back and forth between the residence. This is an unconventional approach, but it works well for some families. For more on this sort of parenting plan, see Chapter 7, Parenting Plans.

This is when it is important to take an honest look at what is best for the children. Some parents try to ease into a breakup by attempting to live separate lives and move into an extra bedroom. If you're putting the children first, that's not a good idea. Staying in the home may give that parent the upper hand financially or during a custody battle, but it will not make your children feel safer and secure if they have to watch their parents fight it out as they go through their breakup. Moving out does not have to be a permanent solution, but it will prevent your children from witnessing more fighting, thinking that's it's normal for people to interact in that manner and setting the stage for them to recreate the same behaviors when they get older.

Keep the Lines of Communication Open With the Children and Their Other Parent

❝ *We simply can't get along. No matter what I say, she argues with me. It's to the point I see her name come up on caller ID and I just hit, 'Can I call you later?' I never do. I just can't deal with her.***❞**

People who want to get along do. People who don't want to get along, don't, and this is the most apparent when you are transitioning from married to single. Those who want to get along look for new ways to communicate and problem-solve in the name of their children. Those who do not want to get along continue to communicate as they did when they were together, which wasn't productive and led them to the position they are in now.

Normally, you would walk away from someone you don't like. You wouldn't stay in touch with that person and look for ways to better communicate. Parents don't have that luxury. They must talk with the other parent if they share custody. Granted, they can have the same reaction as the father in the scenario, and not reply and avoid the other parent, but that behavior puts the child right in the middle. If parents who share custody aren't talking with each other, they are most likely using their children to pass on information.

"Tell your dad I'm going to be 15 minutes late dropping you off."

"Tell your mom the child support check will be late this month."

Using the children as messengers can have a disastrous effect. First, to prevent an argument, the children will not pass on accurate information. So essentially, the parents are teaching their children to lie.

Second, to avoid being a messenger, a child may avoid communicating with the parent who originates the message. For example, teens may screen their calls and not pick up when they see the parent calling.

If your teen is holed up in her room and rarely comes out to talk, she may be avoiding being asked to pass on a message. Check your communication style, and if you are using your child or teen as a messenger, stop!

Breaking Old Patterns of Communication

What is needed between newly separated parents is a new way of communicating. It starts with changing your thinking. What does thinking have to do with good communication? What you think about before your conversation sets the stage for how you approach the problem. This is called a *conditioned response,* based on past experiences—and being angry with your child's other parent, causing you to avoid a conversation with that person, is a conditioned response at its best.

> *I have to pay child support every month. It drives me crazy. Each time I write the check, I want to grab her by the throat.*

This is an actual quote from a father who came to me for co-parenting help. I asked him what he thought about as he wrote the check.

> *I think about her with that guy she left me for. I think about the fact that this is all her fault. I can actually see her laughing at me, and I get angrier each month."*

> I responded, "Of course you are angry about all the things *you just explained, but you are writing a check for child support, not spousal support. The check is for your child, to make his life better. Everything you just told me was about your ex. Your resentment is misplaced. Picture your child's face as you write the check, not his mother's. See him smiling, possibly wearing the new clothes that check bought him. Let yourself feel eager to see him, and see if you are still as angry as you are now.*

He did, and the next time I saw him, he admitted it was still difficult, but it definitely improved his mood simply by changing what he thought about as he wrote the check. The added benefit was because his anger was somewhat diffused, he was now able to talk more civilly with his child's mother.

Here's a personal example of how breaking old thought patterns can improve your communication.

My ex-husband shared equal custody with his children's mother, 1 week with her, 1 week with us. We had what I now call "best family syndrome." Each of us feared that the kids would prefer to be at the other's home, with the "best family." Life was pretty stressful in those days, and both homes were convinced that the other had an ulterior motive, some kind of strategy to win the kids' time and affection. This fear put us into a state of constant conflict.

Even though there was a set visitation schedule, fall break was not included in the kids' parenting plan. The timing changed year to year—one year it was at the end of October, one year it included the Thanksgiving holiday—and because no one could figure out exactly when it would be, it was left out of the negotiation at the time of their divorce. It was agreed whoever had the kids that week automatically had them for the entire break. The kids' father and I wanted to stick to the regular schedule because they were with us that week. Although we didn't plan to go out of town, we planned some special day trips, but I just knew their mother would want to change things in some way, because the kids were home all week. As fall break grew closer, I got more anxious.

I'd stop working at about 4 o'clock in the afternoon and straighten up the kitchen to prepare the evening meal. I regarded this as my alone time. The kids were doing homework, their dad wasn't home yet, and no one was around to distract me. Washing the dishes had become a calming ritual. Truth is, I have a mild case of a circulatory issue known as Raynaud phenomenon. My hands are always cold. After typing all day, I looked forward to soaking my fingers in the warm water.

Each afternoon as I started to wash the dishes, I'd start to hash things over in my mind. I'd run hot water into the sink and think, "I know exactly what she will do. She's going to try to take the kids to the beach during the break." *I'd start to scrub a pot, and with each swish of the sponge, I'd think something like,* "And she's going to call us up and ask if she could have the kids for the majority of the break." *I'd rinse the pot, thinking,* "We can't afford to take the kids on that kind of vacation." *(She just had her two, but we had 4 children—her two and our two as well.)* "Tickets to the boardwalk and so many meals out…and my daughters will be sad because they will not *be included." With each step of the cleanup, I'd lay on another layer of worry. One day, I found myself dreading to walk into the kitchen. Yes, I hated doing dishes, but this was something more—and I had been here before.*

That's when I took a good hard look at my thought process while cleaning up. With each step, I became angrier—I could feel it— and I realized I was subconsciously connecting my angry thoughts with the dish ritual until all the joy was gone. No longer did I look forward to the feeling of the warm water on my hands. I was just angry.

This was a huge revelation to me, and I realized at that moment that if I had thought myself into being angry, I could think myself out of it. I vowed to change what I thought about as I went through the motions. Instead of anticipating all the irritating things I thought the kids' mother might do, I concentrated on my love for my family.

The irony in this story is I used to hate to do dishes and I had used the same reframing technique to get me to the place where I enjoyed doing them! Mentally, I had turned my dislike for doing the dishes into a calming ritual once I stopped working. Here I was again.

I knew the next step was to check my thinking about how my daughter might be slighted by a decision my "bonuskids'" mom might make. I put myself into her shoes and felt the frustration of always having to coordinate efforts with someone else when I wanted to do something with my kids. I had to stop connecting her decisions for her children to what happened to my child. Although we were raising the kids as siblings, that was our decision. I had to realize that she did not have to consider my biological children when she made decisions for her children. Understanding that, I decided to change my focus to how grateful I was to be in my bonuskids' lives at all. I thought about how happy I was that they fully accepted my daughters as their sisters—and how it took their father and their mother to create such wonderful kids. Bottom line: I changed my preconceived notion about what might happen from angry to grateful.

Over the next few days, I reclaimed my enjoyment of afternoon ritual, but, because of my new attitude, the next time I talked with the kids' mother, I didn't have one bad thing to say to her—and, ironically, she never requested extra time with the kids. Instead, we offered it to her! As she stood at the doorway to pick them up to go to the beach *for the day,* she asked the kids, "Would you like your sisters to come along?" She referred to my kids as her children's sisters! What a turnaround!

Changing your thoughts about others will change not only your own mood but also the way you approach them the next time you see them. You cannot control how someone else thinks, but you can certainly control your own thoughts, and when you control your thoughts, you control your life. You break the chain of negative thinking, which opens the door to positive responses from unexpected places. Everyone wins—especially the children in our care.

Building a Working Relationship With Your Ex

Once you've learned to control your negative approach to communicating, you will see how much easier it is to build a working relationship with your child's other parent. Begin with the following actions:

▸ **Approach this as a business relationship.** Let's say you have a disagreement with a coworker. Would you react the same way as you do when you disagree with your ex? Probably not. Flying off the handle, threatening, or even acting irritated is usually not tolerated. When you disagree with a coworker, it is important to keep your emotions in check and find a solution quickly, so that you can continue to work together. Use the same approach when dealing with your child's other parent.

▸ **Look for a mutual goal.** In this case, the mutual goal would be to successfully co-parent and raise well-adjusted kids, even though you are no longer a couple. Once you and your children's other parent realize you are allies, not enemies, it will be easier to make the necessary concessions to get along. If you don't have a mutual goal, you will continue to put your individual needs in front of your children's and blame each other when you can't co-parent.

▸ **Develop empathy.** Put yourself into their shoes. This will allow you to focus on your feelings but also consider what the other parent may be feeling. Empathy for someone else's plight can be the catalyst for creative problem-solving.

For example,

66 *The kids were with their father for a straight week during fall break, and it was difficult to not see them. It made me realize how difficult it must be for their father when he doesn't see them for almost 10 days between his assigned weekends. With this in mind, when he asked for a regular dinner visit on Wednesday nights, I suggested Tuesday and Thursday nights instead.* 99

▸ **Cultivate respect.** When people feel disrespected, they are not invested in finding solutions. An easy way to offer respect to your child's other parent is to ask that parent's opinion. Many transitioning parents are afraid to ask their ex's opinion because they see it as a loss of power. If you are concerned about

power when transitioning from spouse to co-parent, you see it as a battle—
and have already lost. Asking one's opinion is a gesture of respect. You can
always respectfully disagree.

▶ **Pick your fights.** Everything is not a crisis. Take a breath, and count to 10.
Be proactive in your approach to problem-solving, not reactive.

▶ **Always look for a compromise.** When a problem must be solved, come to the
table with a solution. That gives you a place to start in your negotiations.
Then, as part of the solution, if both offer concessions (compromise),
no one loses—and your children will always win.

Creating a Welcoming Environment for the Kids

*66 When my daughters come back from their dad's home, they
constantly tell me that their dad's house is nicer than mine. They
complain about my carpets, they complain about the bathroom
lighting, and they complain that they have to share a room, but
at their dad's, everything is better; plus, they each have their own
room. I have to admit, I'm struggling, but I'm doing the best I can.
He knows all this and doesn't see it as a problem. 99*

Everyone feels the financial effects of divorce. Moving from a 2-parent household,
when both might work, to two 1-parent households is costly and a huge transition
for everyone concerned. The good news is that most do their best to offer what
they can to their children. The bad news is that the children in question are doing
more than just comparing homes; they are voicing their frustration about their
parents' breakup. In the scenario, Mom is taking it personally, while Dad may be
delighted that the girls prefer his home—and neither parent is really hearing what
the children are saying.

When a child prefers one home to the other, it's a huge red flag. It means the
parents are not communicating, and this is a common problem in the first few
months after separation. No one wants to talk with each other. Parents are jockeying for position, trying to get on their feet, and just expect their children to
fall into place, not realizing that Mom, for instance, is getting adjusted in a new
home, and Dad is also—and the kids are going back and forth. The parents think
they are getting organized, but the kids are in constant chaos.

Even though it's difficult to reach out to your child's other parent, particularly
when emotions are high right after the split, that's exactly what parents must
do. One of my favorite bits of advice is "People who ask for help usually get
it." No one loves your children as much as you do—except maybe their
other parent.

I know asking parents to ask each other for help is a different approach than usually suggested, but if you truly put your children first, it's the most logical approach. It's about how well-adjusted your kids are, and both parents are responsible for that.

What Does "Help" Look Like?

Using empathy when problem-solving basically means putting yourself into the other person's shoes and seeing whether that makes it easier to find a solution. Everyone has to put their own interests aside and look for workable solutions. For instance, that might mean that you ask your co-parent to watch the kids while you go to a meeting or, if you see she's working long hours, possibly offer an extra dinner visit so that she can feel as if she's "Mommy." Talk about it. Make it easy on each other if you can. Co-parenting is difficult, and if you can help each other, your kids will be better for it. Even though you are now apart, you are still all in this together.

What if You Can't Co-parent?

Although I am personally an advocate of co-parenting and have seen some miraculous turnarounds when parents put their children first, there are those who simply cannot co-parent. Whether the reasons are deemed legitimate— mental health concerns, abuse in the past, or possibly addiction issues—as a result, there are ways to disengage and parent alongside, rather than in conjunction with, your child's other parent. You can keep each other informed; usually, you can communicate by email rather than chatting. Specific days are assigned to who will attend the children's extracurricular activities, back to school night, or parent-teacher conferences. This is called *parallel parenting*. Everything is kept separate—but it's really not because you continue to share the same child.

Parallel parenting is said to relieve the stress of co-parenting—for the parents. I'm not sure it relieves the children's stress. Parallel parenting still requires a parenting plan to be in place, assigning the same days as might be assigned to parents who co-parent. The children are still required to go back and forth between their parents' homes, but they are forced to live between parents who are so angry with each other that they can't problem-solve on any level. As a result, the children are reminded of the animosity their parents feel for each other every time they change homes. It's a very stressful way to live and can be a form of emotional abuse if parents cannot refrain from openly demonstrating their disdain for each other in front of the children.

Because all parenting plans are recommended to the court "in the best interest of the child," I have gone as far as saying that I could not in all good faith suggest an equal custody parenting plan for parents who hold such animosity for each other.

I have explained how detrimental it is to require the child to travel back and forth between parents at such odds and how, under these circumstances, it would be healthier to establish a primary parent and assign every other weekend to the other. At times, parallel parenting may be necessary and required by law. When a *restraining order* or an *order of protection* is in place that specifies parents may not talk with each other, parents must parallel parent. Restraining orders may also be adjusted so that the parents have "peaceful contact regarding the children." In these cases, the parents are not to interact except when there is an emergency regarding the children or when the parenting plan requires an exchange. Rather than come into contact with each other, parents who parallel parent often set up the child exchanges "to school and from school" on their designated custody days.

Talking With the Kids About the Transition

I often hear parents say they want to keep their stresses away from their children, and that is understandable, but it's all in how you present it. The kids know that this transitionary period is difficult. They are living it times 2—while *both* parents strive to start over. Aspects of life are hard, and to present it all as rosy is doing your children a disservice. It helps children prepare for life by seeing their parents take on difficult tasks. Don't be afraid to let them know how hard both of you are working. Make your goals known and what you are doing to achieve them. Don't make the kids feel guilty—that's counterproductive—but don't be afraid to let them know that you both work hard and are now independent from each other but also working together in their best interest.

Your children always need your reassurance that everything will be OK. You can't tell them enough how much you love them or be supportive of their other parent by reinforcing that parent's love for them as well.

Here are other words that may help them with the transition.

▶ "We are not doing this because you did anything wrong."
▶ "This was not your fault."
▶ "We were unhappy with each other, not with you."
▶ "This is about *our* problems. We are not divorcing you."
▶ "You are part of both of us, and we both love you very much."
▶ "We will both be your parents forever" or "We will always be your Daddy and Mommy."
▶ "*We* will never leave *you*."

One of my favorites is "We will still be a family, just a different kind of family. Dad will live in one house, and Mom will live in another. You will spend time with both of us."

How Much Should You Really Share With Your Children?

66 *I have a 14-year-old son who lives with me. After being divorced for 3 years, I am finally in a loving relationship, and even though my son has been my confidant, I sat him down and explained that my partner is moving in, and, in the future, he will play that role. My son said that he understood completely, even acted happy for me, but then decided to move in with his father—a man with whom he has not had a close relationship for many years.* **99**

It's difficult to know exactly how much to share with your children, particularly if they are a little older—and I'm not talking about bad-mouthing or blaming the other parent for the demise of the relationship—I'm talking about volunteering information about your own journey. When children, no matter their age, know their parent is floundering, they feel insecure, especially during a breakup, when both parents may be struggling.

However, telling your problems to your child lets your child know only that you or your co-parent do not have the foggiest idea what to do either. Children need to feel as if their parent will protect them in a time of stress. Confiding in the children makes them feel as if they must take care of you. It should be the other way around.

To make matters worse, in the scenario, the mother put her child in direct competition with her new partner by telling her child he isn't needed anymore. She may have thought, *"It's time for him to be a kid again. Let me take this weight off his shoulders,"* but what he probably heard is "She obviously likes him best. Look how easily I can be replaced." Of course the child looks for somewhere else to belong—the logical alternative is Dad's house.

Mom has no idea how her actions will prevent her son from getting close to her new partner, nor does she realize that her own relationship with her son has been jeopardized.

When parents need someone to talk with about adult decisions, for example, should your new love sleep over, should you blow your life savings on that trip to Fiji, or should you invest in mutual funds or Intel, consider talking with a therapist, an investment counselor, or maybe your travel agent, not your kids. They don't have the emotional or intellectual sophistication to consult on your drama or help you make decisions.

Room to Room

On a more practical note, a great way to help the children adjust while transitioning from one house to another is to make sure their bedrooms are inviting and a place they can call their own. Let them pick out the colors, possibly the comforters they want, and anything within your budget that allows them to express their individuality in their new spaces. If they must share a room, make sure they have their own corners, or even just a shelf, if that's all the room there is, but they must feel as if they have their own spaces.

When my kids had to share a room—which was often—I always assigned a wall to each child. I let my kids paint it any color they wanted and put up the pictures they wanted. That was their side of the room, and they were responsible for keeping it orderly. The decor was questionable. We wouldn't win the Good Housekeeping seal of approval, but the kids had their own spaces and they looked forward to returning. That was the goal—not which parent won the Best Home award.

Observing the Children During the Transition: Do We Need a Custody Evaluation?

A custody evaluation may be performed when high-conflict parents are so at odds during their breakup that they must depend on a judge to finalize the decision for the parenting plan they will use. If a judge needs help in making that decision, the judge may order a custody evaluation. The evaluation is performed by a therapist, most commonly a psychologist who is licensed to conduct tests that pinpoint various personality traits and parental mental health.

Some courts offer in-house evaluations performed by staff. These evaluations may not be as detailed as those performed by licensed psychologists, but they will still offer additional information designed to aid the judge in making a decision.

All evaluators have their own style, but most evaluations follow a similar pattern.

The evaluator will

- Interview both parents, 2 or 3 times, in various situations, and both individually and together. The interviews will be by appointment—possibly in the evaluator's office or at the parent's home, but the interviews will not be a surprise.
- Interview each child, once or twice.
- Observe parent-child interaction.
- Gather collateral information from teachers, child care providers, doctors, therapists, CPS (if there has been past CPS involvement), and other people who can offer information about how the parent and child interact.
- Review the court file, which will supply a documented history of the case.

When an evaluation has been ordered, it is not to be taken lightly. Make yourself and your child available for interviews and be as open and honest as possible. Do not try to sway the child by suggesting she says anything other than how she feels. An experienced evaluator can easily spot when a child has been coached, and that will work against you. If you find yourself questioning the evaluator's tactics or feel prejudiced against your position, report that to your attorney or your mediator before the evaluation is being accepted by the court.

Having Realistic Expectations for the Future

Rome was not built in a day, and neither is a new working relationship between parents who are no longer together. There will be bumps during the transition, but conflict is also the catalyst for problem-solving. I often tell parents who have just broken up, "If you plan to co-parent, not much changes. You aren't living together, and you aren't sleeping together, but your approach to parenting and your responsibility to your children remain the same whether you are together or apart. How well you do that is up to you."

6

Co-parenting Our Children

The best security blanket a child can have is parents who respect each other.

JANET BLAUSTONE

So You Want to Co-parent?

The need to co-parent was born out of necessity. Although all states recognize the welfare, or "best interests," of the child as the primary concern in the resolution of custody disputes between parents, the laws have changed over the years, from supporting that a child's primary care is best offered by the mother, or the tender years doctrine, to joint custody, when both parents have equal say in how their children will be raised after a separation or divorce. If you have an equal say, cooperation is needed to problem-solve, and that is how the concept of co-parenting after separation or divorce was born.

Laying the Groundwork for Successful Co-parenting in Today's World

Some think it's ridiculous to consider that parents who could not get along while together can get along well enough to successfully co-parent their children after they break up. But research continues to indicate that our children's physical, mental, and emotional well-being is affected if ongoing conflict occurs during a relationship. If the conflict continues after the breakup, that's even worse. This is the primary reason parents who are no longer together must put old issues aside and focus on their children's needs. They must do it intentionally and without judgment. No holding grudges, no being spiteful. They must stand back in the face of conflict and use their children's best interest as criteria for all decision-making.

There is nothing new about this approach, but it's rare that parents actually put their own issues aside and look for ways to problem-solve in the best interest of their children. Even after close to 40 years of attempted co-parenting, parents still approach custody as a battle, a power struggle over time and money. "I'm fighting for my kids!" Or, even worse, "I promised my kids I'd fight for them." Now you've put your children right in the middle of the battle, asking them to choose whose side they are on—and that's certainly not making what's best for them your primary concern. True co-parenting takes work—and compassion, understanding, empathy, and thinking outside the box to solve problems creatively. We are providing the tools necessary to do just that here in this chapter.

Why Is Co-parenting So Important?

Joint custody parenting plans force a child to live in 2 homes. Just by the nature of joint custody, it asks children to check their allegiance each time they leave one parent's home and go to the other's. It's natural for people to compare, so when children go back and forth between parents, they subconsciously consider what room they like best or which parent cooks the best meals. Children often compartmentalize their approach to cope with the back-and-forth. In my own children's case, I found that the foods they ate at one home were not the foods they ate at the other. I was surprised to find that at my house, my "bonusson" (stepson) liked frozen spicy burritos for snacks. At his mother's home, he ate fruit cocktail. When I bought him fruit cocktail to eat at our home, he looked at me as if I was mistaken—"I don't eat fruit cocktail here," he said. He had compartmentalized his food choices—burritos at our house, fruit cocktail at Mom's.

Everything we do sets the stage for our children's future. They watch us and learn by example. When parents argue, they're teaching their children to problem-solve by arguing. When parents openly work together to find solutions, they are teaching their children to do the same. It doesn't matter whether the parents live together or apart. Children learn by example and learn to problem-solve creatively if they are shown how to do it.

However, here's the rub: when parents raise their children under the same roof, cooperation is implied. If there is open disrespect, a mother or father or other caregivers might chime in, "Don't talk to your father (or mother) like that!" Once a breakup occurs, there's no incentive to support the other parent. Under the same conditions, the now-divorced parent's response could very easily be "I understand, honey. I used to hate it when he yelled at me like that too. Ignore him."

By responding in this manner, you're telling children that disrespecting their other parent is acceptable behavior—and it is not. Whether parents are together or apart should have no bearing on the way a parent responds to a child's disrespect of the other parent. It's your job to support your co-parent, not undermine that parent's importance. In fact, it is at this time that it is even more important to openly demonstrate cooperation and respect for each other. It teaches our children self-respect and integrity. Without that display of support, children have no model for respectful interaction and can easily learn to play one parent against the other. They then take this behavior into their adult lives and attempt to manipulate friends, partners, co-workers, or others they perceive to be in authority.

First Things First: Check Your Mind-set

Rarely do parents who are no longer together anticipate a comfortable and conflict-free relationship with their former partners, and just thinking about talking with an ex can put you into a bad mood. Your mind-set, or how you think about an interaction before you see each other, can set the stage for problem-solving and finding positive solutions.

When we feel anger, hurt, or betrayal, we want to lash out, to put those miserable exes in their place—and if we have kids together, that's the last thing we should really do. You can't parent on the defense. You must co-parent and work together if you want healthy children—whether you live together or apart.

Conflict does not have to have a negative impact on communication. It can also serve as a catalyst for problem-solving. How we respond in conflict determines whether the argument will be solved or spin out of control. You have to decide: Will you perpetuate the fight by answering back in like insults, or will you enter the interaction with a desire to find a solution in the best interest of the children in your care?

Here's an analogy I've often used before to help drive the "check your mind-set" concept home.

Let's say rock climbing is one of your favorite activities. It's something you have done for years, and you look forward to getting the exercise. One range of mountains you really like to climb. You like the wildflowers in the spring, the way the rocks smell in a light rain, and the way the light jets across when the sun is ready to go down. All these things make you look forward to the next time you climb that mountain.

But the last time you took on the climb, you fell. You broke a few ribs and had trouble breathing. No one was around, and you had to climb down the mountain by yourself and drive yourself to the hospital. Every time you took a breath, you remembered the fall. Broken ribs take quite a while to heal. It would be a long and painful recuperation.

When your ribs finally healed, you were not eager to return to your favorite mountain. You remembered falling, feeling your weight crack your ribs as you hit the ground and how the pain made it difficult to breathe. The wildflowers were still there. The light rains still made the rocks smell the same way you remembered, and the sunset was still as dramatic, but the way you thought of your favorite mountain had shifted. Now you associate climbing that mountain with uncertainness and pain.

Like your fall off your favorite mountain, the memories associated with a breakup are rarely nice ones, but it is important to see how those bad memories frame your interaction with your ex. You remember those bad times, just as you remembered your fall from the mountain; what your co-parent did to you or what you did to your co-parent, as well as the thought of interacting on any level, sets the stage for future communication. You hear your co-parent's voice on the phone and look for ways to cut the communication short or not talk with your co-parent at all.

As a result, when your kids walk into the room, you might say, "Call your mom (or dad) and tell her (or him) that we are going to be late (or I need my check; you fill the blank)." You've just disrespected your co-parent and put your child right in the middle of the 2 people your child loves the most. We can't do that to our children if we want them to feel safe—and they must feel safe with both parents, not just one, to make them healthy and whole. The concept of co-parenting is working together in the best interest of our children. It makes no difference what went on before. Your children are still here after the fall. They need your guidance, and it doesn't matter if you fell along the way.

This is when I hear…

66 *It's not me; it's him (or her). We just don't get along. I try to co-parent, but he (or she) won't cooperate.* **99**

That statement is about you, not your kids. The truth is, people who want to get along do. People who don't want to get along don't. Co-parenting is not for the faint of heart. Co-parenting is forever. You have to choose to do it well.

Negative Thought–Negative Response Chain

But there's more…you've often heard that communication is a 2-way street. Both players must cooperate to get the best results. If one puts up a barrier, there's no way to get past it. That person controls the situation and you are done. But one person can change the course of bad communication if that person is committed to positive interaction. You must set the example over and over again and not give up because 1 or 2 times you are met with snarky remarks. To break the negative thought–negative response chain of behavior, you *must love your kids more than you hate your ex.* That will allow you to change your attitude about your ex before interaction. When you do, you will be surprised how that change will improve your ability to communicate and problem-solve together.

Here's a personal story I'd like to pass on that drives this idea home.

My father was an "older father" and possibly the funniest man I have ever met. He was 43 when I was born, very old-fashioned, and over-the-top strict, as well as, at times, made racist comments. I had a lot of trouble dealing with the way he saw things, and we were at odds for most of my life.

Needless to say, it was difficult for me to be around him, and being the headstrong young woman that I was, rarely would I let his observations go without comment. We bickered regularly, and it was difficult for other family members to be around us when we were together.

I'm not telling this story because I am bitter about my upbringing or to pass on that my father was a mean and cruel man; there was another side to him that was absolutely delightful, and that was the problem. Our inability to get along hurt both of us, and that is why the rest of the story is so important to my point.

> One day, when my father was 71 years old, it hit me that he would not be with me forever. I realized his choices were his choices and formed as a result of his own life experiences. My choice was to love him as he was. I made a secret pact with myself that I would hug him hello and goodbye and tell him I loved him each time I saw him, and, lo and behold, we never bickered again. Never. He stopped commenting on my choices, as well as stopped making rude remarks in my presence, and for the last 8 years of his life, we were the best of friends. All those years, I thought I was the one on the defense; evidently, so did he. I changed my attitude, and, as a result, his responses changed. From the moment I made the decision, there was a shift— because I wanted to get along with him. I never discussed it with him. I simply changed my behavior.

My point? You can co-parent with your child's other parent if you want to. Something bigger than yourself must serve as the catalyst to make the shift— and in this case, it's the well-being of your children.

Getting the Response You Want From Your Co-parent

Set the Stage

Good communication doesn't just happen. You must set the stage, which means each time you meet, you must approach each other with a clean slate. Rather than take anything personally, make your new life mantra "In the best interest of *our* children," and repeat it to yourself until you have conditioned yourself to both expect and participate in positive problem-solving with your co-parent.

To get the response you want, keep your emotions intact.

Solution-Based Problem-solving

Years ago, when I worked for a photographic company, I had a problem in my sales territory. It was so bad I decided to ask the vice president of sales for direction. He just smiled and said, "Jann, you know this territory better than anyone else. What do you think the answer is?" I told him my ideas and his reply was then, "I agree wholeheartedly with your suggestions. Next time, when you see a problem, come to me with your idea for a solution as well. Then we have somewhere to start. We can negotiate from that point and compromise, if necessary, to get to the correct end result."

I have used this approach ever since and have applied it in many different aspects of problem-solving and negotiation. Here it is used as a model for problem-solving with a co-parent.

Four-Step Plan to Problem-solving

Step 1. Identify the problem.

Step 2. Weigh the obstacles.

Step 3. Suggest a solution—and don't be afraid to ask for help in finding that solution.

Step 4. Listen for the compromise.

Here is the problem-solving plan in action.

Ramona and Jason broke up 2 years ago. They have a son, Trevor, who is 6 years old. They can't seem to talk with each other without it spinning out of control. The fights are getting more furious, and Trevor often hears everything they say. The current issue is that Jason lost his job and struggles to stay up on child support. Trevor plays T-Ball and needs new baseball pants. Both parents express concern that money is tight.

Let's compare approaches and see which approach creates the best result.

Approach A

Ramona: *Trevor needs new baseball pants.*

Jason: *His old ones are just fine.*

Ramona: *They're size 6. He wears size 8 now!*

Jason: *I pay child support! And I just got laid off! What do you want from me?*

Ramona: *What! You lost another job? How many is that in the past 2 years? Everything is always my responsibility! You'd better send me a check!*

Rather than discuss the real problem, which is Trevor needs new baseball pants, their argument morphed into an argument about child support and Jason being a flake.

Approach B

Ramona: *Trevor needs new baseball pants.*

Jason: *He can still wear his old ones. I can't afford new ones. I just got laid off from work.*

Ramona: *I can only imagine how concerned you are about money since you were just laid off, but you always land on your feet. You're never out of work for very long.*

Jason: *Thank you. I have an interview next week, and I should make quite a bit more than I did at my last job.*

Ramona: *I know both of us care about Trevor. He's growing so quickly and really needs new baseball pants. How can we approach this, since we're both short on cash?*

Jason: *Can we split the cost of the pants?*

Ramona: *That would really help. They cost $37.50.*

It goes without saying that approach B produced the desired results—and it was because Ramona followed the basic Four-Step Plan to Problem-solving to the letter. She set the stage, and Jason followed her lead.

1. Ramona identified the problem: Trevor needed new baseball pants.

2. She weighed the obstacles: Money was short for both parents. Jason had been laid off, and the baseball pants were expensive. Neither parent could afford the baseball pants.

3. She asked for help in finding a solution: "How can we approach this, since we're both short on cash?" But there is an important component to how she presented the solution.

   First, she asked for Jason's opinion on how to solve the problem. This demonstrated respect by allowing him to contribute his ideas to a solution as well.

   Second, she consulted her communication toolbox (see the "Communication Toolbox to Help Us Better Communicate With Our Children During Separation or Divorce" sidebar in Chapter 4, Helping Our Children Cope) and used empathy to lay the groundwork when talking with Jason: "I can only imagine how concerned you are about money...." She put herself into Jason's shoes and let him know she understood his plight, but they still had to find a solution. This laid the groundwork for negotiation.

4. She listened for the compromise: Jason suggested they split the cost of the baseball pants. Ramona felt this was an acceptable solution to the problem and they agreed.

More Help Communicating

How Do I Get My Co-parent to Stop Disrespecting Me?

❝ *But I have changed my attitude, and my co-parent is still the same. How do I get him to stop disrespecting me? He won't return phone calls or texts.* **❞**

When you ask "How do I get…?" in essence, you are asking, "How can I make this person do what I want?" You can't make anyone do anything. You can change only yourself. Referring back to the story about my father, you can change only *your* thoughts and therefore what *you* anticipate and how *you* respond. Lead by example. That means if your co-parent texts you, text your co-parent back. If it's an angry text, do your best to keep it on the subject of the children. If you hate when your co-parent is late, don't be late. If you want the kids' clothes back after their time with you, return the clothes when it's time to return them. Don't be spiteful or hold grudges. It just perpetuates bad behavior. Treat your ex as you would like to be treated, and never ask your child's other parent to do something you wouldn't do. That's taking the lead. That's putting your children first and is the beginning of a positive co-parenting relationship.

Bad-mouthing

❝ *My ex won't stop bad-mouthing me, and I'm afraid my child is beginning to believe the lies!* **❞**

In the past, the most common recommendation to curb bad-mouthing was to stay quiet to prevent retaliation, but experts are now suggesting a different approach. Gently confronting the issue seems to get better results. The key is how it is done. Staying calm is imperative. Tact and timing have never been more important. Bad-mouthing, at its core, is rooted in insecurity, anger, revenge, spite, and jealousy, and when confronted, the parent is often surprised that what is being said is regarded as bad-mouthing. "I'm just telling my child the truth" is a common response. But parents must weigh whether "the truth" is what is really being passed on or they are being vindictive at their child's expense. Sometimes a bad-mouthing parent just needs to be educated and that will be enough to stop the bad behavior, but if that's not enough and just fuels the fire, you may have to take a more proactive approach. Teach your children to make judgments based on what they know to be true— not on what they hear.

A Positive Way to Confront Bad-mouthing

For example, an angry mother tells her child that his father really doesn't care about him: "That's why he left." The devastated child confides in his father, "Mommy said you don't care about me." To address the comment directly, a divorced father might respond as follows:

"Sometimes when you hear something bad all the time, you may start to believe it, even if you knew in the beginning it wasn't true. I know Mommy often says I don't care about you, but I love you very much, and if you are afraid or worried about absolutely anything, we can talk anytime. I will always tell you the truth."

As children and teens grow toward adulthood, they inherently know that bad-mouthing is wrong and can speak for themselves. A 20-year-old young adult of divorce who had been badgered by parental bad-mouthing all his life finally had enough. He confessed, "The last time my dad said something bad about my mom, I told him to stop immediately. I was polite, of course. After all, it's my dad, but I came right out and told him how uncomfortable it made me feel when he said rude things about my mom. I told him that she never said bad things about him, and it would be nice if he acted the same way."

When You Must Clarify the Truth

There is also a gentle approach to clarifying the truth when incorrect information is passed between homes.

Let me give you a little background to this story so that you can see how easily the solution is applied.

> *Justin was a 5-year-old boy who went back and forth between his divorced parents' homes. It was a difficult breakup, and Justin's dad moved on quickly. It is not uncommon that parents attempt reconciliation at least once after the breakup, and that's just what Justin's mother attempted to initiate about a year after the separation. But Justin's father was now in love with Janelle and had no interest in reconciling with Justin's mother. When Justin asked his mother why she and Daddy no longer lived together, Justin's mother angrily replied, "Because of Janelle!" The truth was that Janelle had nothing to do with the split, but Justin's mom felt that must be the reason why she and Justin's dad were apart—and that's what she told Justin when he asked what happened. When Justin returned to his father's home, he told his dad, "Mommy said you aren't married anymore because of Janelle. I hate Janelle!* 99

Now the bad-mouthing not only has affected Justin's relationship with his father but is interfering with his ability to accept Janelle—and the offending information is untrue.

My favorite response in these types of situations is to use the word *mistaken* in your explanation.

First state the parent passing on the information is *mistaken*: "Honey, your mother is *mistaken*."

Then state the truth: "I met Janelle 7 months after Mommy and I stopped living together. She had nothing to do with our breakup."

Dad didn't bad-mouth in response. He explained in one word, *mistaken*, that Justin's mother simply didn't have all the information.

❝ *I am as nice as I can possibly be. It doesn't matter. My ex is still a jerk.* **❞**

Your co-parent may be a jerk, but don't get caught up in the manipulation, because then you're acting like a jerk too. Your kids don't need 2 jerks for role models. Live *your* life, and be positive. And certainly don't say your co-parent is a jerk in front of your children. Children have shared loyalties, and the inner conflict the bad-mouthing creates severely confuses them. Your kids will be drawn to the one who is setting the right example. Kids do not want to be around negativity.

❝ *Oh, but my kids don't hear it.* **❞**

But you know that kids *over*hear their parents talking even when we try and be quiet. Without knowing it, your child could hear you on the phone or hear a passing comment you make to a friend or relative. I've had clients who have profanity words listed in their cell phone caller ID, so when their ex calls, the incoming phone call comes up a*****e or b***h. Most children can read well enough to sound out the words by 6 or 7 years of age. As parents you know there will be times when your children will want to or need to call their other parent when they are in your care. Kids know how to use cell phones sometimes better than their parents do. Can you imagine how your children would feel if they saw profanity listed in your phone for their other parent who they love very much?

When your children read these words and realize that the words represent someone very important to them, they can be devastated. As a result, they may want to stop seeing the parent who bad-mouthed their parent. Confused by the sudden change, the bad-mouthing parent often blames the other parent for sabotaging the relationship—and that's not the case at all.

Be careful. Bad-mouthing affects children in ways you may not realize. It undermines their self-esteem and makes them question their importance. Children inherently know they are half Mom and half Dad. If you bad-mouth their other parent, they will personalize it. Even if they don't say anything to you, it has registered. Something as innocent as "Your mother is always late, and it drives me crazy!" can affect *their* self-esteem. Watch their facial expressions when something negative is said about their other parent. They most likely will not be smiling. Unfortunately, there may be no reaction at all, but that doesn't mean they aren't feeling bad. It means they have learned to not show their feelings. Or, even sadder, they have been taught to be emotionless about their feelings.

How? Children learn to curb their responses to protect themselves. If you have reacted negatively to their vulnerability in the past, say, you have gotten angry when they mention that they had fun with their dad or that they miss their mom, they learn to suppress their reaction to the anger to protect against what they perceive as a negative emotion—not anger with the other parent but anger with them for identifying with the other parent.

Co-parenting tip. For your children's sake, consider the old adage "If you have nothing nice to say, say nothing at all" when speaking about their other parent.

Possibly the worst thing a divorced parent can say is something such as "You're just like your dad (or mom)!" in an angry or disgusted manner. Your child knows you do not like his other parent, and using a negative tone when you're talking about his mother or father or other caregivers is essentially commenting on *his* DNA, his essence, or the traits he's picked up. When you talk negatively about your co-parent, you're talking negatively about your child. As a result, don't be surprised if your child slowly makes excuses to not return to your home. You don't ever want to put your child in that situation, nor do you want to cause your child undue stress or anxiety.

Bottom line: if your ex is a jerk, it's your co-parent's decision to act in that manner. You can always lead by example and be the positive influencer. Every family needs a hero. *You* can be that hero.

❝ *I hate my ex. I can't wait until my child is 18!* **❞**

This is usually said when parents are sick of arguing with their co-parents. In their frustration, they think once their teen reaches adulthood, the need to co-parent will end and they won't have to speak with the other parent again.

I always find that statement amusing. In truth, a separation or divorce changes very little in "parenting" your child. Oh, you may move out, and you may get a new partner, but your responsibility to your children remains the same as when you were together. Your children will grow up, perhaps go to college, get a new job, and maybe find a partner....

It is at this point I have been known to ask my clients a series of very important questions. In a way, it's a setup because I want it to register that their involvement with each other doesn't necessarily stop once their teen becomes an adult. Some parenting responsibilities will certainly diminish, but they never go away completely.

The conversation goes like this....

> **❝** *So, tell me, do you think your children will ever have children of their own some day?"*
>
> *Most say, "Of course."*
>
> *I know that's what they are going to say, so I just smile. "Well,"
> I continue (their ex is usually sitting beside them), "Meet Grandma,
> and Grandma meet Grandpa.* **❞**

The faces I get are priceless—but it always hits home. They then realize that parenting, and, as a result of a breakup, co-parenting, is forever. That person you seem to hate so much is just as much your child's parent as you are. That parent loves your child just as much as you do. Your co-parent will not go away when your teen becomes a legal adult. Your co-parent is a permanent fixture in your child's and then teen's life; therefore, that person is a permanent fixture in your life. You can choose to see that person as an enemy or, for the sake of your child you both love unconditionally, an ally.

Co-parenting in Action

Don't Shoot the Messenger

"Shooting the messenger" is a metaphoric phrase used to describe the act of blaming the bearer of bad news. When a child passes on something that the receiving parent does not want to hear, who will hear the negative response? The child, and a child asked to pass on upsetting information will eventually learn to alter or buffer the information to dodge any oncoming bullets. Basically, you are teaching your children that it is essential to lie to keep the peace.

Here's a common situation when shooting the messenger would apply: Your son is being bullied at school. You've exhausted all the regular avenues in an effort to solve the problem. You have talked with the teacher, the principal, and possibly the other child's parents, but the bullying has continued to torment your child, and now it's affecting his school attendance, his grades, and, most of all, his emotional stability.

Short of calling the police, if you were *not* co-parenting, you might…

Arbitrarily pull him out of the existing school and enroll him in another school. When your son's other parent picks him up for their time together, that parent might ask, "How's school?" Your son would then inform his parent that he has changed schools and his new teacher's name is Ms Castro. Your natural reaction would probably be anger. "What do you mean you changed schools!" The child doesn't know what to do. His parent is angry about something to do with him but about which he has no control—and he was the bearer of the bad news.

This situation is a perfect example of why the phrase "Don't shoot the messenger" is so well-known.

Co-parenting tip. Never make your child a messenger. When making an important decision or if you find the need to pass on information, consult the other parent first, then present the decision to your child as a united front.

Change Your Approach

True co-parenting changes not only the approach to problem-solving but the final outcome. If you were truly co-parenting, you would have been keeping your child's other parent apprised of the situation from the beginning. Your co-parent might have even gone to the school with you to approach the principal to get the bullying to stop. As a result, after some conversation weighing the pros and cons, together you might decide that it is in your child's best interest to change schools. This may or may not require a change in the parenting plan, but it might entail the child living with the other parent more often so that he can flourish in a better school environment. If that's true, true co-parents would make the change, taking nothing personally but also being open to negotiate more time for the parent with whom the child lived previously, possibly during spring, summer, or winter breaks.

Co-parenting on the Defense

66 *Because I traveled for work, my son has always lived predominantly with his mother, but I changed jobs a few years ago, and we have shared our son's time equally. He recently started telling me he does not want to return to his mother's home. Last night, I could barely get him into the car. I'm a little worried, but I don't want to say anything to his mother. I know it will start World War III.*99

It is difficult for co-parents to discuss that their child would rather be at one home than the other. As a result, it often takes a while before the subject is properly addressed, and, as time passes, the co-parents become even more estranged. The animosity builds as the concern becomes "I'm going to lose my son!" and, because fear is at the root of the discord, the parents begin to "co-parent on the defense."

Co-parenting on the defense can be an early warning sign of *parental alienation.* Let's look how the alienating behavior might begin.

> *A child's father takes him to the beach for a weekend. The child goes back to Mom's and tells her what a wonderful time he had with Dad. Mom is secretly jealous and afraid the child will like Dad best, so for the next trip, Mom takes the child to Hawaii for a week. Weeks pass, and Mom thinks the child would love to go to a football game; Dad hears about her plan to go to the game and buys season tickets. Both parents one-up the other to ensure the child prefers to be with them.*

The scenario came to a head when these 2 parents came to my office for co-parenting help. "I'm convinced he does this just to 'get my goat,'" the frustrated mom admitted when I was explaining the concept behind co-parenting on the defense. "The truth is," she continued, "I'm afraid the boys won't want to come over anymore if I'm too strict. They'll think my house is no fun and will want to stay with their dad."

I couldn't have said it better myself. This mother perfectly pinpointed her fear that her children might prefer their dad's home—and Dad admitted he felt the same way. As a result, both parents disciplined inappropriately, and both started buying the kids gifts or trips to ensure they liked their home best.

Neither parent realized both of them were in the midst of a malicious game of tug-of-war. Their need to one-up each other was brought about by their own insecurity and fear of losing the boys' affection. The boys were right in the middle—something that, when asked, neither parent wanted.

"I didn't realize I was trying to alienate the kids," the mother confessed. "I just felt powerless and I knew I had to do something. I thought I was fighting fire with fire."

"When I bought those season tickets," the dad admitted, "I knew I had 'won.' I just didn't realize how much all this was really hurting the kids."

I was surprised the father used the word *won* in his explanation. It was a war alright, and both parents felt it.

How Do You Stop?

There's a way to stop all the defensiveness, but both parents have to take an active role in correcting their behavior. First, admit you are contributing to the problem and realize the reason you are acting like this: fear.

Next, acknowledge your part and stop the behavior immediately. Even though co-parents in this position rarely trust each other, you must call a truce for the sake of your children.

Then, look for ways to share the children's time comfortably and support each other's parenting time. For example, make sure the other parent is invited to your children's extracurricular activities so that your children can see their parents have stopped fighting and are committed to supporting them together as co-parents.

Next, to not fall into old behaviors, look for a co-parenting counselor who can help you set appropriate boundaries and offer tools to continue to successfully co-parent your children in the future.

Finally, stay vigilant and if you start to feel insecure again and are drawn to repeat old behaviors, return to co-parenting counseling to keep you on the straight and narrow.

The potential for parental alienation was spotted early in the scenario, and the necessary precautions were taken before severe damage was done to the children by either parent. However, parental alienation can be severe, and it can permanently damage the relationship between parent and child.

Co-parenting tip. Our children must feel safe with both parents, not just one of them, to make them healthy and whole.

Are You an Alienating Co-parent?

Here's a quick checklist of potentially alienating behaviors. Do either of you see yourself in any of these behaviors?

- You call your son right before bed so that he can fall asleep knowing how much you miss him.
- Right before he leaves to go to the other parent's home, you get a touch of sentimentality and wave goodbye with tears welling in your eyes just long enough so that he notices.
- You buy him a puppy, a kitty, a new video game, concert tickets, or another gift and call him at the other parent's house just to let him know it's all waiting for him when he gets home. "Your puppy misses you so much" is classic manipulation.
- You put down the other parent, such as lifestyle or choices, or bad-mouth that parent ever so slightly to gain your child's allegiance, or you allow your child to do the same.
- You ask your son to pass along information to his other parent and rarely talk with the other parent yourself. (You make him the messenger.)

Parents must examine their true motivation when they do something as underhanded as sadly calling a child right before bed to say, "Oh, I miss you so much." In response, the child feels guilty for not being with that parent—even if he just loves being at the other parent's home.

Parental Alienation

66 *My ex is doing her best to undermine my relationship with my child. She has even begun to call my child's stepfather 'Dad' and is referring to me by my first name. We can't talk about anything, and it's very stressful to interact in any way. It's getting so that my daughter won't even come over to my home for dinner. I only live 10 minutes away and it's like its 10,000 mi. After a failed attempt at mediation, my ex recently asked through her attorney if I will give up my parental rights. I don't know what to do, and I'm beginning to think that it will be better for my daughter if I just let her stepfather adopt her and I move away.* **99**

The scenario sounds like the beginnings of what many professionals refer to as *parental alienation*. Unfortunately, the psychological community is still at odds about whether parental alienation is actually a syndrome, in itself, or reactive behavior, when manifesting with other mental health concerns. Whether it is, or it isn't, the label is not important. Some definite behaviors are associated with alienating one's child from the other parent that we see over and over again. These behaviors were first discussed at length by Richard A. Gardner, MD, in his book *The Parental Alienation Syndrome* more than 20 years ago.

Although quite a few years have passed since Dr Gardner's first observations, and many of his theories are now in question, much of the current research on what is referred to as *parental alienation* still incorporates Dr Gardner's original theories. He determined that there are levels of alienation—mild, moderate, and severe—and hypothesized that "Parental alienation is characterized by a cluster of symptoms that usually appear together in the child, especially in the moderate and severe types."

Dr Gardner goes on to offer a list of behaviors that are consistent with what has been labeled as parental alienation. I also offer further explanation in parenthesis of what the behaviors look like in everyday life.

1. Begins a campaign of denigration (makes visitation unbearable by systematically undermining the other parent)

2. Weak, absurd, or frivolous rationalizations for the deprecation ("Your father really doesn't love you.")

3. Lack of ambivalence (The other parent is all bad and everything is that parent's fault.)

4. The "independent-thinker" phenomenon (believes "I am the better parent" and, as a result, refuses to return phone calls or texts and doesn't tell or lies to the child about when the other parent calls)

5. Reflexive support of the alienating parent in the parental conflict (believes "I am the only one with all the information and it is impossible to problem-solve together")

6. Absence of guilt over cruelty to or exploitation of and sometimes both with the alienated parent (sabotages the relationship by telling the child untruths or intimacies about what led to the divorce that the child has no business knowing or does not inform the other parent of doctor's appointments, dentist's appointments, school conferences, or parent-attended sports activities)

7. The presence of borrowed scenarios (openly blames the breakup on the ex's new partner, even if the new partner wasn't in the picture during the breakup, or refers to the noncustodial parent by first name rather than "your mom or dad" and refers to the stepparent as "Mom" or "Dad" or other parental-sounding names)

8. Spread of the animosity to the friends or extended family and sometimes both of the alienated parent (bad-mouths the ex to friends and acquaintances)

Let's see how this might all translate into real life....

Most of us have been raised to believe that the "best home" has a mommy and a daddy and children. Society is working to change this theory, and different family models are slowly becoming accepted, but that is taking time. When a relationship doesn't work out and the parents break up, some custodial parents find new partners but want to recreate that "best home" scenario, doing everything in their power to undermine the ex so that they can once again live as one happy family.

Things can get very unpleasant if the parent who is being aced out fights back. As a result, the custodial parent then pulls out all the stops and begins the campaign of denigration laid out by Dr Gardner and systematically attempts to undermine the other parent's influence. It's essentially brainwashing, if you want to label it as such, and it's very difficult to combat once the campaign is in full swing.

In the midst of the chaos, few parents admit their attempts to alienate or what those attempts really do to their child. But the truth is, their actions contribute to severe psychological problems in their children. The constant badgering can be the reason behind anxiety and adjustment disorders, anger problems, and problems with self-esteem and the ability to feel centered and secure for the rest of a child's life. It can also lay the groundwork for unsuccessful relationships in the future. The child has no model for kindness, positive interaction, or problem-solving with a partner. These children have a model for hate, and that's what they may recreate in their future relationships. Eventually, if enough time goes by, the child becomes so alienated from the noncustodial parent that, in frustration, the noncustodial parent gives up and goes away. But don't do that. Your child needs both parents in life, and the minute you stop trying to be a parent is the minute your ex can say something such as "See? Obviously, your Dad (or Mom) doesn't care."

Eight Steps to Combating Parental Alienation

It is unfortunate that we must address the concept of parental alienation at all in *Co-parenting Through Separation and Divorce*. The whole theory behind an "intentional or unintentional deterioration of a child's relationship with one of their parents" is contrary to the mind-set we are trying to promote. However, parental alienation is real, and, for the sake of your child and your relationship, you must consistently confront it head-on if you are faced with it.

1. Do not give up on or stop seeing your child. Even though you might feel defeated, make sure your visits together are well planned and full of adventures to keep your child busy when you are together.

2. Allow friends to accompany your child on visits. This achieves a few things.
   - It allows you to meet the children your child is attracted to for friendships.
   - It allows you to see how your child interacts with peers.
   - It keeps the child busy during any downtime.
   - You have a witness to any manufactured situations that really didn't happen.

3. Keep a journal and record all the days and times you were denied your regularly scheduled time with the child and the reason behind it. If you must return to court, you will need a record.

4. Make sure your child is in counseling and the counselor knows that you are open to joining your child in session.

5. Make it clear to all concerned (the other parent, your child, your child's counselor, and the court) that you do not want your time with your child reduced.

   Truth be told, reducing parents' time with their child rarely solves the problem. The problem is not the schedule; the problem is the parents' inability to work together in the best interest of their child. That will continue whether the parents' time with their child is adjusted or not.

6. No matter how overwhelmed you become, do not give up your parental rights.

   If an attempt to alienate a child can be proven—and this is done by extensive inter-views with a psychologist during a custody evaluation—common practice is for the court to first mandate reunification therapy, when experienced counselors attempt to advise the parent and the child to reunify the child with the alienating parent. It would also not be out of the question if the court awards primary custody to the alienated parent and supervised visits to the alienating parent. Reason being, sometimes the vendetta is so intense that removing the child from the influence of the alienating parent is the only recourse to stop the attempted alienation.

7. Parental alienation is difficult to oppose on your own. If you must return to court for help, don't attempt to represent yourself. Find a family law attorney who specializes in combating parental alienation.

8. Don't be afraid to seek help from a co-parenting counselor—someone who can work with both parents for the good of their child. Unfortunately, parental aliena-tion attempts can be so insidious that things often go too far for conventional co-parenting counseling to help, but therapists who specialize in this subject are available to concerned parents for advice and direction.

Supporting the Child's Time With the Other Parent

66 *My daughter tells me she doesn't want to go back to her mother's when her time with me is up. I told her mother, and she says she tells her the exact same thing. My daughter would never lie about something like that!* **99**

That your child tells you she doesn't want to leave does not necessarily mean she prefers your home. It means exactly what she is telling you. She doesn't want to leave—and she may very well be telling her mother the same thing because she doesn't want to leave her either. Consider that your child may be torn between the 2 people she loves the most, and, when she has settled in, she doesn't want to pack up and go to the other home. Consider that she's not lying, and neither is Mom. They are both telling you the truth.

The **incorrect** responses to "I don't want to leave" or "I don't want to go" are

▶ "I know, honey, but you'll be home soon."

You've just undermined your child's relationship with her other parent by implying that you are the "real" parent and your house is "home." In this situation, children are just biding their time at the other parent's house until they get back to where they belong.

▶ "You have to go, because it's a court order" or "The judge says you have to go."

A child's mother and father or other caregivers are her greatest source of security. If you tell children that someone other than their parent can make decisions about their welfare, you have just given up your parental power and your ability to make the children feel secure and protected. Essentially, you just told your children that someone has more power over them than their parent.

The **correct** response is

Be empathetic but firm, and support the child's time with the other parent: "Honey, this is your time with your father. He loves you and looks forward to seeing you."

Co-parenting tip. Do not attempt to bribe the child or smooth things over on behalf of the other parent: "If you go without an argument, we can go out for pizza when you get home." Even though you may be trying to help, that undermines the other parent's importance.

If your child truly likes it better at one home, that's a huge red flag that co-parents are not on the same page. Rather than let your ego be stroked, because you are positive your child likes you best, it's time for both of you parents to put your heads together and figure out a way to make the transition from house to house easier on your child. That may mean changing the parenting plan or simply changing your attitude at the exchanges. Remember to talk with your child and see whether she can share how she feels. Maybe your child is bonding with step-siblings or the neighbor kids and now doesn't want to leave because she won't see them for another week. Whatever the issue is, stand back, take a look at what you are both doing, compare notes, and make the changes necessary for your child to be happy and well-adjusted at both homes.

Coordinating Discipline

Toddlers and Elementary School–Aged Children

66 *My 5-year-old is beginning to become defiant when I ask him to do something. My concern is that I am far more patient than my co-parent and we discipline in a completely different way. I do not approve of spanking.* 99

Coordinating disciplinary techniques is far more important than you think. If one parent disciplines and the other doesn't, the child will gravitate to the parent who is more lenient and will take advantage of that situation. Your child may likely want to stay with the parent who is less lenient. So if you can't get on the same page with discipline, you are setting one or both co-parents up for failure, and, ultimately, that hurts your children.

66 *But nothing works!* 99

Parents need to ask themselves how well physical punishment actually works. Usually, the parent admits, "Not that well." That answer matches what we've learned about spanking over the years. Even when physical discipline stops a behavior in the short term, in the long term, it consistently worsens behavior. Children who are spanked are more likely to strike others, having learned that hitting is how you solve problems and get what you want. They are also subject to levels of anxiety, depression, and aggression higher than those in children who are not hit, all of which ultimately worsen behavior.

Instead, positively praising the behaviors you like to see from your children will go a lot further. When you have to come up with a consequence, it will have much more impact in a setting where you're usually positive. As a rule, behavioral specialists suggest that you shoot for a 10:1 ratio of praise to correction.

Ignoring undesired behaviors works well when it's a practical choice. Tantrums are a classic behavior that responds well to being ignored, but so is any other behavior that's intended to get your attention at an inappropriate time or in an inappropriate way. When the behavior stops, you can elaborately praise your child for stopping and have a conversation about what your child wants. Your child wants your attention more than almost anything else, and by giving it to the behaviors you like, you'll see more of them.

Using Time-outs Effectively

Most parents have heard of time-out, but few effectively use it. The idea of time-out is to interrupt an undesirable behavior and get the child out of the situation, although when you're super frustrated, it may be as much for you to get a break as for your child. It can be thought of as a positive and effective disciplinary strategy, and, to that extent, the child should spend it in a quiet, not-fun place. For a toddler, that may simply involve holding your child in your lap facing away from you. Children, especially young children, are still learning how to control their behavior. When your child is learning not to pull the cat's tail, moving your child away from the cat for a few minutes makes a lot of sense.

Time-outs should be short, as many minutes as your child is old plus 1 (eg, 4 minutes for a 3-year-old). They're not time for conversation, but you should follow them up with a "time-in," when you briefly remind the child why the time-out was needed: "You can't pull the cat's tail, or he'll bite you." Give her a hug and move on with your day.

Preteens and Teenagers

> **❝**Last year, I bought a cell phone for my son. He's 12 and I thought he was ready for the responsibility, but I caught him surfing sites he shouldn't and have decided to take away the phone for a while. His father is fighting me on it because they spend a lot of time chatting, and I think he feels it fills in the gaps—he cancels his weekends a lot. My son is watching out for who 'wins' this one.**❞**

That the parents in the scenario are discussing cell phone use, rather than Mom just taking the phone away, is great news, but, there's a *little* red flag waving. Can you see it?

Ideally, the co-parents should have talked and agreed from the beginning whether a cell phone was appropriate at this time and what would happen if their child misused the phone. What will the consequences be? Will the phone be taken away? If so, for how long? And, if the length of grounding runs into the other parent's custodial time, will the grounding continue at the other home?

The key to successful co-parenting is to take a proactive stance, not a reactive stance, to child-rearing and to communicate regularly with your co-parent. These parents are obviously communicating, but they're playing catch-up. That may set them up for failure. If they don't agree how to handle a situation before being faced with it, they will ultimately end up fighting about it. And, as this mother has already mentioned in her original query, their child is taking note of who "wins" this power struggle. It won't take him long to figure out how to play the two of them.

It also sounds as if Mom thinks Dad relies a little too much on the phone to stay in touch with his son. If he was a long-distance dad, I would be commending him for regularly using the phone to reach out, but because he's not, it could feel like an easy out to his son. Any form of communication is good, but the best time is spent one-on-one and face-to-face. Parents must remember that their child is more than just a text away. Time spent with your child will never be wasted time.

For the record, I often caution parents about using discipline strategies that involve their children's phone because their children will not be able to contact them when they are out and about.

Case in point: The child can't use his phone but is still participating in after-school sports. Practice runs late or gets out early and he can't call you. I suggest parents designate a "phone place" in the home. When the child comes home, that's where the phone goes and the child can't use it—unless the other parent calls. That is the only exception. If the child leaves for school, he may take the phone only for emergencies, but he immediately comes home after school and the phone goes back to the phone place. (You can disable or check your child's history to verify that the phone has not been used.) If friends are allowed to come over, the phone goes to the phone place as well. (I always allowed friends to come over, but they could not hang out in my child's room. If they wanted to watch TV, they watched in the living room. That was torture at first, but it soon became a blessing.) If the friends can't abide by that rule, they don't come over until your child is no longer grounded.

Although grounding is regarded as an effective disciplinary tool for teens, grounding for long periods of time may be an impractical form of discipline if your child or teen goes back and forth between homes regularly. If you have grounded your teen, but during that time, your teen is scheduled to go to your co-parent's home, there is no guarantee the grounding will continue. As a result of being grounded at one home and not the other, your 15-year-old may call to say he doesn't want to come home for a while. That's why, if grounding is in the cards and you can't coordinate efforts with your co-parent, you may wish to consider that the discipline strategy be in place only until the child or teen returns to the other parent's home.

Finally, do the best you can to coordinate efforts, but if the other parent is not on board, you have to establish rules in your own home that work for you.

Co-parenting tip. You'll figure out a rule that best works for your child, but it begins with communicating with your co-parent.

"I Pay for the Phone!"

❝ *Three months ago, I decided to buy my teenaged son a phone. It costs me $100 a month. Last week, his mother decided that since he got an F in geometry, she would ground him from using the phone. Now I can't talk to my kid and I pay for the phone!* ❞

When parents are in a relationship and raising their children together, they agree about the rules surrounding the children's use of any phone, laptop, or tablet before it being purchased. The children would also know the rules and they would understand that their beloved phone would be the first thing to go when the rules are broken. Period, end of story.

Then the parents break up and they forget how to parent. Oh, they think they are being good parents because they offer their kids all the basic necessities when they are at their home, but they forget how to consult each other in the best interest of their children, they stop coordinating efforts, and they make arbitrary decisions that affect their children and their children's time with their other parent. Kids learn very quickly, when faced with this kind of parenting, how to play it all to their advantage.

In the ideal world of co-parenting, it would be nice if the parents could coordinate disciplinary rules—nice because the parents agreed, and think how that would eliminate tension as the child went back and forth, and nice because the child would have the same rules and not have to weigh one's allegiance to each parent each time one left one house to go to the other. But, in reality, divorced parents don't always agree, and when they don't, most dig in their heels and say, "My house, my rules." That's how you end up with problems such as children being grounded from electronics paid for by the other parent.

Your role as a parent is to teach lessons, but when you need to set consequences, the child should never be grounded from the other parent—not from seeing that parent, not from going to that parent's home, and not from communicating with that parent in any way. It does not matter who pays for the phone, laptop, or tablet; when use is being restricted as a learning lesson, parents must put in checks and balances that allow the child to talk with both parents at any time.

In this particular scenario, if the parents were truly co-parenting, their conversation would go something like this.

Mom: *Hello, Michael flunked geometry. I think he spends a disproportionate amount of time playing on his phone than doing homework. I think we should restrict it until he brings his grade up.*

Dad: *That's fine, but I don't want him grounded from talking to me. I pay for the phone, you know.*

Mom: *I do, and that's why I am calling. How would you like me to handle that?*

Dad: *I'll call him every night from 7:00 to 8:00 pm. Make sure his phone is on, please. And he can call me anytime. He just needs to check with you first. When he comes to my home, you're the only one he can talk to until he is no longer grounded. What do you think?*

Mom: *Perfect. I'll let you know as soon as his grades are up, or you can check online to make sure all his assignments are up-to-date.*

Then to implement the grounding, Mother explains to the teen that she and his father discussed his grounding; then she lays out the program to the teen.

Co-parenting tip. The telephone should be used as a tool for communication, not as a weapon to undermine the other parent.

Enlisting Your Co-parent's Help When Disciplining

❝ *My son's father and I get along pretty well, so when our son cut school and was caught skateboarding in a parking lot near my home, I let him know how much trouble he was going to be in when his father found out. We called his dad right then and there, and I let him yell at him. That put the fear in him!* **❞**

I bet the parent in the scenario thought she was co-parenting properly. After all, she reached out to the other parent, she confided in him, and she asked for help in finding a solution—and she gave up all her parental power in the process.

This child lives in 2 homes. The "wait until your father gets home" type of discipline may have worked for a 2-parent household years ago, but now, when so many children go back and forth between Mom's house and Dad's house, both parents may have to take responsibility for discipline when the child is in their home.

Of course, anticipating problems and coming to an agreement before the child needing discipline is the ideal approach, but at times, time is of the essence—the co-parent can't "wait until Dad (or Mom) gets home" because Dad (or Mom) doesn't live there. That's when parents who truly co-parent anticipate the problem, agree to a particular response, and stick to their agreement when faced with the need to discipline.

If, at the spur of the moment, there is a need to deviate from the agreed-on response, those who truly co-parent acknowledge their co-parent's parental power and trust that parent to make good on-the-spot decisions in the best interest of their child.

Suspected Abuse

66 *My child has been sad and withdrawn lately and now tells me she does not want to go back to her father's home. I'm worried there might be something wrong....***99**

When a parent suspects there is "something wrong," it merits investigation, especially if your child is reporting questionable behavior. However, parents must also have age-appropriate expectations for their children's behavior. A parent, for example, who expects a 2-year-old to sit still and be quiet during a visit does not really get the concept of being 2. A parent who comments that a fussy infant or toddler is being "bad" also sends up red flags; young children are never bad. Before we continue, let's clarify what is regarded as *abuse*. There are different kinds of abuse, and each requires a little different action plan.

Defining Abuse and Neglect

It's natural that separated and divorced parents will introduce some differences between their homes. At one house, a child may get plenty of sleep, and at the other, he may stay awake half the night. The food may be healthier; the car, safer; and the home condition, better at one place or another. There's a line, however, between less-than-ideal parenting and abuse or neglect. While that line can be fuzzy at times, it helps to start with some basic definitions.

Physical Abuse

When doctors, psychologists, and law enforcement personnel think about child abuse, we use 4 broad categories. It's not unusual in cases of abuse that a situation includes more than one. Physical abuse usually comes to mind first but is not limited to when physical punishment goes awry. For example, an angry parent loses control or is possibly under the influence and takes things too far. The American Academy of Pediatrics strongly discourages parents from using any kind of physical punishment, including spanking, slapping, hitting, kicking, forceful shaking, or using any foreign object (eg, spoon, belt, switch) to hit a child. We now know that these techniques don't work as effective discipline, often worsening behavior in the long term. More important, hitting a child causes permanent psychological damage. When parents say, "I was spanked, and I turned out fine," it is important to acknowledge their observation but also remind them that every child is different, and physical punishment harms most children.

Importantly, not all physical abuse leaves marks, and "marks" are the determiner for agencies to intercede. If a child comes home and says, "Dad, Mom spanked me!" or, "Mom, Dad hit me!" that's not necessarily abuse, and reporting it may be ignored. It is not illegal to spank your child—and if the parent who spanked determined that spanking was an appropriate disciplinary tactic at the time, that's the parent's right as a parent. It is illegal to spank your child so hard that you leave bruises. *That* is when an agency will intercede.

Spanking is not the only form of physical discipline that can be harmful. Some parents may poke their child in the chest, yell, squeeze their child's arms uncomfortably, or push their child. Threatening physical violence doesn't leave any marks, but it can be terrifying to a child and create long-lasting psychological scars and is highly discouraged.

Emotional Abuse

At the other end of the spectrum is emotional abuse, which may also be referred to as *emotional neglect*. Separation and divorce are already traumatic experiences for children, with lifelong psychological and even physical consequences. Add to that that we as parents are rarely at our best during these events, experiencing our own anxiety, depression, and frustration. The combination raises the risk that parents will lash out at children by yelling, insulting them, blaming them, or simply being emotionally unavailable. Emotional abuse doesn't have to be directed toward the child to be abusive; witnessing physical or emotional violence between parents or a parent and a new partner counts. As with physical abuse, it can be difficult to define when a behavior crosses the line from lousy parenting to actual abuse, but sometimes, sadly, it's not that difficult to tell.

Here's an example.

> *A father walks into the house after work with a 12 pack of beer, puts them into the refrigerator, and sits down in front of the TV. It is obvious he has already had a few before he walked in the house. Jared, aged 12 years, and Janelle, aged 14 years, are waiting for him in the living room. He was supposed to pick them up after school for their weekend time with him, but he forgot. School is around the corner, so they walked to Dad's.*

> *"Get me a cold one!" he yells to Jared, but Jared has his earphones on while playing video games and can't hear him. "Get me a beer!" Dad yells at Janelle. She takes a beer from the refrigerator and hands it to her father.*

> *"Your good-for-nothing brother thinks he's too good to get me a beer. He'll get his later! You're the good child. Come here and give your dad a hug."*

> *Dad drinks 3 more beers and falls asleep in his chair. The kids are left to fend for themselves. They order a pizza to be delivered. When the pizza arrives, Dad wakes up.*

> *"What the hell? Who ordered pizza?"*

"We did, Dad. We're hungry."

"Do you make the money around here?"

Dad throws his credit card at the delivery driver and puts the pizza onto the counter. He then walks back to his chair to settle in for the night.

"Janelle, get me another beer...."

Dad falls asleep while drinking the beer. Janelle takes her pizza to her room. Jared continues to play video games.

The next day, Dad wakes up and while he's straightening up the kitchen…

"Neither of you says anything to your mother about what goes on around here. What goes on here stays here! **"**

People who abuse kids often tell them, "Don't tell." If you hear yourself telling your child, "What goes on here stays here," that qualifies as emotional abuse. You are expecting your child out and out lie—or lie by omission—to make value judgments based on your demand for dishonesty. A child must then consider to whom the child's allegiance lies—"Whose side am I on? Mom's or Dad's?" That's emotional abuse.

Children experiencing emotional neglect learn that their needs are not going to be met and may give up entirely on sharing their feelings with others or even identifying those feelings in themselves. The symptoms often don't manifest until adulthood, when survivors find themselves unable to trust others or form strong relationships. They may feel unusually disconnected, unfulfilled, or empty. These are feelings all of us struggle with at times, of course, but the difference is in degree, the extent to which these feelings interfere with one's ability to find life satisfaction.

It may be difficult for you alone, without the help of a professional counselor, to address your co-parent's emotional neglect. If you have a good relationship, you may be able to suggest ways for your co-parent to be more responsive to your child's emotions, starting with simply asking your child how he's feeling or helping him name his emotions when he appears happy.

Sexual Abuse

The idea of sexual abuse horrifies everyone. Because it can be difficult to detect, the specter of sexual abuse haunts many parents in situations of separation and divorce, when they have doubts about the environment in the other home. Sexual abuse does not have to involve contact; it may include inappropriate exposure to sexual situations as well. Sexual abuse that involves contact falls into 2 categories:

contact without penetration (ie, fondling, masturbation) and contact with penetration (oral, genital, or anal alone or in combination).

Child sexual abuse does not discriminate. It can affect any child at any age. Some findings often alarm parents but are actually normal and do not mean that a child has been sexually abused. These include vaginal bleeding in the first week after birth and masturbation in the toddler and preschool years. Red rashes are common around the anus and the vagina in childhood and usually do not suggest abuse. Herpes and genital warts can be sexually transmitted, but they can also occur without any sexual contact whatsoever, and neither can be used as evidence that a child has been abused. Straddle injuries of the groin can and do occur, often on bicycles or playground equipment, but usually, children who experience such injuries are old enough to describe exactly what happened.

Some other behaviors, on the other hand, raise serious red flags and deserve further investigation when they occur before adolescence or when they become inappropriate or intrusive. These include

▶ Putting the mouth on genitalia

▶ Asking to engage in sex acts

▶ Masturbating with an object

▶ Inserting objects into the vagina or anus

▶ Imitating sexual intercourse

▶ Making sexual sounds

▶ French-kissing (with the tongue)

▶ Undressing other people

▶ Asking to watch pornography

▶ Imitating sexual behavior with dolls

The nature of sexual abuse makes it especially challenging to investigate, and the criminal implications of sexual abuse make it particularly important to diagnose accurately. For this reason, some medical professionals, called *certified medical examiners,* are especially trained in making this diagnosis. Not every county or municipality has trained certified medical examiners on-site, but if they are available, they are the only people who should conduct an examination. Otherwise, the examination may be performed by a professional in your child's pediatric office or the local emergency department. Credible allegations of child sexual abuse should be investigated by the best qualified medical professional available, always in conjunction with law enforcement and child protective services (CPS).

When Is It Not Abuse?

Melissa walked into her daughter's room to find Jillian and stepbrother, William, both 4 years old, naked from the waist down. Jillian was crouched over William's penis, staring at it intently.

"Oh my god, Jillian! What are you doing?"

"I'm looking at William's thing, Mommy. **99**

Experimentation

Our children are human, and they experiment. You set them up for failure if you leave them unattended without adult supervision. However, 2 four-year-olds looking at each other's private parts would most likely not be of concern to CPS, but it would be suggested that the parents not leave the children unattended. An older adolescent boy or girl experimenting with a child of 3 or 4 years would be of concern.

Neglect

The fourth broad category of child maltreatment involves neglect, the failure of a parent to provide for a child's basic needs. Neglect may be physical, nutritional, or medical. Emotional neglect falls under the heading of emotional abuse, but, of course, it's both. Neglect can be difficult to pin down in some cases, but in others, it's glaringly obvious.

For example, CPS may make a finding of "general neglect" if not enough food is in the home, if the home has no running water or the electricity has been turned off, if food or animal feces have not been disposed of properly and the home is infested with roaches or maggots, or if there is a refusal by one parent to not meet medical needs, such as not giving a medication. They may also make a finding of general neglect (caregiver absence) if an adult is not present and toddlers are left alone with 5- or 6-year-old children. (For a more in-depth discussion of child neglect, see Chapter 9, Is My Child Safe Over There?.)

What Do I Do if I Suspect Something Is Wrong?

Abuse or neglect of any kind is concerning, and if a child tells you something troublesome, believe the child. But, rather than immediately accuse the other parent, start your investigation by asking that parent about what the child is reporting, and if you don't get an answer that makes you feel comfortable, that's when you get the authorities involved for help.

This is when many parents question this advice: "Wait a minute, my child comes home telling me that his mother hit him, and I'm supposed to call her and ask her about it?"

Absolutely. That's what co-parents do. And they reach out and help each other as well, because they both love that child. We must remember, many things that are legal are still not good ideas, and hitting a child is no exception, but a disagreement about discipline merits a discussion. This is *your* child. *You* will have to determine if this is a spanking or a beating. Is it discipline or abuse? If you honestly can't decide, agencies such as the police and CPS can help you.

"My Child Told Me..."

> 66 *My child is telling me that her uncle touches her after everyone goes to sleep and she is afraid. Her uncle lives with her mother. I called her mother to tell her what our daughter is reporting, and she said she thinks our daughter is exaggerating. I'm afraid to send her back to her mother's home. What recourse do I have?* 99

If a custody order is in place, you can't arbitrarily decide to keep a child at your home. You must abide by the court order; however, there is recourse. You can apply for temporary custody orders with the court. Most often this is done in conjunction with a referral to CPS. While CPS is investigating, a judge will consider your request, and if it is granted, you will receive sole custody and not have to return the child until the investigation is completed. Courts know how serious something such as this can be; therefore, a judge will intercede quickly. A hearing will take place and the judge will finalize the decision to change the parenting plan or to keep it as it is.

Is It the Truth or a Lie?

> 66 *My child tells me all sorts of things that go on at his mother's home that seem absolutely ridiculous, but I don't want to completely discount what she says. How can I differentiate between the truth and a lie or an exaggeration?* 99

This is a tough one, because children make up stories, especially young children, or they report things incorrectly. Or they report things correctly, but adults misunderstand what is being passed on. Just because our children speak doesn't mean we understand their language. An infant or a toddler obviously can't tell you what happened, nor can a child with a developmental delay that affects his understanding or speech. Children younger than 4 years have little ability to tell reality from fantasy, so it can be nearly impossible to judge how true their stories are. Children younger than 6 years have little understanding of time, so while they may be able to tell you *what* happened, don't count on them telling you *when* it happened, unless it was tied to a special event, such as a birthday or holiday.

Case in point: During mediation, an angry father reported that his 4-year-old told him he caught his mother sleeping with her boyfriend. The father was furious, and because the parents rarely spoke, he did not check in with Mother after the incident was reported to him. He simply returned to court to try to change custody. As we spoke together in my office, it was discovered that the mother and boyfriend had fallen asleep in front of the TV after the children had gone to bed, and after having a bad dream, the child woke up to find them asleep on the couch. All he could tell his father was "Randy was sleeping with Mommy." No change in custody was made, but we can all learn a valuable lesson from this. Our children tell us something they perceive and innocently report it as a child. We take that innocence and tack on our adult skepticism and perceptions, and, all of a sudden, the meaning of their story changes from innocent to sordid.

Even older children may not get their stories straight for a variety of reasons. Children are loyal to their parents, even abusive ones, and they may not want to get their parents in trouble. They may also lie to keep themselves from being punished or because they sincerely feel that they deserved whatever abuse they sustained because they were "being bad." Adults and other children often discourage kids from tattling, so they may believe that honestly reporting abuse makes them a snitch or a narc.

Parents can take cues from doctors, social workers, and law enforcement personnel who are trained to avoid asking leading questions. Instead of asking, "Did your mother's boyfriend hit you?" we ask, "How did you get that bruise on your cheek?"

When You Suspect Abuse

1. Call the police.
2. Call child protective services.
3. Apply for temporary custody orders.

If you question whether it really is abuse, report it and let the agency decide whether it merits an investigation.

Co-parenting tip. A young child's perception can be skewed, and the ability to communicate what is seen or felt can be questionable as well. A child of 3 or 4 years may have trouble communicating what happened to him. A child of 6 or 7 years, or 9 or 10 years, has a very clear memory of what happened and can articulate it very well.

Parents who live under the same roof often disagree. It goes without saying that co-parents who live apart will do the same. Even if you get along, when you are faced with a problem, it's hard to know exactly what to do to find a solution—together. That's why one of the primary things I suggest to parents in preparation to co-parent after their breakup is to establish a *forum for conflict resolution* to aid them in problem-solving; otherwise, they will just problem-solve the way they always did, when they were together. Some fight. Some clam up. Some avoid and withdraw. Some call names and threaten. Some cry. None of these tactics help parents figure out how to solve a problem. If one did, they would probably still be together. A problem-solving plan can be put into place before there's an issue, and then they will know exactly what to do when faced with a possible disagreement.

Many couples who break up know that, and the plan they put into place is to agree to go to a mediator before going back to court. I can't tell you how many court-appointed mediations I have done when I have heard the following conversation:

> **❝** *You said we would never go to court, and here we are. All you had to do was call me."*
>
> *"I did. You never answer the phone."*
>
> *"You could have texted me."*
>
> *"I did. You don't return my texts. I call the kids when they are with you, and you don't ever let me talk to them. It's like they are in a black hole when they are at your house."*
>
> *"I answer your calls."*
>
> *"No, you don't. The only way I can get you to listen to me is if we go to court."*
>
> *"We said we would never go to court! All you had to do is talk to me!"*
>
> *"You don't answer my calls. How am I supposed to talk to you?* **❞**

If this sounds familiar, you are the parents who need a **plan in place to help you**—and it's not just that you agree you will go to a mediator. A plan will head off the need to go to a mediator—it's for the time between "the problem" and the mediator. It's for when you are living the problem.

You will need to agree how you will approach a problem *before* there is a problem and honor your agreement to the established plan. Make it a checklist, and each time you fulfill a step, check it off. The last step unfortunately is **going to court.** If the step has a check, you have attempted it and going to court will not be a surprise. As you work down the list together, it may be an incentive to figure things out with your co-parent, because if you can't, you're giving up your power to a judge to decide about *your* kids.

Good Ex-etiquette Co-parenting Contract

This contract is between _____ and _____.

We acknowledge that we are both good people who are simply unable to live together. We believe that all children have the right to have both parents in their lives, and we shall do everything to support that end. We pledge to negotiate in good faith relying on the 10 Rules of Good Ex-etiquette* as a guide and to use the best interest of our children as the basis of our decisions.

In solving problems or disagreements, we pledge to

☐ Call the other parent on the telephone to discuss the matter privately and respectfully.

☐ Call a meeting with the other parent by using the following means:

   ☐ Telephone: _____

   ☐ Text: _____

   ☐ Email: _____

☐ Hold the meeting in an agreed-on public place. It shall be: _____.

☐ The other parent shall respond within _____ days with an acknowledgment or a suggestion for other dates and times.

☐ We shall not drink alcohol or take recreational drugs 8 hours before our meeting, nor will we consume alcoholic beverages as we negotiate.

Meeting Protocol

☐ We shall address only one topic per meeting, unless mutually agreed-on before the meeting.

☐ We shall display a photo of our child or children at the meeting to remind us to keep our tempers and that we are there to problem-solve, not argue.

☐ The parent calling the meeting shall present the problem with a suggested solution that centers on the best interest of our child or children.

☐ We shall negotiate in good faith, plus stay open-minded to any alternative suggestions made by the other parent.

☐ We promise to be respectful and polite during all negotiations.

☐ We promise to always consider a compromise when searching for a solution.

☐ We agree to sign a final agreement after each meeting as verification of our mutual acknowledgment of finding a solution, plus demonstrate good faith that we shall both uphold the agreement.

☐ If we cannot come to an agreement using the prior steps, we shall go to a mutually agreed-on mediator or therapist to help us address the problem.

☐ The parent presenting the problem shall be responsible for making the appointment and then notify our child's or children's other parent in a mutually agreed-on manner.

☐ We agree to split the cost equally.

☐ If we cannot come to an agreement using a mediator or therapist to help us address the problem, we shall then seek legal means through a court of law.

Co-parent: _____ Date: _____

Co-parent: _____ Date: _____

© 2015 Jann Blackstone, PsyD. Ex-etiquette® is a registered trademark.   *https://bonusfamilies.com/ten-rules-good-ex-etiquette-parents.

Finally, for some couples, sometimes things are just too fresh, and trying to negotiate seems impossible. I recently worked with divorced parents who were so angry with each other they could barely sit in the same room. As we spoke, it became apparent that both were struggling with the hurt of the breakup and they couldn't get past it to negotiate in the best interest of their kids. It's times like this when you really have to just stop—nothing either of you can do will get the other back enough for the hurt that person has inflicted, and if you keep up the conflict, the ones who are truly hurt will be your children. Stop hashing it over. Try your best to make a pact—from this point on, it's *only* about your kids. Period.

7

Parenting Plans

Stay committed to your decisions,
but stay flexible in your approach.

TONY ROBBINS

The schedule in which parents share their children's time is called a *parenting plan*. Most parents want to share equal time with their children, but not all parenting plans are created equal. The parenting plan that is best for *your* child may be an equal custody plan, or it may be that your child lives primarily in one home and sees the other parent on the weekends, sometimes every other weekend. Your parenting plan, also known as a custody agreement, is a plan that outlines when each parent will see the children once they no longer live together. An effective plan is personalized to fit the needs of your family situation and takes the following questions into consideration:

▶ How long have the parents been apart?
▶ How have the parents been sharing the children's time to date?
  – Is there currently, or does there need to be, a primary caregiver? If so, which parent is most likely to share the children's time and foster a relationship with the other parent?
  – What is the distance each parent must travel to exchange the children?
    • Are there any barriers to exchanges—for example, restraining orders or orders of protection that prevent the parents from interacting?
    • Extracurricular activities?
  – What is each parent's work schedule?
  – What is the age of each child?
  – Does any child have special needs?

Let's take the considerations one by one and explain why they are important when forming a parenting plan.

How Long Have the Parents Been Apart?

If the child in question is 9 months old, for example, but has rarely seen one of the parents, overnight visits may not be considered appropriate until a bond has been established. The bond would be created through a step plan, starting with hourly visits, progressing to 4 hours in a day, then to all-day visits, and then to 2 all-day visits in a row, and then those 2 days would become an overnight. An agreed-on duration for each step would be established, say, 6 visits for each step, and, starting from scratch, it usually takes between 4 months and 5 months to work up to overnights.

However, if the parents lived together and recently broke up with a 9-month-old infant, the infant would know both parents, a bond would have already been established with both parents, and a step plan to work up to overnights would not be necessary. If, however, a primary caregiver is established, for example, one parent stayed home all day with the child, while the other saw the child after work for a few hours a day, studies have shown that it may not be in the child's best interest if multiple overnights in a row are spent away from the primary caregiver. In those cases, things such as the age of the child and where the parent is living might be a consideration.

For example, the child is 10 months old, and after the separation, one parent is temporarily homeless or is couch surfing with friends. It may not be in the best interest of the infant to set up a parenting plan through which this infant sleeps on the floor or someone's couch. Each situation is unique and needs to be approached in the best interest of *that* child.

How Have the Parents Been Sharing the Children's Time to Date?

When you are building a parenting plan, to keep disruption for a child to a minimum, it's best to start with what the child's schedule was before the breakup and build from there.

Is There Currently, or Does There Need to Be, a Primary Caregiver?

Rarely do parents share parenting time equally when they live together. They fill in when one or the other needs help. If only one parent worked outside the home, the other was most likely in charge of caring for the children. Therefore, the parent whose responsibility it was to take care of the kids might be deemed "the primary caregiver." If this designation is established, it would not be uncommon for that parent to have more time with the children than the other because the children would most likely attend school Monday through Friday from the primary parent's residence.

Who Gets Primary Custody?

A couple of things are considered when a primary designation is established.

1. If a primary caregiver was already established while the relationship was intact.

2. If the parents are at odds, the parent who is most likely to share the child and foster a relationship with the other parent often receives primary custody of the child. But *primary custody,* or more time with the child than the other parent, does not preclude the need to co-parent. To have healthy children after a breakup, parents must consult each other and work together for the sake of the children, no matter what time share has been designated.

What Is the Distance Each Parent Must Travel to Exchange the Children?

It is my experience that it can be extremely stressful for a child to travel longer than a half hour to and from school. Although this is not written in stone and different courts may have different guidelines, if parents must travel longer than 30 minutes one way, then the children are often late for school, they don't live in the same neighborhood as their friends, and the distance from their home to school makes it difficult to participate in after-school extracurricular activities. Therefore, if one parent lives farther than 30 minutes from school, it is likely that the children will live predominantly with one parent when school is in session and visit the other on the weekends and during school breaks.

What Is Each Parent's Work Schedule?

Does either parent work at night or does either parent have to leave for work before the child goes to school? As a result, can the parent get the child to school on time? Who will be supplying child care when the parent is not available? Will the child be attending an after-school program because of a parent's work schedule? All these things are considered.

What Is the Age of Each Child?

The age of each child plays a huge part in how long the child is away from each parent. The psychological community changes their recommendations all the time, but typically, child psychologists suggest a child younger than 1 or 2 years should not be away from the primary caregiver longer than 1- or 2-night overnights per week. Therefore, a toddler would have a completely different schedule than a teenager.

Does Any Child Have Special Needs?

Does the child have a chronic illness or a mental health diagnosis that could influence the parenting plan? Or does the child need a tutor or an individualized education program at school?

Here's the type of question I often receive from one parent attempting to co-parent a child who has special needs.

> 66 *My son has been diagnosed as autistic, high functioning. He also has OCD [obsessive-compulsive disorder], possibly has Tourette syndrome, and can be trying at times, but he's my son and I want to spend more time with him. I'd like to have him 2 days with me, have him 2 days with his mother, and alternate the weekends. His mother and I don't speak, and so I often petition the court to change the parenting plan, but they never do, and I am at a loss.* 99

A lot of red flags are in the scenario—some are obvious, some are not. Let me first address the one that waves the brightest—it's that these parents have a child who has special needs and they don't speak with each other. It doesn't matter what happened in the past; a child diagnosed as having autism spectrum disorder with obsessive-compulsive disorder and Tourette syndrome will be a challenge to raise. These parents need each other's support on this one.

In most cases, when there is a problem, divorced parents rarely reach out to each other. However, although there has been animosity in the past, they both love their child equally. Both are pained when it's difficult for their child to assimilate into mainstream education or when the other kids mimic their child's behavior. Both parents celebrate their child's successes and are saddened by their child's challenges. These parents are not alone while raising their son. And in a positive co-parenting relationship, they realize it even more.

That said, a trait that is often overlooked when designing a parenting plan for a child who has autism spectrum disorder is how much these children crave order and consistency. Children with this diagnosis have trouble with change, so it would not be in this child's best interest to have to follow a parenting plan that requires him to go back and forth every 2 days. Many children with an autism diagnosis also have anxiety, and they may have panic attacks and emotional meltdowns. It is imperative that both parents have a consistent routine in place to help them cope. This may be the reason the court will not consider a change.

At this juncture, the best thing both parents can do is consult their child's doctor and design a plan that incorporates coping strategies they have seen work for their son. Another goal would be for the co-parents to develop a better working relationship so that if Dad wants more time with the child, he can pick up the phone and say, "I have the afternoon free and I'd love to take our son for ice cream." And Mom can say, "Great, come get him." That's a co-parenting relationship that benefits the entire family but especially the child.

"Bird's Nest Custody"

A "bird's nest custody" arrangement, sometimes simply called "nesting," is an unconventional approach to sharing custody of your children, but it works well in special cases—for example, as in William's case—a child with special needs.

William is 12 years old and has been using a wheelchair since he was thrown from a horse at 5 years old. It has been stressful for not only William but his mother and father as well, and they decided to split 2 years ago. William needs a lot of different things to be comfortable, and the house he has lived in all his life has been fitted with hardwood floors, extra wide hallways, and ramps; plus, all the light switches have been altered to allow William easy access. When William's parents discussed how they would share William's time, they realized that asking him to go back and forth between 2 different homes, neither of which was set up for his disability, would be terribly difficult for him, so they opted to "nest," and William sleeps every night at the home that has been adjusted for his comfort and his parents move in and out every 2 weeks.

Nesting works well when everyone is in agreement, and there are a couple different ways it can be approached.

First, understand it is an expensive alternative. Next, the parents need 2 additional residences for when they do not live with William, or they need one residence that they can continue to share in their downtime. This particular approach becomes troublesome when one of the parents gets involved with someone else. Rarely will someone other than a parent invested in a child's special needs move in and out every 2 weeks or wish to share a home with a partner's ex, even if the ex is not present when the new partner is living there. If the new partner has no problem living by oneself every 2 weeks, that understanding simply becomes part of their new life together. But you can see how this particular parenting plan works well only under special situations.

The Child Support Controversy

> **❝** *That's all well and good, but if I saw my daughter more often, I wouldn't have to pay so much child support.* **❞**

Actually, that is true—on paper—but if you had a working relationship with your co-parent, you could probably see your daughter anytime you wanted, if that was your true motivation for the change in your parenting plan.

Child support is calculated by a computer program that takes in to account the amount of time the child spends with each parent while considering income and expenses of both parties. It is not an arbitrary number made up by one party to get at the other party. If your motivation to change the parenting plan is to reduce your bill, rather than increase your time, it is doubtful the court will see a reason to change.

> **❝** *My son called me up and asked if I would split the cost of his karate lessons with his mother. I was outraged that his mother put him up to asking, and I told him, 'No way! Ask your mother! That's what child support is for!'* **❞**

So many red flags. First, neither parent should discuss child support with the children. It will make them feel guilty, as if they are a number, not a beloved child. Any discussion creates a parental hierarchy—"I pay, you receive" or "You pay a pittance, I need more"—and forces the child to take sides: "Which parent is telling me the truth? Is too little paid? Am I a burden?" As a result, the child may identify with the perceived underdog and stop wanting to return to the parent's home who is creating the ruckus.

Second, never ask your child to ask the other parent for money. Again, it puts the child right in the middle. Ask the other parent yourself, come to an agreement, and then present the final decision to the child.

> **❝** *What if there is no decision? What if a parent refuses to help?* **❞**

The "human" thing to do without a decision might be to tell the child that you would love to enroll him in karate, but you simply can't afford it and your co-parent refuses to help, but we have to be superhuman when co-parenting. Of course, you might be resentful, but how will that response help your child? Besides, there may be extenuating circumstances of which you are not aware. Brainstorm. There may be other ways to fund extracurricular activities—scholarships, fundraising, or possibly classes that are taught by volunteers. When your child sees you being creative to raise fund extras, your child will get the message and respect you all the more.

Parenting Plans

Equal Custody and Visitation Schedules: Deciding Whether They Will Work for Your Children

When you choose an equally shared parenting plan, the child spends the same amount of time living with each parent. This allows the child to build a close relationship with both parents; however, an equally shared parenting plan can also be detrimental if the child is too young to be away from the primary caregiver for long periods of time (babies and toddlers) or if there is ongoing parental conflict and problems cannot be discussed easily. This is when parents often turn their children into messengers and communication breaks down. Forcing a child to go back and forth between battling parents is emotionally abusive. If you can't problem-solve together, no parenting plan works well, but an equally shared plan exacerbates any problems in communication the parents may have.

> **❝** *My co-parent and I get along fine. Anything other than 50-50 wouldn't be fair.* **❞**

Wouldn't be fair to whom? If we are making our decisions in the best interest of the children, then we consider them first—and we design a schedule that works best by using what makes their life easier as the criteria for the parenting plan.

With that in mind, if someone states, "I want 50-50!" to a family court judge, the judge's response may be, "I don't know what that means," reason being, the judge wants to know what schedule you would like. Fifty-fifty is not a schedule. It's a concept. The parent is saying, "I want equal time with my children," but that's not necessarily what 50-50 means.

Establishing custody of your children takes 2 concepts into consideration: legal custody and physical custody. *Fifty-fifty legal custody* (joint legal custody) means that both parents have equal legal rights concerning their children. They can both sign legal papers, and they can both make legal decisions for the kids, but it does not guarantee equal time with the children. *Physical custody* refers to where the children actually reside. If you receive equal physical custody, then you have what most parents regard as "50-50" custody of your children.

When 50-50 Schedules Work Best

- Distance between the parents' homes is close enough that exchanges are convenient, and the children can easily attend school from both homes.
- The parents are able to communicate with each other about their children without fighting.
- The children are emotionally ready to switch homes regularly.
- Both parents can easily problem-solve and put the children first.

Here are some common parenting schedules through which the child resides with each parent 50% of the time. You can modify any of these schedules so that they work better for your situation.

The 2-2-3 schedule (Figure 7.1) has your child spending 2 days with one parent, 2 days with the other parent, and 3 days with the first parent. Then the next week, it switches. Please note that the 3:00 pm exchange time has been chosen because it is a common after-school time. If you work later than 3:00 pm and your child is in an after-school program or with a private child care provider, of course the exchange times may be adjusted to fit your family's needs.

Because there are so many exchanges, and the midweek days and weekends alternate back and forth, the prerequisites for this parenting plan to work best are

▶ Infants and toddlers who are not cognizant of time and the days of the week

▶ Younger children who do not have a regular school schedule

▶ Low parental conflict

Sharing different days of the week can make it difficult for school-aged children to stay organized. If parents do not communicate well, then with the constant back and forth, homework may not get done on time, reading records may not be signed, and the children's teachers will not know which parent to contact on what day.

Sun	Mon	Tue	Wed	Thu	Fri	Sat
	3:00 pm				3:00 pm	
			3:00 pm			
			3:00 pm			
	3:00 pm				3:00 pm	

Legend: ▨ Parent 1 ▨ Parent 2

Figure 7.1. The 2-2-3 Schedule

The 3-4-4-3 schedule has your child spend 3 days with one parent, 4 days with the other parent, 4 days with the first parent, and then 3 days with the other parent.

Sun	Mon	Tue	Wed	Thu	Fri	Sat
3:00 pm			3:00 pm			
3:00 pm				3:00 pm		

Legend: ▨ Parent 1 ▨ Parent 2

Figure 7.2. The 3-4-4-3 Schedule

Schedules of this sort are a good compromise when children are younger and unable to stay away from either parent for longer than 3 or 4 days. This schedule can serve as a transition schedule if the ultimate goal is to keep an equally shared custody plan. Consider this plan for children around ages 5 to 9 years or older.

The 2-2-5-5 schedule designates Monday at 3:00 pm to Wednesday at 3:00 pm to one parent and Wednesday at 3:00 pm to Friday at 3:00 pm to the other parent. Each parent would also alternate weekends, Friday at 3:00 pm to Monday at 3:00 pm. When the parent's designated weekend attaches to that parent's regularly scheduled days, the child is with that parent for 5 days in a row. Exchange times can be adjusted to coincide with the parents' work schedules.

Sun	Mon	Tue	Wed	Thu	Fri	Sat
	3:00 pm		3:00 pm		3:00 pm	
			3:00 pm			

Legend: ▚ Parent 1 ▚ Parent 2

Figure 7.3. The 2-2-5-5 Schedule

The alternating weeks schedule has your child spend 1 week with one parent and the next week with the other parent.

Sun	Mon	Tue	Wed	Thu	Fri	Sat
					3:00 pm	
					3:00 pm	

Legend: ▚ Parent 1 ▚ Parent 2

Figure 7.4. The Alternating Weeks Schedule

This schedule works best when the children are preteens or teens. At that age, they are much more social, they have lots of extracurricular activities to attend, and staying at one home for a week does not put pressure onto them to move back and forth during the school week. Most exchanges occur after school on Fridays. This gives the children time to relax at the new home and to possibly get their schoolwork and laundry in order before returning to school on Monday. But the exchange day chosen must be in the best interest of *your* child. Some exchange on Sunday evenings or Mondays after school because it works best with the children's schedule.

The 2 weeks each schedule has your child spend 2 weeks with one parent and then 2 weeks with the other parent.

Sun	Mon	Tue	Wed	Thu	Fri	Sat
					3:00 pm	
					3:00 pm	

Legend: ▊ Parent 1   ▊ Parent 2

Figure 7.5. The 2 Weeks Each Schedule

I see this schedule chosen most often for older teens, perhaps juniors or seniors in high school, when a teen can drive or needs flexibility in the schedule because of extracurricular activities. This schedule also works well for sharing the summer break.

Adding a Holiday Schedule

To help the holidays run smoothly, it's best to have a solid plan in place. Without one, scheduling becomes overwhelming and co-parents may find it difficult to coordinate time with extended family and even gift giving. Staying organized will ensure your children feel safe and secure and, ultimately, increases their ability to accept the changes associated with shared custody. Any day, but especially a holiday, is stressful for kids when they see their parents fighting, floundering, and disorganized.

A holiday schedule is also the place parents might make up a time discrepancy in their parenting plan.

For example, if a parent has Monday through Friday with the child because the child attends school from that parent's residence, the other parent could be assigned spring or fall break each year—or possibly most of the summer—to compensate.

The key, however, to make any parenting plan work is for the parents to be flexible and free to negotiate when a change in the schedule is desired. It's best for your children if you can discuss changes easily—switch weekends, plan vacations, and cooperate in their best interest.

Dealing With Conflict at Exchanges

Exchanges are about the only time a child sees one's parents together after a breakup. If those exchanges are fraught with conflict—parents fighting or bringing their new significant other to antagonize the ex—a child will dread the exchange. Putting your child first means preventing the sorts of conflict that can make your child feel extremely insecure and frightened.

Here's a common problem.

Anthony was 5 years old. His parents were doing fairly well after their initial breakup, but Mom recently started seeing her new boyfriend, Billy, and he goes with her when it is time for Anthony to return to his father's home. This makes Dad uncomfortable and fights often break out. Last time, the police had to be called and Anthony's dad was almost arrested. Anthony was very frightened and quite teary for the rest of the weekend. When it was time to return to his mother's home, Anthony did not want to go. He pleaded with his father to let him stay: "I don't want to go to Mommy's!" When asked why, all Anthony could say was "Billy!"

Hearing that, Dad thought Billy was being mean to his son. Obviously, something Billy was doing was making him not want to go back to his mother's. Dad called Mom, who, in turn, thought the whole thing was crazy. She didn't believe that Anthony didn't want to come home and another fight ensued. Mom thought Dad was putting ideas into Anthony's head and felt the only way to end all this was to go back to court. They ended up in my office, both telling me that Anthony did not want to go to the other parent's home, and both wanted full custody with limited time to the other parent.

After listening to their story and hearing similar ones over the years, I knew it was not that Anthony did not want to leave either home—or that he preferred one home to the other. He was afraid to go to the exchanges. The fighting paralyzed him. At 5, he couldn't tell his father or his mother to please stop fighting. All he could articulate was "Billy," because that's who Daddy fought with at the exchange.

You are your children's protectors. When they are very young, they can't tell you why they hurt or exactly why they are frightened. You must do everything in your power to keep conflict to a minimum. That means that before you blame the other parent for an indiscretion, consult with that parent in the name of your child, and both of you should make the changes necessary to keep your children safe.

Finally, it's important that parents realize that parenting plans are not written in stone and should be adjusted as a child gets older or if the plan is simply not a good fit. Each child is an individual with likes, dislikes, and temperaments all one's own. Some kids have no trouble going back and forth between their parent's homes. Some kids prefer to have a home base and sleep primarily in one bed. A parent should not take it personally if a child asks to sleep predominantly in one bed, especially if things changed dramatically after the parents decided to split. Your child is not saying, "I like Daddy better than you." Your child is telling you, "I hate that you broke up. I like my bed. I like my stuff."

You made the decision to break up. The child has to cope with that decision.

Be observant. Watch how your child responds to the parenting plan you've put into place, and make changes if you have to.

Ask yourself,

▶ "Does my child seem to be adjusting?"

▶ "Is my child sleeping well?" (Sleep disruptions indicate something is wrong.)

▶ "Is my child eating well?" (A change in appetite indicates something is wrong—eating too much or eating too little.)

▶ "Is my child moody?" (Watch for depression or anxiety, particularly in teens. In younger children, depression and anxiety may translate into uncharacteristic clinginess, protesting, headaches, or stomachaches.)

▶ "Does my child invite friends over?" (For children, wishing to share their environment indicates that they are adjusting.)

And if you see your child is not adjusting, do some soul-searching: "Is this the right parenting plan for my child?" If a change must be made, make the change—your children need you to be their advocate. They need you to put your personal concerns aside and make future decisions in their best interest. Would you like the parenting plan you are expecting your child to maneuver? If not, call the other parent and make the appropriate changes, realizing that it's not about who has more time; it's about what we can do to make this lifestyle more comfortable for our children. Now, you are finally co-parenting!

8

Toxic Stress and Its Effect on Our Children

In times of stress, the best thing we can do for each other is to listen with our ears and our hearts and to be assured that our questions are just as important as our answers.

FRED ROGERS

We keep saying that separation and divorce are stressful and that stress taxes not only our coping skills but our children's as well. But what do we really mean by that? How have pediatricians and psychologists come to understand that in some circumstances, stress can be as toxic as any other poison? Let me start with a story.

It's 3, maybe 4 weeks, since I've been on my own, and so far, so good. The kids are getting to school on time with most of their homework done and matching shoes on their feet. Dinners, baths, and bedtimes have been close to on schedule, and the house is as clean as it has ever been. Now, as they say on the shampoo bottle, we just wash, rinse, and repeat. I got this.

All 3 kids have gotten up on time for school this morning, and their teeth are brushed. All we need is breakfast. They are standing in their pajamas in our walk-in pantry, rummaging around. One opens the fridge and starts looking behind everything. "Dad, there's nothing for breakfast."

"What?" I say. "There's all sorts of stuff for breakfast."

"Nothing good," offers my daughter, the oldest and elected spokesperson. "Why don't you ever get us anything we like?

There's no food here."

"No food?!" I repeat, my voice rising. I stomp into the pantry. I pick up a box of oatmeal. "Here! This is food!" I say, hurling it across the kitchen to where the kids are now gathered at the counter. I throw a box of Cheerios, then Mini Wheats, and then protein bars as the children duck and cover their heads. "THIS is food! And this is food! And this is food! It's all food! Now pick one of them up and eat it! We leave in 30 minutes!"

So far, not so good. We're all crying. Needless to say, no one wants to eat. I slump to the floor. I am a highly capable professional, educated in child behavior and accustomed to high-stress environments, and I just completely and totally lost it. What happened?

Stress Test

We tend to think of all stress as bad. "Don't stress out," we tell each other. "I don't need the stress." But as Andrew S. Garner, MD, PhD, FAAP, and Robert A. Saul, MD, FAAP, FACMG, explain in their book *Thinking Developmentally: Nurturing Wellness in Childhood to Promote Lifelong Health,* a life completely free of stress would also be a life free of learning and growth. A growing body of science is helping us think about child development and what different kinds of stresses do to the body and the mind, including the heart, the immune system, and even the brain itself. Some stress is good, some is tolerable, and some is literally toxic. But even for toxic stress, we have powerful antivenoms, if we know how to use them.

Positive stress is brief, mild in intensity, and relatively infrequent. For a baby, positive stress may be falling while learning to walk. A 5-year-old might face a positive stress when her mom leaves her at kindergarten for the first time. A teenager may face a big school project or a final examination. In each case, the stress is manageable, it's part of mastering a new skill, and an end is in sight. So long as we have a safe, nurturing environment, we can quickly return to our baseline physical and emotional states, proud that we have accomplished something new. As parents, we help children cope with such stresses in a variety of ways. We may offer words of encouragement, consolation, or a hug. We might suggest breaking a larger challenge into smaller, more manageable parts. With time and repetition, such positive stresses can help a child build competence and confidence in her abilities.

Some stress is not positive, but it's still tolerable. Compared with positive stress, these tolerable stresses are longer-lasting, more intense, and more frequent. For children, the death of a grandparent or a treasured pet might count. Moving away from friends or attending a camp where they're not quite being bullied, but they also don't feel as if they fit in, are other examples. In the absence of safe, stable, nurturing relationships, these types of stresses may have long-term consequences, but with strong support, they usually don't. At the same time, nothing about these stresses is motivating. They may not lead to any improvements in a child's competence or confidence.

Toxic stress, on the other hand, is more severe, chronic, and more frequent. This type of stress takes children beyond the limits of their coping skills, and it leaves a lasting impact on their bodies and brains, down to the levels of their genes. Toxic stress actually affects how the brain matures, altering the number of neurons that grow, the connections between those neurons (synapses), and how fast different regions of the brain can communicate with each other. The sum of these effects is that early stressful events can keep children from fully developing the very parts of their brains that help them cope with stress itself, a cruel feedback loop that can lead to more impulsive and aggressive behaviors, which, in turn, cause more stress. Understanding and breaking this cycle is the key to helping your children (and you) flourish in the face of one of life's greatest stressors.

What Are Adverse Childhood Experiences?

For decades, doctors, psychologists, and sociologists have known that children who face more difficulties early in their lives experience worse outcomes later. As early as 1957, composer Leonard Bernstein dedicated an entire song in the musical *West Side Story* ("Gee, Officer Krupke") to the concept. Listening to the lyrics more than 60 years later ("I'm depraved on account I'm deprived"), they actually sum up subsequent research remarkably well. But writing a song about a phenomenon is a far cry from opening up a new frontier in medical science. That had to wait 41 years, for Vincent Felitti, MD, of Kaiser Permanente and Robert Anda, MD, of the Centers for Disease Control and Prevention to publish their findings in the Adverse Childhood Experiences Study, comparing the health of more than 17,000 middle-aged, middle-class Kaiser Permanente patients with their recall of stressful events they faced as children.

The Adverse Childhood Experiences Study inquired about 10 adverse childhood experiences (ACEs) that participants experienced before their 18th birthdays.

- ▶ Emotional abuse
- ▶ Physical abuse
- ▶ Sexual abuse
- ▶ Mother treated violently
- ▶ Household substance use
- ▶ Household mental illness
- ▶ Parental separation or divorce
- ▶ Incarceration of a household member
- ▶ Emotional neglect
- ▶ Physical neglect

While hardly a comprehensive list of all the stresses a child could face, the questionnaire provided a chance to look at how 10 discrete events might affect mental and physical health. The results shocked researchers. More than a quarter of respondents reported being exposed to physical and substance use in their households. One in 5 recalled sexual abuse, parental separation or divorce, and parental mental illness. Similar studies repeated with under-privileged populations have confirmed that rates of ACEs rise with economic or social disadvantage.

The bombshell finding, however, was how strongly these childhood events were related with health outcomes throughout adulthood. Adverse childhood experiences correlate with physical ailments such as cancer, heart disease, lung disease, and liver disease. They track with sexual health issues such as early intercourse, teen pregnancy, sexually transmitted infections, and sexual dis-satisfaction. Perhaps more predictably, ACEs increase the risk of mental health problems, including anxiety, depression, hallucinations, panic attacks, and anger issues. When it comes to general social functioning, adults with a history of more ACEs experienced more problems with relationships, work, and stress management.

In trying to understand these relationships, researchers wondered whether children who feel stress might grow up to engage in more high-risk adult health behaviors, such as smoking, drinking to excess, eating a poor diet, becoming sexually promiscuous, or using illegal drugs. After all, these are all behaviors that provide temporary relief from psychological distress, even if they cause more problems in the long run. In fact, there is a correlation between ACEs and these behaviors, but researchers are able to control for these effects. Even after they factored out things such as smoking and obesity, ACEs still contributed independently to heart disease, suggesting that they affect the body in deeper ways.

Once researchers understood the importance of ACEs, they recognized that there must be more than the original 10. We now know that adverse events include poverty, bullying, witnessing violence inside or outside the home, belittling behaviors from parents, and living in a violent neighborhood.

If you are a parent, it's tempting to read these findings and start counting up the ACEs your own child has faced, including separation and divorce, and to despair. It's critical, however, to understand that adverse childhood experiences are not fate. These negative outcomes apply to whole populations of people, but how they will affect an individual child—your child—varies widely, and you have significant power over what happens. Some kids thrive despite facing odds that would floor most of us. Others seem to flounder with even minimally chal-lenging situations. Some of the difference lies with the child herself, which we explore next, in the Affiliation Gives Hope section. Some factors, however, rest within your control as a parent. This is where we find hope as parents, that while, yes, our children are going through an extremely stressful time, there are things we can do to help them cope and even thrive.

Affiliation Gives Hope

What Are Affiliative Factors?

The opposite of ACEs are called *affiliative factors*. Another term for these factors is *positive childhood events*, or PCEs, essentially the opposite of ACEs. These are behaviors that help children form strong connections to the people around them and teach them to cope with adversity. The most important affiliative factor is having at least one engaged, attentive caregiver: a safe, stable, nurturing person the child knows she can turn to for support and love. Other factors include access to health care, quality early education services, and ample opportunities to play. These PCEs are just as important as ACEs, so if we want children to thrive, we not only have to protect them from ACEs but must provide them with as many PCEs as we can.

Children with more affiliative factors grow up to enjoy better health, higher academic achievement, better employment, fewer divorces, less depression, and lower incarceration rates. If toxic stress is a poison, you can think of affiliative factors as the antidote. To learn how to deploy this antidote, it helps to understand more about what toxic stress does to the body and the brain and what steps you can take to help.

Freeze, Flee, Fight, or…Hug?

Stress starts in the brain, so to understand toxic stress and how to fight it, we have to look at how the brain processes danger. The amygdala is the part of the brain that functions as our danger sensor. Whether we're falling down a hill, being chased by an angry dog, or staring at a test question we don't understand, our amygdala is processing the threat and implementing a response. You can think of the amygdala as the "gas pedal" of stress, designed to rev us up and get us ready to respond. Our responses fall into 4 broad categories.

One stress response is familiar to anyone who has driven enough dark country roads: to freeze. This is what a literal deer does in the literal headlights, and it's what many of us do when faced with more abstract fears: Stand still. Do nothing. Hope it goes away. The brain slows the heart rate and stops you from moving; you may even feel your muscles stiffen, unable to budge. That time your mom caught you with your hand in the cookie jar, and asked what you were doing, and you just stood there holding a cookie and staring at her? It's like that.

The second response is to flee. If you've ever run away from a playground bully or hidden in the bathroom to avoid a difficult conversation, you know what this feels like. Fleeing makes a lot of sense when we're facing a physical danger, such as a wild animal or a flood, and our amygdala helps by stimulating the pituitary gland in our brain to tell the adrenal glands over our kidneys to pump out chemicals, including epinephrine and norepinephrine ("adrenaline") and cortisol, that rapidly increase our heart rate, breathing rate, blood pressure, and blood glucose level so that we can get moving.

The third response is similar to the second, fight. When the threat is physical and you're trapped, your only choice is to turn around and hope you can beat it. This response relies on the same chemicals and the same physiological changes as flight. Whether you're hitting or running, you're going to need all the energy your body can supply.

The fourth response, however, takes a different path, and that is to affiliate. If you ever crawled in your Dad's lap during a thunderstorm or held a friend's hand during a scary movie, you know this response. Affiliation relies on a completely different hormone, oxytocin, which does not have the same effects on heart rate, breathing rate, blood pressure, and blood glucose level as epinephrine and norepinephrine. If the first 3 responses to stress are all about hitting the gas, affiliation is about applying the brakes. When we're dealing with chronic stress, such as with family separation, affiliation is the most constructive and least damaging response, and it's one we want to foster as much as possible.

Once an immediate threat has passed—for example, the dog has stopped chasing us, we have reached high ground—fighting and fleeing are not helpful, and the brain has "brakes" to shut down the stress response. When epinephrine, norepinephrine, and cortisol remain in the bloodstream for a long time, they contribute directly to problems such as heart disease, diabetes, and poor immunity. Over time, they even affect how genes are expressed and how the brain grows. In the brain, the hypothalamus and the pituitary gland play a role in decreasing the stress response immediately, but the long-term job goes to the prefrontal cortex, the part of the brain that lets us think through the threat and analyze what we can do once we're calm. The prefrontal cortex is the ultimate "brake pedal" for chronic stress.

Here's the frustrating thing about toxic stress, especially when it occurs early after a child's birth: it affects how the brain develops. Children subjected to chronic stress actually grow a larger amygdala and a smaller prefrontal cortex, giving them more gas and less brakes. These changes leave them more apt to fight and flee and less able to control their behavior than they might otherwise be. Kids undergoing chronic stress require even more patience and understanding, which is a lot to provide when you yourself are under the same strain.

Back, then, to the goal of combating toxic stress. We want to shift our kids' brains from a fight-or-flight reaction to a relational reaction, when they can slow down, reflect on what's happening, and learn to adapt to their new situations. As you might have guessed, the relational reaction depends on strong relationships. Next, we talk about how to build those.

What Happened to You?

Our new understanding of ACEs and toxic stress has transformed the practice of pediatrics and of medicine as a whole. In the past, we doctors saw ourselves almost as mechanics for the body: identify the problem, offer a solution, and move on. Every encounter started with the question "What's wrong with you?" Now, however, we understand that our patients exist in a whole ecosystem of stresses and affiliative factors and that these factors have profound effects on their physical and emotional health. The question is shifting from "What's wrong with you?" to "What happened to you?"

Even a condition as seemingly physical as asthma depends on countless environmental factors, from toxic stress to poor diet, to the presence of tobacco smoke in the home, to a family's ability to afford and administer long-term medications. When we look at learning or behavioral issues, such as attention-deficit/hyperactivity disorder and anxiety, the environmental impact only grows. We can't treat any of these problems without understanding a lot about the child's environment and the stressors that affect the whole family.

The good news is that the more we learn about toxic stress, the more we understand the sorts of things that can help. We can think of these affiliative factors as coming from 3 realms. The first is outside the child: the social supports provided by family members and the community. For every successful child, you can find at least one adult who believed in that child, one person willing and able to provide a safe, stable, nurturing relationship. When a community is strong, it can have a whole battalion of such people, from teachers and coaches to faith leaders and extended family members. Every person a child can turn to for love and affirmation provides a safe haven from toxic stress.

The other 2 protective realms come from within the child, but they must be taught and nurtured. One, mindfulness, involves an ability to frame what's happening in the moment and to put it into context. Most anxiety, for example, focuses on what *might* happen in the future, not on what is happening right at this moment. When a child is worried about next week or next year, we can redirect her to experience what's happening now: Is she safe? Is she with someone who loves her? Does she have a teddy bear, book, or blanket that makes her feel better? Even moments of discomfort become more manageable when we approach them mindfully, just feeling what they are and turning away from our instincts to flee and fight.

As parents, we naturally find our children's unhappiness deeply uncomfortable. Our instinct when we see our children crying or upset is to rush in and try to fix the situation. Whether the ice cream has fallen off the cone or a guppy fish has died, we want to make the sadness stop, and fast. This instinct, while protective, can also deprive children of the opportunity to become comfortable with feelings that are critical to their understanding of life. Fred Rogers, the genius behind

Mister Rogers' Neighborhood, understood this concept profoundly. Before Mr Rogers, children's TV had focused on encouraging children to be happy through comedy and escapism. What made Fred Rogers special—the thing that made his program critical to my own childhood survival—was that he instead encouraged children to name and accept their less happy feelings. He talked about feeling angry and sad and afraid and reminded children (and their parents) that these feelings are also a normal part of life. In addition, he discussed constructive ways to cope with them. When we feel our own discomfort with our children's negative feelings, we would do well to imagine donning Mr Roger's iconic cardigan and exploring those feelings with them rather than searching for the magic wand that will make those feelings disappear. Like Mr Rogers, we can talk about what we do when we feel bad, and by doing so, we help our children build their own emotional skill set.

Mindfulness also includes emotional intelligence. Children are naturally sensitive to the feelings of those around them (especially their parents), but sometimes their attention must be directed toward naming those feelings and coping with them. Chances are that if you're going through a separation or divorce, you're experiencing some strong emotions. Rather than try to hide what you're feeling, it's OK to tell your child, "I'm sad right now. I won't always be sad, but I'm thinking about some things right now that make me sad." Then ask, "How are you feeling?" From there, it's easy to turn the conversation to what both of you can do that help you feel less sad.

The third protective realm also comes from within the child, but you will also need to help with building this realm, and that is healthy adaptation. Healthy adaptations are the things we can do that redirect our energy and attention away from toxic stress and toward being constructive. They include exercise, journaling, and artistic pursuits, such as music and drawing. Each of these activities provides natural answers to the question "What can we do to feel less sad?"

One way to find a constructive, creative outlet for your child is to ask a simple-seeming question: "If you didn't have to do anything else, what is one thing you'd love to do all day long?" This question may take repetition and redirection. For example, the first answer might be "Play violent video games." "OK," you say, "what else?" Sometimes, practical constraints may require redirection as well. If the first answer is "Buy a pony and ride her," you may have to point out that you live in a city and that a pony isn't in the cards at this moment. But, with exploration, chances are that you'll find an activity that is practical for you and your child, at least in some fashion.

Building on these protective realms is another creative endeavor for you. Every one of these efforts, from talking about feelings to going on a bike ride, to drawing pictures, will engage you and foster your own creativity and healing. You'll quickly find that it's impossible to help someone else without also helping yourself. Speaking of help, therapists are increasingly trained to support you and your child in building these protections. Trauma-sensitive care is a new, popular approach to therapy that takes into account the damage that toxic stress wreaks and works to counter it in multiple ways. Trauma-sensitive therapists are trained to ask, "What happened to you?" and to address whatever answer comes.

What Can I Do Right Now to Fight Toxic Stress?

First and most important, you'll need to ensure that your child's basic needs are met. All of Chapter 6, Co-parenting Our Children, is dedicated to exploring what you can do, but you'll want to ensure that your child has access to safe shelter, sleeps well every night, gets plenty of exercise and play, feels that she is physically safe, has appropriate medical and dental care, and has an appropriately supporting and challenging educational environment. Separation and divorce can provide challenges to each of these needs, but as we go, we walk you through some strategies that should help.

Next, your child will need the support of caring adults, starting with yourself. Relationships that help children share 3 primary properties: they are safe, stable, and nurturing. If you have reached a point of stress when you cannot be all 3 of these things, seek out others who can, starting with your co-parent. Caring adults may include grandparents, aunts, uncles, adoptive parents, and even your best friend, essentially anyone who is just crazy about that kid. Ideally, a child would encounter caring adults not just at home but also at school and in the community. Caring cannot be overdone, and different people will offer different strengths.

Children, like adults, feel best about themselves when they have a sense of purpose. All of us like to feel as if we're contributing. For toddlers, building this sense can be as simple as enlisting them to help put the toys away after playtime. Watch how your toddler loves to imitate your household chores! Give her a big hug afterwards, and let her know that she really helped you.

Older children can and should do more around the house, within the limits of what's safe. They can also become involved in their communities. Check out local charities and houses of worship for opportunities to help at a soup kitchen, a hospital, or a housing effort. They can use their talents to send cards to children who feel sick or to prepare holiday gifts for the less fortunate. We are hardwired to help others, and such efforts can be especially helpful when we ourselves are facing hardship.

Teens may be able to do even more, volunteering at local hospitals or raising money for medical missions. They can mow a neighbor's lawn if the neighbor feels sick or help a relative move furniture. The more we see outside ourselves, the more content we are being in our own skin.

Becoming a "Good Enough" Parent

I make a living giving people parenting advice. Have I ever met a perfect parent? Not yet. Am I myself a perfect parent? Did you read the first pages of this chapter? Clearly, I am not. Honestly, no one knows how to define a *perfect parent,* and, even if we could, that's not what your child needs. She needs you, imperfect as you are, doing your best. When we stop worrying about being the perfect parent, we can focus on being a "the best parent we can be" parent.

What does that take? Just the 3 things we mentioned earlier, in the What Can I Do Right Now to Fight Toxic Stress? section. Be safe. Be stable. Be nurturing. *Safe* means you don't hit your child, you don't belittle your child, and you don't knowingly put your child into dangerous situations. *Stable* means you're there, both physically and emotionally. It doesn't mean that you're by your child's side every minute, but it means that when you leave, you return when you said you would, and you don't disappear without warning. It means that when your child needs you, she knows she can count on you to respond. *Nurturing* involves all the basic needs we described, but it also means believing in your child and helping her believe in herself. You are there with high expectations for what she can do and also with a high degree of responsiveness to her emotional needs. This combination of expectations and responsiveness has shown to help children grow into their best selves.

It is true that many of us parent the way we were parented. Our own parents were probably good enough as well, which means they weren't perfect either. We have learned a lot about parenting in the previous generation, and you are now in a position to take the best parts of how you were raised and combine those things with the best current information on how we can help our children succeed. Accept that you will sometimes make mistakes, and when that happens, you'll have to just keep going and remember to do it better next time. We all learn. One way to think about this issue is to ask yourself, "What kind of parents do I want my own children to be when they grow up?" Then, model for them what that might look like.

As you plot your way forward, it may help to reflect on any ACEs you may have faced. Did you have to struggle with poverty, violence, or substance use in your home, or did you have to struggle with parental separation or divorce? These struggles will have left their impact on you as well, making it harder for you to always be the best version of yourself. Every technique we talk about using for your child is a technique you can also use to care for yourself. Take time to invest in the relationships that you find safe, stable, and nurturing. Explore your own mindfulness and build your own emotional intelligence. Find your own creative outlets in exercise, journaling, and artistic expression. You'll be strengthening your own coping skills while setting an example for your child to follow.

A variety of barriers can make it harder for us to deal with our own stresses and to parent as well as we'd like. Educational disparities and economic inequality can pose serious challenges to finding adequate housing, food, and health care (see Chapter 3, What Do Children Need to Be Healthy?, for some suggestions). Neighborhood violence can increase stress and deprive children and parents of opportunities for play and exercise. Discrimination and racism can add a level of stress to acts as simple as shopping for clothes or driving down the street. None of these challenges have simple solutions, but sometimes it helps simply to name and acknowledge the factors outside of yourself that make your successes count double.

Addressing Spiritual Needs

The word *spiritual* may seem surprising cropping up in a secular book about parenting and divorce. Here we are talking about a set of universal spiritual needs as identified by Mark Bartel, a pediatric chaplain who works with children at the Arnold Palmer Medical Center in Orlando, FL, who have terminal illness. Bartel has spent nearly 30 years helping children and their parents address the greatest stress of all, death, and he has some observations that transcend any particular faith or religion. What Bartel has learned in this most difficult position can help us cope with the lesser but still weighty stress of separation and divorce.

Bartel's first spiritual need is love. Love in this context includes affection but also compassion, meaningful relationships, forgiveness, and a sense of self-worth. As you struggle with your child's needs and behavior, not to mention your own, it's worth running through this list and imagining how each element might apply to the love that you're teaching and modeling.

His second spiritual need is faith or worldview. If you practice a religion, you may already feel that you have a firm grasp on this concept, but even the very devout sometimes struggle to connect with faith, and fewer people are participating in organized religion. By *faith*, Bartel means a personal philosophy, a sense of wonder and humility at the world, and a practice of prayer or meditation. We know that simply stating our gratitude and sitting quietly with a still mind can help us with our mood and with stress.

The third element in Bartel's concept of spiritual needs is hope or vision. This is a belief that life has meaning and purpose and that if we face our challenges with courage and perseverance, we will be able to pursue that purpose. Hopelessness is one of the most pronounced features of depression, and reminding your child that she will find purpose and meaning in life can grant you both a critical sense of hope at a difficult time. We already considered some practical ways to help children of all ages connect with a sense of purpose.

The next aspect of spiritual need in Bartel's model is virtue and ethics. We each define what it means to be a "good" person, and much of parenthood involves imparting those concepts to our children, through teaching and through modeling. There is no better way to do this at any age than to "catch your child being good." When you see a behavior that makes you proud, don't stay quiet; let your child know how happy it makes you and why: "You noticed that your friend was sad, and you offered her your teddy bear. That makes me really proud."

Finally, Bartel identifies beauty and renewal as a spiritual need. Beauty can involve appreciating what's around us, from the clouds out the window to the ants marching down the sidewalk. Art and music are ample sources of beauty, when we appreciate them and when we participate in making them. Bartel, to my delight, also identifies humor as part of beauty. Psychologists recognize humor as a positive coping mechanism, and anyone who has ever joked one's way through a trying ordeal knows that we feel better and more connected, if only for a moment. When things are tough, consider making up a silly story about what's going on or how it could be worse: "We had to leave the old neighborhood, but, at least where we moved, there aren't so many lions." We can't fight, flee, and laugh at the same time.

Catching "All the Feels"

Children are emotional sponges, but they are also emotional loudspeakers. Compared with adults, they have a lot of amygdala and not as much frontal lobe, which means their emotions come on full force, with little modulation. When they are joyful, they can barely contain themselves, and witnessing that contagious delight and excitement is among the best parts of being a parent. When they are sad, they cry, often hard, and when they are angry, they yell, stomp, and even bang their heads on the floor. It can be a lot to deal with as a parent, especially if you're feeling fragile yourself. At times, we all wish we could mute the loudspeaker, if only for a minute.

Periods of toxic stress amp up the amygdala and suppress the frontal lobe, so your child's emotions are likely to be even more intense. Rather than teach your children to suppress those feelings, you can instead help them identify what they're feeling and then channel their strong emotions in positive ways.

This process starts with a step that is deceptively simple: naming what your child is feeling. It seems easy enough, but consider how in touch with your own emotions you are as an adult. Are there ever times when you've looked up only to realize that you were feeling something you had not acknowledged or even realized? One of the hardest questions my therapist asked me during my separation was "How do you know what you are feeling?" I don't know; I just do? But I didn't, and I had to learn to pay attention to my own face, heart, hands, and stomach to understand and name my emotions.

For children, this insight is even harder to gain. If you watch educational TV with your child, you'll notice a surprising amount of content directed toward this goal: "What do you do when you're sad? What makes you angry?" You don't have to be a furry puppet or an animated character to ask your child these questions. Start just by naming what you see: "You're not talking as much as usual, and you didn't eat your lunch. Are you sad?" "The way you slammed that door and threw your toy down makes me think you're angry. Why?" or "Your eyes are big, and you're shaking; are you scared? What about?" Naming and validating these emotions starts the process of acceptance and reflection, and from there, you can help your child deal with them.

Once your child identifies her emotions, she needs a way to deal with them. John Gottman, PhD, in his book *Raising an Emotionally Intelligent Child* notes that just as with adults, children's coping skills can be unhealthy, neutral, or healthy adaptive. As a parent, your goal is naturally to help your child learn to use healthier coping skills with time. You can probably imagine what unhealthy coping skills look like: yelling, tormenting a sibling, breaking things, throwing fits, overeating, or playing hours of violent video games. None of these behaviors are desirable, but as you're trying to redirect, remember what they are: coping skills. Your child is taking the emotions that come with an enormous stress and doing what she can to diffuse them.

More neutral coping skills are not violent or harmful, but they don't add anything to your child's life either. Most of them are passive, such as playing endless hours of less violent video games, watching TV, or listening to music. Compared with throwing fits, these activities are a major improvement, but they don't evoke much in the way of joy or passion.

Healthy or adaptive coping skills add something to your child's life and may even help others as well. These include some that we've already discussed, such as exercise, making art or music, and helping others. They can also include meditation (yes, even young children can learn to meditate), reading, and working on puzzles or games. In each case, your child is learning a new skill and developing competence and confidence, great antidotes to toxic stress.

Another way to think about children's emotions has been popularized by W. Thomas Boyce, MD, in his book *The Orchid and the Dandelion: Why Some Children Struggle and How All Can Thrive*. Dr Boyce notes that some children are naturally more responsive than others to the positive situations and the negative situations around them. Less emotionally responsive kids, the "dandelions," seem to be able to survive situations of adversity that most children would find daunting. These children keep an even keel, no matter what life throws at them.

While this type of personality serves to protect children from emotional damage, it may also mute their response to delight and stimulation, leaving them in a sort of academic and artistic middle ground.

More emotionally reactive children, the "orchids," respond more strongly to negative environments and positive environments. When adversity strikes, they may be particularly vulnerable to emotional damage and toxic stress. When, on the other hand, they find themselves in highly nurturing environments, they are uniquely capable of thriving, producing transcendent works of science, art, or literature. Naturally, each child falls somewhere along a spectrum, with many having some dandelion traits and some orchid traits. The key is to know that your own child's emotional reactivity is neither good nor bad. Dandelions and orchids both possess certain gifts and certain vulnerabilities, and it's your efforts at understanding your child and providing the emotional response that she needs that will determine how she endures.

Practice Forgiveness

As we said earlier, the stress of separation and divorce don't just affect your children; they affect you too. As a pediatrician, I would never counsel a parent to respond to a concern over breakfast by screaming and throwing cereal boxes at a child's head. Ten years later, my children still remind me of that fiasco occasionally, usually when I'm enjoying a particularly proud-of-my-parenting moment. That morning, I was sad, frightened, and doubtful that I could continue at the pace that co-parenting required of me. My frontal lobe disengaged, my amygdala sensed a threat (my kids doubted my ability to provide for them), and I responded with aggression. At the same time, my children weren't reading the room; they didn't sense my rising frustration and anger, possibly because I didn't really sense it either. We were all under the influence of toxic stress. Sitting on the kitchen floor, I was frightened of the person I had become. I knew that I had to do better. But how?

Doubting your parenting is exactly how you become a better parent. First, listen to yourself. When your child is expressing distress, either verbally or by acting out, how do you respond? Are your words supportive and understanding? Harsh and controlling? Do you grab her? Spank her? When we are stressed, we turn to a fight-or-flight reaction, rather than reflection and affiliation, and we do the first thing that comes to mind, which is often not the best thing. Start by taking a breath. Just a short pause will give your prefrontal cortex time to wake up and formulate a better response. For a complete discussion of positive discipline techniques, look at Chapter 6, Co-parenting Our Children. But first, remember to breathe.

Second, think about what you can do to help your child foster positive responses to toxic stress. Can you take time to read with her? To play with her? As we said earlier, financial and social constraints can feel as if they're closing in on you when you're living through separation and divorce, and you'll need to call on every resource you can find. Remember that in Chapter 2, How Do I Begin?, we talk about how to mobilize those resources so that you have more time and energy to focus on your child's needs, which include focusing on your own needs.

Third, consider what is reasonable to expect of your child at this age and under this degree of stress. The most frustrated parents I see are those whose expectations of their children exceed their children's developmental abilities. Will a 2-year-old sit still and quiet for 5 minutes? Almost certainly not. A 5-year-old? Maybe. If you find yourself constantly frustrated with your child's behavior, a pediatrician or therapist should be able to help you determine what sorts of behaviors are truly concerning and what might just be normal for your child's age and situation.

In many cases, rewards and consequences can help a child learn certain behaviors, but let's consider a child with dyslexia. No amount of incentives or discipline consequences will get that child to read. She needs specific therapy for her dyslexia and help with her reading. Now think about a child who feels anxious and stressed and who is acting out. When anxiety and stress are driving a child's behavior, anxiety and stress are the things that need to be addressed.

One of the most effective methods for combating our own toxic stress is to practice forgiveness. In the midst of a separation or divorce, you may not feel like forgiving anything. Your anger and frustration are probably peaking, and you're likely thinking more about revenge. Consider, however, about how much of your energy these feelings are consuming. Does your ex really deserve that much real estate inside your mind? What example is this simmering rage setting for your child? We don't forgive others because they deserve it. We forgive them because when we do so, our own lives improve. Forgiveness is a muscle that takes time to build. Start small, for example, with your child. When she frustrates you and makes you angry—and let's be honest, she will—use the breath that you take to set the stage for forgiveness. With time and practice, it will become easier.

Part of being a forgiving parent is simply persevering. When you find yourself slumped to the floor among the spilled cereal, it's tempting just to stay there. To admit defeat and never stand up again. But you are your child's pillar. You'll have to stand. You'll have to sweep up the Cheerios and Mini Wheats and protein bars, pull out the milk, and ask, "What would you rather have for breakfast?" You will never be the perfect parent. But every day, you can get a little better. Together, you and your child will learn to make this stress less and less toxic. The antidote is you.

9

Is My Child Safe Over There?

Precaution is better than a cure.

EDWARD COKE

Among the most frightening aspects of separation and divorce is the loss of control you face over your child's environment. "But I don't know if my child is safe over there!" is something professionals constantly hear—and because each home and situation is different, we have decided to devote an entire chapter to assessing and ultimately creating a safe environment for your children.

It's All Different Now...

When parents share their home, they at least have the illusion that they know who is coming and going and what is happening with their children at all times. However, once parents separate and their children go back and forth between the parental homes, during stretches of time their children are under someone else's roof and out-of-sight. Especially given the distrust and suspicion that usually accompanies separation and divorce, it's no wonder that parents in these situations worry about their children's well-being. That suspicion often worsens if the ex has a new partner or even just a new set of friends. Children, too, already face heightened anxiety about transitions, and they may worry about their safety as much as or more than their parents.

❝ *How do you know when to worry and when to relax?* **❞**

Knowing when to worry and when to relax is a great question, and it is difficult to answer if you don't trust your co-parent's ability to parent properly and worry whether the kids are safe.

Let's Define *Safe*

You would think coming to an agreement about what is safe would be easy. After all, it seems obvious when a child is safe. Not necessarily. What is safe to one parent may not be safe to the other, and that difference of opinion can cause friction when co-parenting.

> **66** *My son's father is an avid motorcycle rider and thinks it's safe for our 10-year-old son to ride on the back of his motorcycle. My son loves it and looks forward to it, and every time I bring up how unsafe it is and how I don't want him to do it, he says, 'Well, Dad says it's safe.' I've talked to my ex about it, and he just laughs at me. 'You know I've been riding for years' is all I get. I'm petrified every time my son goes over there, and now his father is proposing a long ride to a national park. I guess I just don't trust his dad's judgment—and my son knows it.* **99**

Distrust in one's ability to assess safety does not begin with a breakup. That distrust was most likely there while the parents were together, but some sort of consolation was made to ensure that the relationship continued. Once the parents split, however, that distrust continues unchecked, and when there is a disagreement, there is simply no incentive to take the other parent's concern to heart. That's when co-parents butt heads.

> **66** *I can do what I want when the children are with me!* **99**

Technically, that you can do what you want when the child is with you is true—as long as the child is not hurt or encouraged to break the law. However, in the best interest of the children, co-parents must come to agreement about exactly what *safe* is and then abide by that agreement when the children are with them. If they don't, they are undermining their co-parent, and that single-handedly can be a contributing component to a child's insecurity and inability to adjust after a breakup. As in the scenario, that blatant disregard for the mother's concern asks the child to choose between Mom and Dad. Who has better judgment? In this case, the child chose Dad, and, as a result, Mom's position was diminished, and she was made to look like a silly worrywart. This approach then affects the child's attitude about Mom's ability to make all decisions, and from that point on, every decision Mom makes for the child will be scrutinized, weighing Dad's perception of safety against Mom's perception of safety. Of course, this is just an example; in actuality, the entire scenario would be just as damaging if reversed—and the disagreement could be about doing anything "dangerous," from living in a perceived unsafe environment to rock climbing, equestrian jumping, or even surfing, for that matter.

So does that mean that the more conservative parent runs the whole show and gets to dictate policy and let the co-parent know what that parent can and cannot do? Of course not, but it prompts a private discussion between co-parents with compromise at its center.

How Do Co-parents Who Disagree Compromise?

Compromise starts with respect, something that may be hard to find between co-parents with a tumultuous history.

> 66 *How can I respect him (or her)? He (or she's) the one who left!* 99

Or…

> 66 *He (or she) is the one that cheated…* 99

History plays a huge part in our ability to put things aside and make decisions together in the best interest of our children. And it's understandable if the past interferes with your ability to get along; however, once you have kids, it's not about you any longer—and it's even more important to take this observation seriously after a breakup. When the children are required to spend time with both parents, it's the parents' responsibility to make that as easy on the children as possible, not throw up emotional roadblocks that make them question where they should live and whom they should believe. After doing some honest soul-searching, if you can't respect your co-parent, do your best not to not openly demonstrate that disrespect in front of the children. If it's any consolation, you do that for your children. Not your co-parent.

The next step to compromising with your co-parent is to do some background investigation. Have all the facts before you negotiate or else you are negotiating according purely to emotion, and that rarely gets the response you want. In this case, what are the laws in the state in which you live regarding a child as a passenger on a motorcycle?

Doing some investigation, you will learn that the laws regarding child passengers on motorcycles are vastly different from state to state. Some states have an age requirement. Some states have a height requirement. Some states leave it up to the judgement of the parent or primary rider. All require the child passenger wear a helmet and proper protective gear. Alaska, for example, does not require the primary rider to wear a helmet, but it requires the passenger to do so. Know the laws regarding the decision you are trying to make, and if your child does not meet the requirements to legally ride in your state, the question of whether your child rides is moot.

> 66 *I don't care what the law says. I can take my child anywhere I want.* 99

That you can take your child anywhere you want is true to a degree; however, if you are breaking the law and your child is hurt, you may be charged with child endangerment, and in those cases, child custody is often revoked or only supervised visits are allowed, which would defeat the purpose of this entire disagreement.

But there's more. That kind of response can make a co-parent feel as if any conversation is a lost cause. When parents feel as if nothing they say will be taken seriously, that's when they seek help from the courts. As a result, a judge will be making decisions for your children, not you or your co-parent.

If you anticipate that there may be a disagreement before any compromise can be made, it may be helpful to refer to your communication toolbox, first mentioned in Chapter 4, Helping Our Children Cope. There it was used as a reference to better communicate with our children. Here we use the same principles to better communicate and learn to compromise when problem-solving with our co-parent.

Communication Toolbox to Help Us Better Communicate With Our Co-parents During Separation or Divorce

- **Patience.** Set the stage for each conversation by mentally counting to 10 before you speak. It doesn't matter if you are already calm—make it a ritual so that when you are under stress, you are sure to count to 10 first.
- **Empathy.** Put yourself into your co-parent's shoes. You will respond appropriately if you anticipate what your co-parent might be feeling: "I understand you want to share your love of riding with our son."
- **Ask questions.** Talking it out is important. Ask open-ended questions that do not find fault or put your co-parent on the defense. Rather, promote positive interaction with questions that help your co-parent explain personal point of view. Instead of "I won't permit it; our child is unsafe!" try "What will you do to ensure our child's safety?"
- **Active listening.** To prove that you are listening and understand, paraphrase what was said: "Thank you for hearing me out. I hear that you are doing A, B, and C to make sure he's safe. What do you think about adding D?"
- **Reframe.** Present negative observations as positive. This is not a disagreement but an opportunity for negotiation and compromise in the best interest of your children.
- **Humor.** Using gentle humor often helps you address even the most sensitive issues and keeps things in the proper perspective.

What Are the Components of the Compromise?

If the laws in your state allow a child to ride, the decision is not whether the child will ride with Father but what, as a co-parent, can be done to secure his safety while on the ride.

Here are some suggestions.

1. Make sure he has a helmet that fits properly and appropriate safety clothing for the ride.

2. Install a backrest for added safety.

3. To ensure the child does not fall asleep on the back of the motorcycle, have an agreement for how long the daily ride might be.

4. Agree on a check-in time for the child to keep the other parent up-to-date on his adventure. This allows the child to express excitement and appeases the other parent's concern.

5. No riding in bad weather.

6. No alcohol on the day of the ride.

How Can I Present the Compromise to My Child?

Normally, a child would not be involved in any discussion; however, these parents have already involved him in this disagreement. Therefore, this is an opportunity for them to *reframe* their disagreement as a compromise. It also allows them to openly demonstrate respect for each other, even when they don't agree.

The disrespectful approach: *"Your mother is driving me crazy. I can't take her whining about your safety any longer!"*

The respectful approach: *"Your mother and I are very concerned about your safety on this ride. I have assured her that I have taken all the precautions I can to keep you safe. We have agreed that (and list the agreement)."*

More Safety Concerns

Housing

When Your Co-parent Leaves the Children Alone

> ❝ My children's mother and I share custody of the kids during the week and alternate our weekends. She works for 3 hours in the afternoon each Saturday the kids are with her, and she leaves them home alone for this period of time. They are 10 and 13. I don't think it's safe. She says they are fine. Isn't there a law about leaving children alone? ❞

As in the motorcycle scenario, one co-parent thinks the situation is safe, while the other co-parent disagrees. And, again, finding the solution is in the compromise.

Remember, start with an investigation to get the proper background information. In this case, what is the legal age a child may be left unattended? Once again, there is no cut-and-dried answer. Laws are different from state to state, with only a few states offering an exact age requirement. It goes without saying that common sense suggests a baby and a toddler are too young to be left alone, and there will be legal ramifications if done so. Where the rules get blurry are the ages of the children in question in this home alone scenario. Montana offers the following observation when ruling about the age a child can be left alone: "There is no magic age when children develop the maturity and good sense they need to stay home alone. Mature children in a neighborhood with several adult friends home nearby may be all right for a few hours. For younger children, one hour may be too long. YOU need to decide if the time alone is too much, based on your child and your situation."

So, again, if this mother ascertains that the children are safe when they are in her care, there will be no legal ramifications if they are left alone. However, a couple of things could be put into place in the name of a healthy compromise that might help ease Dad's concerns. It starts with a discussion. Remember to refer to your communication toolbox: use patience, empathy, questions, active listening, compromise, reframing, and humor when attempting to solve a problem with your co-parent.

Can you find a healthy compromise with your co-parent?

1. How far away do the parents live from each other? Would it be possible for the mother to drop the children off and pick them up from Father's home on her way to and from work? If this is done, there should be some agreement that Father not make plans that would prevent the children from returning to Mother's home once she is done with work without their mutual agreement. And, if Father helps with child care, it would be agreed that this is done in good faith and will not be used as ammunition to change the parenting plan or child support.

2. Are house rules in place?

   – Will friends be allowed to visit during the time the children are left alone?
   – Do the children have access to a telephone in case of an emergency?
   – Are adults or neighbors next door who the children know and can call for assistance in case of an emergency?

3. Have you talked with the children? Do they prefer to stay at their mother's home, or would they feel more comfortable if other arrangements were made?

Weighing these considerations prior to facing any disagreement sets the stage for better communication on all fronts. Having a plan that both the child and the co-parents agree to in this situation allows everyone to know exactly what to expect.

Roommate in the House

66 *Money is tight and my children's father needed a roommate to make ends meet. My daughters are 4 and 6. Their dad found this guy on Craigslist. I know nothing about him, and I don't think it's safe over there now. I don't want my daughters to spend the night!*

I worry that he could hurt the girls when everyone is asleep. **99**

A roommate is an understandable concern; however, it is doubtful that a court of law or other agencies will stop visitation because your co-parent has a roommate, unless the roommate is a convicted sex offender, openly uses drugs or alcohol and it has been deemed the children are in danger as a result, or is possibly violent. If that is the case, that parent's judgment is truly in question, and the co-parent's concern is merited.

That said, roommates are a possible reality, so it's best to lay the ground rules before advertising for one. Decide between yourselves what are the deal breakers concerning finding a roommate. And, finally, because a co-parent can't stop the other co-parent from getting a roommate, here are just a few suggestions for compromise.

1. Conduct background checks and references for all potential roommates before they move in.

2. Put rules into place that you both agree on when leaving the children alone with this new roommate.

3. Your co-parent may not have the final say-so about your choice of roommate, but make it a point to introduce your children and your co-parent to the potential roommate *before* that person moves in.

4. If your children are unsafe at night, they are probably unsafe during the day. Mutually agree on safe checks and balances, and put them into place at both homes.

It's natural that there will be some differences between divorced parents' homes. At one house, there may be a specific bedtime, and at the other, she may be allowed to stay awake half the night. The food may be healthier; the car, safer; and the home condition, better at one place over another.

Along the same lines, co-parents may have difficulty assessing safety when first moving to a new home. There may be a swimming pool that one believes is dangerous, while the other believes it's not, or there may not be enough beds, or no beds at all, and children have to sleep on the floor. This does not necessarily mean the children are being neglected. Neglect is subjective. What is questionable housing to one is not questionable housing to another. If accommodations keep a child clean, warm, and fed, an agency will most likely not interfere in a child's time with a parent. I've worked with a client who was homeless and living in his fifth wheel camper. When he had the children, he took them camping—it was their big weekend excursion—and much to their mother's credit, she never told the children their father was homeless. The children never knew and have fond memories of the summer they went camping every other weekend with Dad.

Some parents are homeless and are not fortunate enough to have a camper to pose as their home. In those situations, accommodations may not be safe, and the parenting plan may have to be adjusted until the parent can arrange for proper accommodations for the children. In these situations, a parent may retain joint legal custody, but physical custody may be adjusted until those proper accommodations are put into place.

A Different Kind of Compromise

For many, stories of sleeping in campers or on the floor may seem far-fetched, but sleeping arrangements at the other parent's home are a common safety concern for co-parents.

Take Ginny and Linda, 7-year-old twins whose parents separated 6 months ago. Dad had moved into an apartment but hadn't had time to shop for furniture. He had the bare necessities, and Ginny and Linda had told their mother they were sleeping on the floor. Mother was up in arms and threatened to take Dad back to court, until Dad took the time to explain to his co-parent how he handled the situation.

> **❝** *Each weekend, after I pick up the girls, we go to the store and I let them buy snacks. The girls love microwave popcorn, so we make a big deal out of it and use lots of butter, in a big bowl, and sit on the floor. I have no furniture, but I do have a TV. We spread a blanket down in front of the TV in the living room, and each girl picks out a movie to watch. We lie on the floor, eating popcorn, watching Netflix, and falling asleep together. I don't have any furniture yet, but I love my girls, and I'm doing the best I can.* **❞**

After the girl's mother heard that, she consulted her co-parenting communication toolbox and stopped expressing concern. She put herself into her co-parent's place (empathy) and realized how important it was that Dad spend time with the girls. She listened to his explanation and allowed him to reframe sleeping on the floor and what that meant—he wasn't being neglectful, he was having a special time with his daughters while they were eating popcorn and watching movies together. Dad bought beds a few months later. It took just a little patience to allow him to get settled. No adjustment was made to the parenting plan.

> **❝** *After we broke up, I stayed in the house with my ex and our children. I knew my kids' mother wouldn't be able to afford the house payment and it would offer the kids some sort of consistency until their mother could get settled. She tells me the kids have their own rooms in her new place, but I don't think that's true. I'm concerned the kids just aren't safe over there.* **❞**

Granted, co-parents should not dictate policy at the other home, and there should be a certain amount of autonomy once they break up, but offering as much information as possible will help your co-parent relax and build trust in your judgment and parenting skills. If your co-parent has a question about accommodations, consider offering pictures of the children's room. Or, if you have a more casual relationship, invite your co-parent to see your home firsthand. The more information you can offer each other, the better—for your communication and for your ability to co-parent together.

Suspicious Bruises and Breaks

❝ *My son came home from his mother's home with a huge bruise on both inner thighs. When I asked his mother about it, she was vague and didn't have a clear-cut reason for what had happened. I'm so worried my child is not safe with his mother, and I don't want to send him back. I called the police for advice, and they said I had to send him!* **❞**

When a child custody order is in place, you cannot decide on your own free will that your child should not see the other parent. With no order, it is your word against your co-parent's and police have nothing on which to base that a child must be returned. This is the reason it is suggested that parents always have a custody order in place. If parents want to deviate from that order by mutual agreement, that's fine, but if you do that for a length of time—say, on your custody order your weekends ended on Sunday, but you mutually agreed that it would be easier on the kids if the weekend ended "to school Monday morning"— you should both have a signed agreement stating the change and file it away as proof. If you would like the change to become permanent, you must return to court and have the parenting plan officially adjusted.

❝ *Oh no, we have to stick to the custody agreement. It's the law!* **❞**

Yes, sticking to the custody agreement is the law, but many custody orders include language that states if the parents mutually agree, they can change any aspect of the custody order they like. This was done because family court wants co-parents to be able to comfortably negotiate changes. They want you to fill in for each other and help each other co-parent your children. As long as a change is mutually agreed on, parents can legally make any change from the parenting plan that they like.

In view of all this, if you spot a suspicious bruise or break in the skin, remember: kids fall and hurt themselves all the time. Many toddlers seem to have bruises on their foreheads, which simply indicate active play. Other injuries, however, can almost come only from abuse. Infants who can't walk, for example, also can't fall, and there's pretty much no way for them to break a bone. Here is a list of injuries that could raise concern that a child is being mistreated.

Warning Signs That Indicate Someone Might be Mistreating Your Child

- Hair pulled out in patches
- Injuries to the teeth or the inside of the mouth, which suggest being punched in the face
- Bruises on the face except for on the foreheads of toddlers
- Bite marks unless they clearly match the mouth of a young sibling
- Bruising of the thighs or buttocks, which rarely occurs from unintentional injuries but often from spanking
- Marks in the shape of a foreign object, such as a cigarette, stick, or cooking utensil
- Bruising over the softer parts of the body: abdomen, neck, ears, face, or upper arms

If you see anything suspicious on your child, you do not have to carry the weight on your shoulders, trying to prove whether it is true or not true. Your best allies are a trip to your child's pediatrician for verification of your concern, the police, and child protective services for help with an investigation. You may also want to apply for temporary custody orders with family court until your suspicions are proven or disproven. But be careful; the courts frown on parents applying for such orders under false pretenses, so if your concern is not legitimate and you are applying for temporary orders out of revenge, you could lose time with your children. Safety concerns are real, and they should always be reported. False reports made to manipulate the system indicate attempted parental alienation and should be investigated as such.

When Parents Have Different Morals

66 *My ex has a different woman at his home every weekend, and my 13-year-old daughter can't stand it. He drinks too much and is far more affectionate with these women than makes her feel comfortable. She loves her dad, but she comes home feeling humiliated. I never thought he would act this way in front of our daughter! He's changed so much since our divorce. I don't know who he is anymore. He's so unpredictable, and my daughter just doesn't feel safe over there!* 99

After being together for years, many settle into a calmer, relaxing lifestyle than when they were dating and forget about the wild, crazy days when they first met. Go back in your memory banks—did you drink together to excess when you first met? When no kids were around, did you throw caution to the wind and simply act a little crazy? Your ex may not be as different as you think.

That said, kids don't like open displays of affection between their parents even when they are together. You can only imagine how a 13-year-old teen might feel if she is witness to open displays of nondiscretionary affection between her parent and other people she does not know. Also, when things are particularly confusing, such as immediately after your parents split up, there is an allegiance issue to consider. It takes a while for kids to accept their parents are no longer together. Open displays of affection with someone other than their parent too soon after a breakup can feel like additional betrayal. Kids don't rationalize it by thinking, "Oh, it's OK now, they've broken up." They look to their parents for comfort and predictability. They don't want their parents to be sexy or impulsive. They want to know exactly what will happen and how any change will affect their life. If the teen in this scenario can't depend on her dad to keep her safe, she will not want to return. Quite frankly, constantly flaunting that kind of behavior when it is obvious that it makes a child uncomfortable could easily be categorized as emotionally abusive. Consider what your child is feeling and act appropriately.

Once again, the answer is compromise.

Of course, this parent's behavior is questionable and in bad taste, but, once again, it is not illegal. These parents simply don't agree on what is safe for their daughter. When there is a clear difference of opinion, the only answer is compromise.

Consulting the co-parenting communication toolbox, let's start with empathy. It's common knowledge that there is usually very little intimacy before a breakup. Both men and women may feel unattractive and taken for granted because of the constant turmoil leading up to the split. Quite a few fear that no one will ever again find them attractive and fill their dance card as soon as they become single. This is understandable, and if you both put yourself into each other's shoes, you both might understand the longing to feel desired again. But the kids still see you as their parents, not sexual beings. They need you to protect them and be their parents.

There's more. It's also time for the "dating" parent to check that motivation. Empathy is a wonderful motivator for compromise, but there may be more to Dad's behavior (in this case) than meets the eye—hurt, anger, and revenge may be at the root of his bad judgment. If he felt rejected during the marriage, the overt dating could very well be his way of putting Mom in her place: "You don't want me? Well, hundreds of women do! Watch this!"

It's important to note that any example used in these scenarios can be reversed: either parent could be dating indiscriminately, while the other looks on. The common denominator is always the child. The child must go back and forth between homes. Without saying a word, this child is being asked to be a messenger and pass on information: "Your mom didn't want me, but let her know how many other women do...." Children rarely see it that way. Some shut down. Some openly rebel. Both emotions prompt a child to not want to return. Plus, if a child is especially attached to the dating parent, he may even feel as if that parent is choosing *anyone* (because this person has no real relationship to his parent) over him. The hurt and resentment that breed can affect a child's feeling of self-worth and the parent-child relationship forever.

The compromise? Date, but date with discretion. This may not sound like much of a compromise to some, but it is: if this co-parent did not compromise, he might continue his current dating behavior in front of his daughter because dating is not illegal, and he could make that argument if asked to defend his behavior. In truth, co-parents can't forbid each other to date or even move in with someone "too soon," but they can formally agree to compromise—to not flaunt their sexuality in front of their children and to introduce their children only when the date becomes a partner. That compromise starts with a conversation, and that conversation should happen sooner rather than later.

Addiction

Lucy is the mother of a 7-year-old daughter, Carley. They are very close; however, Lucy has been struggling with an alcohol problem for the past few years and has gotten 2 DUIs as a result. Her driver's license was revoked, and her time with Carley has been reduced so substantially that Carley is becoming withdrawn and depressed. Sam, Carley's father, sees the change in his daughter and wants to do something, but he is also concerned about Lucy's drinking. Lucy just got her driver's license back, can drive without restriction, and wants to take Carley more often, but Sam is afraid for Carley's safety while driving with her mother.

Addiction is a common problem, and, again, because there is no exact right or wrong answer in this situation, compromise is the best solution. If Lucy has a working driver's license, she can transport anyone she wants, but is that in Carley's best interest? Will digging in her heels set the stage for a working co-parenting relationship? Consider the following conversation Lucy and Sam had in my office, and see how a compromise was reached.

❝*I have to see Carley more often, Sam. It's not good for her to be away from me for so long."*

Sam agreed, but he was also a little resentful: "Lucy, I get it, but this is your fault and it's my job to keep Carley safe."

Of course, that made Lucy angry: "Are you saying I don't want her safe? Come on, Sam. You know better. I've been sober for almost 6 months! I would never hurt Carley!"

I could see this might spiral out of control, so I intervened: "Is there a compromise here? What can you suggest, Lucy, that would keep Carley safe and, as a result, you could see

*her more often?" She thought for a second. "How about if
I agree that I won't take her in the car alone, Sam? Would
that work?"*

*Sam looked at me for reassurance. "It's your agreement, Sam.
Lucy is looking for ideas, a compromise. Think about it.
What exactly do you want? Tell her."*

*"I want Carley to be safe and Lucy to stay sober," Sam said
matter-of-factly.*

*Lucy sighed loudly. "OK, how about we go back to our original
parenting plan if I agree not to transport Lucy by myself for
another 6 months? That will be an entire year sober. How's that?"*

*"If we do that," Sam said, thinking about what she had proposed,
"how will she get to school in the morning and who will pick her
up after school when she is with you?"*

*"I will arrange for her to take the bus in the morning and carpool
in the afternoon for the next 6 months."*

"Will that work for you, Sam?" I asked.

"Yes, I think it will. **99**

And so there's your compromise. Carley can spend more time with her mother, and the checks and balances are in place to ensure her safety.

66 *OK, Lucy," Sam added, "we will try this. I want to support you in
your sobriety, but if you relapse, the agreement is off. I can see Carley
needs you, and I want to make this work, but she is my main priority."*

"She's mine too, Sam. Thank you. **99**

They left my office with a signed agreement.

All the scenarios are situations when each parent holds an opposite opinion of what is safe for their child. The final situation is no exception.

Staying Adherent to Prescribed Medication

66 *Our son has ADHD [attention-deficit/hyperactivity disorder] and
is on 10 mg of Adderall each day to help him focus. His father does not
believe he has ADHD and refuses to give him his medication on the
weekends he is with him. My son is so rambunctious without his
meds I'm afraid he will hurt himself. His father thinks I'm being
ridiculous. My son is not safe over there!"*

Different kinds of medication are given to children with an attention-deficit/ hyperactivity disorder (ADHD) diagnosis. Some are stimulant based and some are not. Most children with ADHD experience symptom improvement while taking a stimulant-based medication, such as methylphenidate or amphetamine. If one ADHD medication doesn't seem to work—or if it works at only an extremely high dose—the doctor may prescribe another drug.

There is no evidence that any particular medication is best. "Treatment of ADHD should begin with an oral stimulant, either an amphetamine or a methylphenidate-based formulation," reports the November 2006 issue of *Treatment Guidelines,* a highly respected newsletter for physicians about prescription drugs. "None of these drugs is inherently more effective than another.... The choice of a specific drug should be based on its rapidity of onset, duration of action, and effectiveness in a given patient."

The controversy surrounding the pros and cons of taking a break from ADHD medication, specifically stimulant-based medications, has been well-documented. Some believe that it is good for the child to take a break because a common adverse effect is a decrease in appetite, and not taking the medications for a while will allow the child's appetite to return. Ultimately, taking children off ADHD medication may cause their ADHD symptoms to reappear, but they won't get sick as a result or experience other adverse effects.

On the flip side, ADHD medication helps children stay focused and reduces disruptive behavior. These students stop getting into trouble for interrupting class time or wandering around in class, and then their self-esteem is, once again, restored. If children stop taking their medication, it may take several days or possibly weeks for it to resume being effective. Remember, most of these medications are stimulant based. Imagine yourself drinking 3 cups of coffee in quick succession one morning and then you don't drink any at all the next morning; then you drink 3 cups of coffee over and over again, because your parents can't get on the same page about medication.

Parents in this position should not diagnose the child themselves. If the child is under the care of a physician and has a true diagnosis, parental ego aside, both parents must sincerely watch how the child responds when taking medication and, under the direction of the child's pediatrician, keep the child medicated or find other (alternative) treatments to allow the child to flourish. To play with his medication in this manner is, for want of another word, abusive.

All the way through this chapter, the solutions offered are compromises designed by the parents based in respect, patience, and the ability to listen with empathy, as well as sprinkled with a touch of humor. These are the tools in their co-parenting communication toolbox that allowed them to reach out to each other, find their own unique solution when one was not obvious, and problem-solve in the best interest of their child.

> 66 *But what if you can't compromise? What if your co-parent simply does not see the danger and does not want to cooperate?* 99

Of course, at times, lack of compromise may happen, and there are various avenues co-parents can take to help finalize a decision. Here is an example of just this sort of situation....

When You Feel Your Co-parent Is Using Bad Judgment

> 66 *Our daughter is 6 and has very bad asthma. Her father does not believe her asthma is that bad and thinks nothing of smoking in the house or while driving in the car. When she returns from his home, she can barely breathe and must be on her nebulizer to get a deep breath. It's frightening to see her fight for air. She's not safe over there!* 99

Or...

> 66 *My ex parties a lot and does not stop when the kids are around. This makes me very uncomfortable, and I'm afraid the kids are not safe when she is under the influence and around her party friends.* 99

As in many of the scenarios already given, the questionable activity (substance use such as drinking and smoking) is not illegal, so the disagreement lies in a difference of opinion on how to approach the activity when the children are present. Initially, the smoking parent agreed to simply stop smoking in the presence of the children and thought that would be enough of a compromise to end the disagreement. The co-parent didn't say, "I'll do what I want when the kids are around"; he acknowledged that the behavior should be adjusted when children are nearby. This approach works well for partying too. A partying parent simply agrees not to partake around the children; however, at times, a co-parent simply changing her behavior is not enough. That's when doing that background research will help and then you can legitimately offer information that will substantiate the need for a change.

For example, a co-parent who smokes has a child with asthma. The co-parent may not know that even the residuals of smoking around someone with asthma could be troublesome; simply not smoking when he or she has smoked in the home previously may not be enough to prevent an asthmatic reaction. Cigarette smoke lingers for hours and is known to permeate carpeting and furniture. Your co-parent may not realize that the lingering odor could be enough to set off an asthma attack in a child with an extreme condition. That means smoking outside may not be enough to prevent a problem when a child with asthma is in a home where people often smoke. It's becoming so obvious that smoking contributes to breathing difficulties that some states in the United States have even passed laws forbidding adults to smoke in cars when children are present.

So, in this situation, there may be no compromise, per se. If the condition is bad enough and the offending parent still refuses to make the appropriate adjustments, the next step would be to ask your co-parent to accompany you to an appointment with your child's pediatrician. There, the doctor could explain, in no uncertain terms, the dangers of smoking around a child with asthma. If the offending parent still refuses to listen, the pediatrician can write a letter to the court explaining the dangers and reporting that your co-parent refuses to consider this during individual time with the child. Under those circumstances, if the proper precautions are not taken, a judge could very well adjust custody.

The truth is, co-parents can always return to court if they can't come to a prior agreement, but the ultimate goal is to build the kind of co-parenting relationship through which problem-solving and compromise are second nature and the threat of returning to court is merely a thing of the past.

10

Is There Someone New?

Your experiences are not limited to what you created in the past.

GARY ZUKAV

When Do I Tell My Kids and My Ex I'm Starting to Date Again?

In the aftermath of separation and divorce, people's attitudes to romance run the gamut, from "Never again" to "Woo-hoo!" Regardless of where you fall on this spectrum, at some point, you're likely to start dating again. This development will profoundly affect your emotional life, and you may be eager to share it with your children. Before you rush to do so, however, let's look at where your kids are emotionally.

First, your children will be yearning for stability. Kids thrive on routine; they love knowing what to expect today, tomorrow, next week, and next year. The disruption of separation or divorce throws everything into question. The more they can establish some sort of predictable routine, the sooner they will regain a sense of comfort with their new lives.

Second, no matter how often you reassure them, almost all kids hold on to hope that, someday, their parents will get back together. They will often blame themselves for the split and will constantly look for clues to validate that the 2 of you will hopefully reconcile. I remember vividly that when my children's mom and I were standing together at school events or when we would exchange the children, they would literally take our hands in theirs and try to get us to touch.

No matter how painful your prior relationship, no matter how obviously unsuitable your ex is for you or for the family, your kids will still be imagining some scenario in which everything goes back to the way it was before, only better. It's going to take them a long time to accept that you're moving forward, not backward. This pattern of self-blame and mourning may repeat itself every time you introduce a new partner into your children's lives, so you'll want to be quite cautious about when and how that happens.

Third, your children are going to need a lot of reassurance and attention. Sometimes they'll ask for these things from you directly, by crawling into your lap, bringing you a book to read together, or simply asking for you to be present with them. At other times they'll seek your attention in ways that are less appealing, by throwing fits, getting into trouble at school, or screaming that everything is your fault and you've ruined their lives. Either way, what they're telling you is that they feel insecure, and they need your attention and reassurance that everything is OK and they will always be loved.

Your children are also likely to be curious about what sort of new partner you will find. Will it be someone who reminds them of your ex? Someone very different? Will that person fit into their lives? Will that person love them like a parent or find them to be a distraction or an annoyance? Your children will be emotionally raw, alternately eager to bond with a new parental figure in their lives and prepared to reject anyone who might compete with them for your attention or even try to replace either parent.

So what about your needs? Naturally, you're going to have an easier time dealing with the stresses of parenting if you, too, are feeling loved and supported. It's hard to overstate the blow to your self-esteem that comes with separating from someone you had hoped to love forever, even more so if the separation wasn't your idea. Discovering that someone else finds you attractive and wants to spend time with you can provide you with a burst of joy, reminding you that indeed, people are out there who value what you have to offer in a relationship. The first time this happens, you'll probably want to share the news with the world, especially with the people closest to you, your children.

Don't. Not yet. Just as your children are adjusting to their new normal, so are you. You are growing and changing, learning what it means to be you without your ex. If a hobby, an interest, or an aspect of your personality felt squelched in your old relationship, chances are that you're rushing out to explore that part of yourself. If an aspect of your ex's behavior or attitude grated on you endlessly, you are probably looking for someone who reminds you of your ex as little as is humanly possible. While your first new relationship might indeed be the one to last a lifetime, it's more likely that you're going to experiment with a few relationships before you get a good sense of who the new you really is and what sort of person will best complement you and your children.

This is a normal, healthy part of your recovery, and it's appropriate that you're excited about it. But it's not time to tell your kids. It takes a while to get to know another person, and the flush of new romance colors everyone's perceptions. It will take a lot of conversations with prospective partners before you know how they will feel about taking an active role in your children's lives. How were they raised? Do they have children of their own, and, if so, what sort of relationship do they have with them? How do they feel about other people's children? What are their ideas about household rules and discipline? You might dive right into these topics on the first date, but it's probably going to take quite a while to really learn what sort of a person your new partner will be around your kids. Take some time to sort these things out before you put your children through this inevitably emotional experience.

When Is the Right Time to Break the News?

If you have spent the time to really get to know a new partner and you think this person might become more deeply involved in your life, ideally, your co-parent should be the next person to know. Your kids should never be in the position of breaking the news to the other parent. When they ask your co-parent, "Have you heard about…?" they should be able to say, "Yes, I know." It's especially important to have this conversation before you start living with a new partner.

How you go about delivering this news depends a lot on the nature of your relationship with your co-parent. Ideally, you're on good enough terms to meet in person with your co-parent and your new partner present. If circumstances make such a meeting impossible, a call, an email, or a video call may work instead. It may be tempting during this conversation to recount all the ways that your new partner treats you better than your co-parent did, but that's not what this conversation is about. Instead, it's an opportunity to let your co-parent hear about your new partner from you rather than from your kids. The conversation does not have to be long or involved; keep it focused on the future and on your commitment to always placing your children's well-being first.

As you can imagine, your co-parent may not be as excited about this new relationship as you are. There are likely to be questions about the suitability of your new partner to be around the children. Your co-parent may use this opportunity to open old wounds and revisit past slights and insults. People who have been close to each other are experts at hurting each other, if they choose to. You, however, are moving forward with your life. You don't have to take this bait, and this conversation is simply to provide information, not to refight old battles or defend yourself. Take the high ground and keep coming back to the facts: this is the person you're seeing, and it's getting serious and you thought your co-parent should know before the kids. If the conversation becomes overly emotional, feel free to acknowledge your co-parent's pain and suggest that you take up the subject again when everyone is calmer.

Dating After a Breakup

There is always a period of adjustment after a breakup as a couple transitions from being together to being single. This transition time can seem even longer for couples who break up amicably. In these cases there seems to be no rush to sever ties and both may send mixed messages that confuse the parties, the friends, the extended family members, and especially the children.

> 66 *My ex and I split up about 6 months ago. We were married for 10 years and share custody. Last week, the kids came home from his house and told me, 'Daddy had a woman spend the night.' I was horrified! I didn't think he would ever do that! What do I do?* 99

Although it's probably the last thing you want to do, if you find out about someone spending the night from your kids, it looks as if you may have to talk with your co-parent about his dating behavior. Be careful with your approach. Preface that conversation with something such as "I'm not making judgments about the way you conduct your life. I'm concerned about our children," and then state the problem. Make sure you don't bring your leftover baggage into it, and be tactful when you describe the new person in your co-parent's life. He'll be more open to a conversation if you refer to her as "your new relationship" or even use her first name; just don't make derogatory comments. Make it clear that your concerns are about how seeing him intimate with another woman so soon after the breakup affects your children. Give honest examples if the kids have mentioned something. Don't exaggerate or make things up. As you explore new relationships, remember that you're modeling behavior for your children. Especially when you have teens in the home, be aware that they're watching how you and your new partner behave and are likely to use your behavior as a script in their own romantic relationships.

Jealousy and anger aside, you shouldn't be surprised when your co-parent eventually moves on. For your kids' sake, agree in the beginning as to how you both will present a new relationship if one develops, and then stick to that agreement. As strange as it may sound, your ex can be your biggest ally. When, for example, your child comes home announcing that Mommy or Daddy has a new partner, a well-informed co-parent will not have to act surprised; instead, that parent can offer an informed response. Think that's crazy advice? What do you think a child would rather hear: calming reassurance or angry surprise?

Consider How Your Dating Behavior Looks to Your Children

I've worked with quite a few clients who are in denial about how severely their behavior with new partners affects their kids. First, they think the kids don't know. They do. Next, they think the kids don't understand. They do. And finally, they think the kids will get over it. They won't—at least not in the near future—and if you are flaunting behavior that makes your children uncomfortable, no parents should be surprised when their children say they don't want to visit. Children are embarrassed by their parents' sexuality. They're doubly embarrassed by their divorced parents' sexuality. Children don't necessarily know how to act or what to say. They simply may feel awkward about it.

> *Thirteen-year-old Amanda was very close to her mother after her parents broke up. They had very frank conversations about sex, and Mother emphasized abstinence. The relationship grew even closer when Amanda's father started to date. Amanda found her father's dating habits "disgusting." She said she felt uncomfortable around her dad because he was openly affectionate with different women, and when he finally found someone he truly liked, Amanda refused to interact with her on any level. Father didn't realize that his previous behavior actually sabotaged any relationship his girlfriend might have with Amanda. He blamed Amanda's surly disposition.*
>
> *Amanda's mother started to date Bill and thought she was being discreet, but Bill visited one afternoon when Amanda was at school and a used condom wrapper was left on the headboard. Amanda saw it when she got home from school and went crazy. "You're doing exactly what you told me not to do!" Amanda would not even look at her mother, and whatever relationship she had formed with Bill ended immediately.*

What the parents did in the scenario contributed to the problem without their knowing it. They neither discussed nor agreed about how to handle dating after their breakup. Their oversight only undermined their own relationship with their daughter, plus any relationship their daughter might have with their prospective partners.

66 *What can I do to fix it?* **99**

First, let's look at exactly what happened.

Once divorced, parents often make their children their confidants. They relax, enforce the rules less stringently, and believe their children will make the right choices because they are "pals." In this case, Mother had been preaching abstinence, something she was not practicing herself. The "say as I say, not as I do" philosophy reinforces disrespect in your teen. Amanda felt betrayed when she found out her mother had been lying to her.

Second, the mother-daughter boundaries blurred, and Amanda regarded her mother more as a friend. As a result, Amanda felt she and Mom were on the same level and what was fitting for an adult was also fitting for her.

Truth is, Amanda felt betrayed by both parents and she felt she had no one to trust. She began to act out and became pregnant at 15 years of age.

Bottom line: all this points to a frank conversation with your child's other parent—and an agreement about how dating will be handled. Most parenting plans give both parents enough private time to date when the kids aren't around. Flaunting your sexuality will alienate your children. Put parenting first when your kids are around and when they are with your co-parent, then you can have your private time.

What if There Was an Affair?

In some cases, your new relationship may have begun before your old one ended. The new relationship may be the reason the old one ended. If that is the case and your co-parent is already aware of this relationship, an introduction is unnecessary and may be potentially painful, at least at first.

If, on the other hand, you're the parent on the flip side of this situation, you may find it particularly difficult to deal with your co-parent's not-so-new partner. You may even be eager for your children to know that your co-parent cheated on you or that this new person is the reason they no longer have an intact family. Unleashing this anger onto your children may give you a rush of feeling righteous, but stop and think about what it will do to them. They are still going to love their other parent, because that's what children do. They may also need to learn over time to accept this new person as a stepparent. Railing against this new person as a home-wrecker or your co-parent as a cheater is just going to make the process harder for everyone. Your children are not keeping score, no matter what age they are. They are trying to cope with a new and profoundly difficult change in their lives. As hard as it may be, share your outrage liberally with your adult support network, or keep a journal to track your anger, but spare your children.

> 66 *OK, I've gotten to know this person well, and I think this person would be good with my kids. What now?* 99

Once you feel that a new partner is potential co-parenting material, introduce your children to your new "friend" slowly, starting with activities everyone can enjoy, such as a trip to the park or dinner and a family movie. Don't be alarmed if that first venture is an awkward one, but be on the lookout for red flags, such as your new partner being unpleasant (or worse) toward your children. Even if things go better than expected, remember that this new relationship between your partner and your children will mature slowly, and all parties will need a lot of time to relax around one another.

In this early stage of dating, it's important to maintain boundaries. Your new partner and your children may enjoy spending time together playing, reading books, or going on outings, but you should be clear with all parties that your new partner is not yet a part of your family. Sensitive duties, such as discipline, bathing, and child care, are still your responsibility, not your new partner's. As eager as you may be to finally have someone to share not only the challenges but the joys of parenting, you'll want to proceed slowly until you are really convinced that this person deserves a place in your home.

> **❝** *I think my new partner is wonderful, but the kids have been slow to warm up. Should we still move in together?* **❞**

In short, no, do not move in with your partner if the kids have been slow to warm up. You may find yourself eager to move on to a new chapter in your life. Your children, however, are still adjusting to this one, and you may need to set the pace a little slower. Remember that even if you felt your prior home life was miserable, it's the life that they knew, and it's going to take them some time to mourn. Your new partner may be amazing in every possible way, but your kids are going to want things back the way they were for a period of time. They're also going to be hungry for your undivided attention, and a new partner can inevitably divide your attention.

> **❝** *I want everyone to get along and be happy. Should I check in with my kids and see if they like my new partner?* **❞**

The success of a check-in kind of conversation is based on your approach. Of course, we want our kids to be happy, and we want them to feel as if they can come to us with their concerns, but initiating a conversation by asking them what they think about your new adult relationship could be a double-edged sword. On the one hand, they may see something you don't see, but their prejudice may be masked as concern because they want you to reconcile with their other parent. If you give your children the power to weigh in on your adult relationship by asking their opinion, it can blur the parent-child boundary, and you may find yourself arguing about staying or going. If they don't like your new partner, are you prepared to walk away? Some are. Some are not, and that possibility could put your children in direct competition with your partner. Your job as a parent is to create an environment where your children feel as if they can come to you with their concerns, but if you're looking for another perspective because you are concerned someone else might see something you don't see, ask your friends, or check in with a therapist, but don't ask you kids. Let your kids be kids.

66 *I don't have a new partner, but my ex does. How do I deal?* **99**

Consider the following scenario.

66 *Leanne and I co-parented just fine until I met Lisa. Then things that seemed to be easy to figure out became World War III."*

"Are we being honest here?" Leanne asked. She took a breath. "Even though we hadn't been together for 3 years, it was a shock when Lisa moved in with Tom. I was blindsided! The kids told me! So I stopped cooperating. **99**

When your co-parent starts to date, it's not uncommon to feel some combination of jealousy, anger, sadness, and territorial behavior. Being a co-parent, however, also means that you're going to have to overcome those feelings in order to serve your children's best interests. No one expects you to cope alone; we've already talked about how to gather your support network around you. But, ultimately, you're going to have to bring a healthy mind-set to this altered relationship, even when dealing with a person you might see as your replacement.

Start with labels you use, because they can affect your attitude. Your ex now has a partner. Not a "new" partner, or a "current" partner, just a partner. Will this relationship last? Maybe, maybe not. But it's what's happening now, and now is the only moment we can deal with.

Every adult in this new situation is likely to feel a little uneasy. Whatever role you had in your child's life, be it provider, nurturer, disciplinarian, or confidant, now another person may be doing some of those things. That is hard to think about, but remember that a child's emotional life is not what economists call a *zero-sum game,* which is to say that every hug your child gets from someone else is not a hug taken away from you. It just means sometimes your child gets more hugs! You are the only one who can diminish your importance in your child's life. You will always hold a special spot in your child's heart, no matter what your co-parent's new partner may bring to the situation.

Also, remember that your new partner is facing something completely new. New partners may feel tremendous pressure to try to earn a child's love or respect and they may respond by being overly indulgent or overly strict. In either case, the key is to develop a strong working relationship with your co-parent and your co-parent's partner and coordinate efforts to problem-solve around whatever is going on with your children.

Moving Forward

The easiest way to move forward is to keep everyone's attention on the child's needs. You may really, really not want to communicate with the new partner, for example. But if that person is responsible for setting up medical or dental appointments, getting your child to sports practice, or attending a parent-teacher meeting, you do your child no favors by withholding what you know. In my pediatric clinic, the second question I usually ask right after "What's going on today?" is "When did the first sign of this illness start?" I'm shocked by how often a parent will answer, "I don't know; I just picked him up from my co-parent's home." This child has been sick for some period of time, and the parents couldn't communicate enough to share when it started! It's not a matter of what you think your co-parent or your co-parent's new partner deserves; it's a matter of what your child deserves.

> 66 *But my co-parent's new partner hates me; I can tell.*
> *What can I do?* 99

It's certainly possible that your co-parent's new partner feels some sort of animosity toward you. Meeting your co-parent's new partner is an incredibly awkward experience, especially early in a relationship. Many people don't know what to say, aren't sure whether they should shake hands, and aren't comfortable making eye contact. All those behaviors can seem hostile, but they may just reflect embarrassment or fear. In addition, does this person really know you? Or is this person just responding to a label, "ex" or "new," and so that's supposed to be a naturally adversarial relationship? You can change that. Be honest and straightforward and explain that you have no desire to perpetuate the old stereotype— that you would like to forge new ground by getting along for the sake of the children.

Jealousy

Dealing With Jealousy of the Past

> 66 *My guy and I have just decided to move in together. I was*
> *cleaning out his garage in preparation to store some things and*
> *came across his wedding album and other family pictures framed*
> *to perfection. I asked him to throw them out, but he refused, saying*
> *the kids might want them someday. I don't want to be reminded*
> *there was someone before me.* 99

Of course, there was someone before you. Just as there was probably someone before him. We all have a past. It makes both of you who you are. It makes your kids who they are. Don't be afraid of it.

It's time to get things into perspective. Consider some of the true definitions of *past* according to Dictionary.com. They are "gone by or elapsed in time" and "of, having existed in, or having occurred during a time previous to the present." That time with someone else that so intimidates you no longer exists and never will again. It had nothing to do with you. You are the present from this point on.

Having said that, if the pictures were pictures of past girlfriends, to whom he has no current attachment, and are on the living room coffee table, expecting him to dispose of them would be understandable. Openly displaying them would be disrespectful and insensitive. But the pictures you describe are pictures of his wedding to his children's mother and family pictures of the 2 of them with their children. Plus, albums such as this not only include pictures of the former couple but also pictures of their parents and other relatives who may now be deceased. Those pictures can never be recreated.

Also, note how the album was stored. It was tucked away in a box in the garage. Hopefully, that indicates how "your guy" views his past—a memory that is tucked away, not of his undying love but of his respectfully acknowledging the union, to be shared one day when his kids have grown and become adults.

On a personal note, I have to admit I still had my wedding album from when I married my daughter's father for years even though I had remarried. It also was tucked away at the bottom of a hope chest. I gave it to my daughter when she announced her engagement to her husband. She cherishes the album, not only because it is the only record of her biological mom and dad together but also because her dad has now passed after a long illness and in those pictures her father was happy and vibrant, laughing with his groomsmen and cutting up on the dance floor. That's the way she wants to remember him. The only color pictures in existence of her great-grandmother and great-grandfather are also included in that album.

Jealous of the New Partner: When the New Partner Fits in Too Well

66 *She's doing everything too well," a divorced mom confided when talking about her ex's new girlfriend. "She's only been around for a few months, and she leaves nothing for me to do for my children. When I try to talk to her about it, she just laughs. I wish she would just bug off and let me take care of my own children. Where did she come from anyway?* **99**

Ironically, mothers confide that if they feel jealous, it's often not over the new partner's relationship with the co-parent but the new partner's relationship with the children. It seems, without warning or the proper preparation, the former spouse is expected to fall in line and share the mom duties she used to regard as sacred. So, from a practical standpoint, when you have a newly divorced mom and her ex's new partner jockeying for position with no idea how to coexist and no communication between the 2 of them…it's a recipe for disaster. They're bound to butt heads.

Using something out of my own memory book, I can offer this story to demonstrate firsthand the changes that must be made to coexist with your ex's new partner for the sake of the children in your care.

A little background first… In my practice, I was often asked for a guide or list to which divorced parents could refer when they had lost patience with an ex—anyone's ex—it doesn't have to be yours. The principle is universal. With all my years of experience, I created a list. The first and primary rule is "Put the children first." The next 9 rules offer suggestions on how to handle bad-mouthing, revenge, spite, holding grudges, empathy, disrespect, and, finally, compromise.

> **"***I remember how furious my husband's ex was when I became her 5-year-old son's room mother. It had only been a few months, and the kids were adapting well, but she was not. She was furious at the prospect of someone else baking brownies for her son's class and feared, because I spent so much time with him, he would automatically prefer me…until, after a lot of soul-searching, she realized her kids loved her, no matter what. The fact that I loved them, and they loved me, had nothing to do with her relationship with them. When she told me, 'I used to really worry they would love you more, but then I decided I would rather have them with someone who truly loved them and watched out for them than a day care center who just lumped them in with all the other kids,' that sent up a red flag—and it was an eye-opener. We were both putting the kids first, and I was doing a good job, but maybe I was doing too good of a job, and that explained her unwillingness to cooperate at times.***"*

When I used empathy in attempting to problem-solve and put myself into her place, I decided I wouldn't like some other woman taking over my children. I wouldn't like to be out of the loop and find out secondhand that my child went to the doctor for a checkup and I didn't even know about the appointment. Even if the appointment was made on their father's time, I would resent not being informed. Why was I always so surprised by her resentment? We needed tools to do this better—for our own sanity and for the sake of the children in our care.

> **"***I want to build a better relationship with this new person, but how do I make it happen?***"*

The first step to build a better relationship is to accept that you are the only person you can control. Chances are that there are all sorts of things you'd like to control about this situation: what happens at the other home, how the new partner views you, or what your children think of this person. However, none of those things are in your control. What you can control is how you behave, what you say, and what sort of attitude you model for your children. Here are some things to consider when you are in a similar situation.

1. **Define your goal.** What sort of interaction would you like to have with your co-parent's new partner? What would that actually look like? A handshake? A friendly conversation? Can you visualize a positive outcome to your next interaction with that person? Instead of looking back on what you didn't like about past interactions, imagine what you might appreciate about future ones.

2. **Don't worry about being friends.** Your co-parent chose this person, not you. Eventually, you may find that you have some things in common, which is great, or you might not. The new partner may not be interested in being friends, and that's that person's choice. It's likely that every day in your work or your social life, you have perfectly serviceable interactions with people who are not necessarily your friends or even your type. If that's as good as this relationship gets, you're doing better than most people.

3. **Remember that your children know who their parents are.** No matter how close they become with the new partner, you will always be the primary parent. Giving up on this competitive fear frees you up to leave behind your jealousy and focus on productive communication.

4. **Clarify your roles.** My wife, for example, is great at schedules and calendars. It's not that my co-parent and I never make appointments for the kids, but both of us are, to some extent, relieved to have someone in their lives whose mission it is that every kid gets to the dentist, the doctor, and even the hairdresser right on time. Are you good at helping with homework? Practicing ball? Shopping for clothes? For each child, there's probably a special role that you play and jobs that are better left to each of the other partners in this situation. That doesn't mean that one parent should be the only one to do that thing, but it gives you room to relieve everyone's sense of competition.

5. **Develop empathy.** Before you get upset about something that happened at the other house, try telling yourself the story from a few different angles. Maybe the kids were late to bed because things got off schedule. Or perhaps soccer practice ran late, and no one was home to make dinner. In difficult relationships, it's easy to imagine that the other person is doing things on purpose to upset you. But, much more often, stuff just happens, and it's not about you at all.

6. **Cultivate respect.** The key word here is *cultivate*. Given the feelings you may have about your co-parent, your relationship, and your co-parent's choice of partner, you may start in a negative frame of mind, and that's an intentional understatement. This process is going to take time and work, and it will happen in small, intentional steps with regular setbacks. The first step is to remember again that you can control only your own actions, your own words, and your own attitude. But if you set an example of respectful interactions, it's going to be easier for your co-parent and the new partner to follow suit.

7. **Express gratitude.** Say, "Thank you," when appropriate. Just as you do with your kids, when you see a behavior you like, reinforce it by noticing and commenting. "Thanks for helping pack everything up and get it to the car" is a great start! Your words will convey respect, *and* you yourself will feel happier and more at peace. Don't force the issue, of course. If you're not truly feeling grateful, sit tight. But chances are that your co-parent's new partner is trying to do something good for your child, in some way, and when you see something, say something.

8. **When you find yourself comparing you and the new partner, just stop.** This one is easier said than done, I know. If there is anything at all you're insecure about, the arrival of the person you may see as your replacement is likely to bring that thing to the forefront. Is this person funnier? Better looking? More financially successful? More athletic? I'm on the short side of average height, for example, so just statistically speaking, my co-parent is likely to date some- one I have to look up to when we shake hands. You have your own strengths and weaknesses, and when those doubts creep in, it's important to remember that you can't even fairly compare one apple to another, much less 2 people. You are your own package, and the relationship you had with your ex is in the past. As far as the children go, you're always the parent. Moving forward, let that person be that person and you be yourself. It's fine.

9. **Ask for the new partner's opinion.** This is another hard one, especially if you don't particularly like this person. But let's play it out. This is another adult who knows your child, who most likely loves your child, and who sees your child in a setting that you don't. That person may surprise you with a fresh perspective on the problem that you actually find useful. Or maybe you don't find it useful at all, but now you've learned a little more about that person's perspective and approach to problems, which may give you new goals to work toward. In the meantime, you've demonstrated respect and begun to build trust. Ultimately, what you do should depend on the discus- sion you have with your co-parent, but by asking the new partner's opinion, you've made another strong step in crafting a working relationship that will benefit your child.

10. **If you do nothing else, just don't make things worse.** Before you speak, mentally consult your communication toolbox. Take a moment to ask whether you're being part of the solution or part of the problem. Are you picking a fight over one thing because you're angry about something else? How in the world does that benefit your child? Are you upset that your co-parent seems happy and trying to ensure that you're both experiencing equal levels of misery? Then it's time to work on your own happiness, not someone else's unhappiness. Keep asking yourself one question: How does what I'm doing help my child feel happy and secure? If you don't have a good answer, it's time to find another path.

Should the New Partner Discipline My Children?

❝ *My co-parent's new girlfriend watches our daughter while he is at work. I don't like the idea of a strange woman disciplining my 4-year-old daughter!* **❞**

It's understandable that parents don't want other people disciplining their children, especially if they don't know them well. But after a breakup, most recouple, and that means our children will be living with an additional parental figure. We could fight it, dig in our heels, and proclaim, "That person will not discipline my child!" But the truth of it is, our partners, like us, will most likely find someone new, and that new someone will live with our child.

Rather than fight the inevitable, it's best to establish rules together among the households and do your best to stick to them. One rule to which I always subscribe is "Parents make the rules; stepparents or new partners support them." In other words, the children's parents establish house rules and their parents' partners support the rules that the parents put into place. This is especially important when it comes to discipline. It's not uncommon for new partners to be the primary caregivers of the children who live in the home, particularly if the new partners also have children of their own. The parental figures must then coordinate efforts and, for the safety of the children, empower the new partners to make decisions and discipline by relying on the rules the parents put into place.

New Partner Alert

When a new partner hears "You're not my mother!" or "You're not my father!" or something similar, it's a signal that the new partner has overstepped one's bounds and is making the children do something their own parent would not make them do. In frustration, the children blurt, "You're not my parent!" This is a time to revisit the house rules, how they were put into place, and how and by whom they will be enforced.

Doing anything well takes practice. It's hard enough to parent and have a functioning family with both birth parents living in the home. The complexity of adding another adult to family life is bound to have its ups and downs, or its mistakes and overcorrections. If, however, all parties commit to putting the child's needs first and to treating each other with empathy and respect, wonderful things can happen. In a best-case scenario, children of separation and divorce can draw from the strengths and experiences of very loving adult in their lives.

11

The Making of a Family

*The bond that links your true family
is not one of blood, but of respect and joy
in each other's life.*

RICHARD BACH

Less than 30 years ago, when divorce rates had peaked in the United States, what was regarded as the "normal" stepfamily was a 2-parent family, male and female partners, now married to each other with one or both partners having children from a prior marriage. But today's family configuration does not necessarily follow that model. More people choose to live together than marry each year, same-sex relationships are commonplace, and many women do not find it necessary to marry to have children. With these changes in what constitutes a family comes the need to adjust our mind-set of what it takes to create a loving family unit.

❝*If someone asked what the most important tip you could offer parents who want to successfully combine their families, what would that be?* **❞**

When parents combine families, they are often so excited to find someone new that they overlook laying the necessary groundwork and present their new relationship to their children as "Look, we are all going to move in together and be one big happy family." It's that whole blended concept. Take a little of your family, take a little of mine, squish it all together, and here we are—the new and improved blended model of family. The *blended* family.

But that's not it at all. In fact, it's quite the opposite.

Understanding that all family members' individuality needs to be cultivated and their history respected is possibly the most important component to successfully combining families. That's one of the reasons you'll rarely hear me use the phrase *new family* or even *blended family*. I use the term "bonusfamily" instead and for very good reason.

Here's why....

First, the concept behind *new family* is considered to be a substitute, a new and improved version of the "old" family, and that's how you breed competition between households. The truth is, even though the parents are no longer together, they are still a family. Parents are still parents; for instance, Mom is still Mom and Dad is still Dad. The children are still their children. New people are added, and the family configuration may change, but Mom stays Mom and Dad stays Dad.

Second, when you blend something together, you lose the individual components. Flour and eggs don't care but people do. It matters to some children if they used to have a room of their own but now have to share a room. It matters to some children that they used to be the oldest but now are a middle child or the youngest. It matters to some children that they are half of each their parents. It matters that they had to leave their friends, or their baseball team, or their cheerleading squad, and move because their parents are no longer together. If there was any sort of trauma that occurred in their past, or a child has special needs, this needs to be considered as well. As in anything, combining components can make the final product stronger **or** compromise its strength. Respecting each family member's history and individuality makes all family members feel as if *they* matter, and because *they* matter, they are more willing to accept family membership.

Here's an example of discounting a family member's history.

Mom and Dad want to move on. They meet someone new, move in, and, to facilitate the blending process, start referring to their new partner as "Mom" or "Dad"—and expect their kids to call their new partner "Mom" or "Dad." The reason may lie with our upbringing. Parents (consciously or subconsciously) think an "intact" or "good" family must have 2 "parents." Same-sex couples face a variance of this issue, but the bottom line is that past parental roles often get usurped by new partners, and this is initiated by the parent in the new relationship.

Kids don't necessarily want to move on. It's their mom or dad you're talking about. When you say, "I want to move on," to a 10-year-old, the child gets scared: "Move on from Mom? MY MOM? Whyyyyyyyy?"

This is particularly troublesome for kids who struggle with the idea that allegiance to one parent means betrayal of their other parent. Plus, parents who feel dismissed because their ex who has moved on will not be as willing to co-parent if they feel their parental position has been disrespected. Angry co-parents who don't want to cooperate = a miserable life, because the kids will continue to go back and forth between their parents for years.

The same principle is true when referring to your new partner's kids as your children's "brother" or "sister." If the kids choose to say that, fine, but *requiring* them to do that asks them to abandon their history *to get your approval,* and that can cause resentment and frustration, extend their period of adjustment, and slow down acceptance of your new partner.

An easy solution? Sit down together and discuss how you will refer to each other. Don't do all the talking. Listen. What do *they* want to call your new partner? How do *they* want to refer to your new partner's children? Allow them to actively participate in creating their future while being careful not to discount their past and they will be more willing to become an active family member.

Why "Bonus"?

More than 30 years ago, when I married a man and fell in love with his 2 children as well, calling them my stepkids just didn't gel. I had done things such as staying up all night with his child battling a 103°F (39.4°C) fever, wiping her brow, and feeding her popsicles to keep her hydrated, and it just didn't seem right to call her a step-anything after all that. I knew she wasn't my biological child, but the feelings were certainly not step-feelings either. I needed a word that more exemplified how I felt about these kids—something far more loving than *step-*.

My kids, both biological and "bonus," needed a new word as well. They were little at this time, in the midst of Disney princesses and elementary school shenanigans, and felt that stepmothers and stepfathers were mean and evil. We cared for each other, and our feelings did not match what we knew about step-relations. *Step-* just didn't work for us.

Blended was the politically correct word of the time, but that pertained only to "family." You couldn't have a blended child or a blended dad or mom, so we searched for a word that better described how we felt about each other. One didn't seem to be out there.

"A Rose by Any Other Name Would Smell as Sweet"

Shakespeare was trying to explain that a name makes no difference; it is the essence of a person, in that case, Juliet, that makes the person special. Although that is true, sometimes, people rely on special labels to find their identity, unite them, and build camaraderie.

For example, people of various cultures unite through their labels and choose to be called one thing over another to depict how they feel about their origin. Some labels are acceptable only within that culture and deemed an insult if someone outside that culture uses the label—because that label unites *them*.

"Bonus" is no different. A bonus is a reward for a job well done. In sales, for example, you get a bonus when you reach quota—your ultimate goal. That was the concept behind "bonusfamily." We recognize that it was a journey and the ultimate goal was getting to a place of acceptance and comfort. The basis was love. Calling my stepkids my "bonuskids"—and them calling me their "bonusmom"—and referring to our family as a "bonusfamily" was designed to be a compliment and sign of acceptance. "Bonus" was our label and united *us*.

At the beginning of this experiment, one of the most common questions I received was

> 66 *My partner and I are not married; would the term 'bonus' apply to our family as well?* 99

Currently, **well more than 40%** of all new babies born in the United States are born to unmarried mothers. Many of these children are born to intact families whose parents have had other children together, plus who have additional children from other relationships. *Step-* implies married, and when you are not, people stumble over how to refer to themselves.

"Bonus" is all-inclusive. The concept can include families whose parents are married but does not depend on marital status as *step-* does. And "bonus" can easily be used to describe all relationships—from bonusfamily to bonusmom, "bonusdad," "bonusparent," "bonuskid," and more. Plus, if you have formed a relationship with someone over the years, for example, your stepmom, and she and your dad part ways, that breakup changes her label. Technically, she's no longer your stepmother, but your feelings for her have not changed. Bonus status doesn't have to change, ever, if you don't want it to. Whether you are married or not, "bonus" is a label of the heart. It's all-inclusive and discounts no one, certainly not someone who loves a child as one's own.

Some people have written to me saying that they think "bonus" is corny or syrupy. I get that. I can say, like with all words, only use it if you like it. If you don't use it, just remember the attitude behind it…acceptance, respect, and love. That's really the secret to any successful relationship.

Laying the Groundwork to Successfully Combine Your Family

In Chapter 5, Facing the Transition: Moving From We to Me, I talked about creating a "survival plan" for your life after separation or divorce. I am of the mind that you need the same kind of plan every time you take on something new, particularly something as monumental as attempting to combine 2 families. In this case, it's a 2-step plan, with both steps centered on your mental preparation. The thought is, after completing the steps, you are then fully prepared for what is ahead. The first step considers your personal mind-set, what *you* envision for your family and, most important, what you envision your role should be to help make your new family a success. The second step includes your partner and asks what you envision as a couple for your new family.

Creating Your Family "Survival Plan"

Step 1. When working with families, I often tell the parents, who I regard as the leaders of the family, to envision a slate on which they write all the bad things from their past relationships—and all their justifications for the bad things—the blame, the fault...everything. Then I tell them to look at it long and hard, for as long as they need to, and erase it. Literally, clean the slate.

Co-parenting tip. As Benjamin Dover said, "It's okay to look back at the past. Just don't stare."

Now write down your goals for creating this new life together. Some of the things I suggest are not what you might think. Remember, we are talking about forming a mind-set for what you envision ahead, so the things I suggest are things such as

▶ I want to contribute to a harmonious family atmosphere. (How will you do that?)

▶ I want to be a source of security and inspiration, not a source of chaos, for *all* the children in my care. (How will you do that?)

▶ I want to support my partner in the ability to positively co-parent our children, and I want my partner to do the same. (How will you do that?)

Keep going. Those are just suggestions. You will have your own, and when you have considered all of them, that will be the new family model tailor-made for your future life together.

Testing the Waters

❝ *My boyfriend and I have 6 kids between us. We are thinking about moving in together to test the waters before tying the knot.* ❞

Moving in together to see whether it will work may not be the way to proceed when children are involved—for 2 reasons. First, things change radically when new people move in. If the changes are undesirable, say, the kids must share a room with someone they don't like (or with someone a lot older or younger), the blame usually falls onto the new partner: "Things were fine before you got here!" If the kids aren't ready, moving too quickly is a surefire way to undermine any relationship your new partner might build with them.

Second, if you move in *just to see whether things will work*, the kids get close to your new partner, and then you realize that your partner isn't a good choice, the kids will face yet another divorce, officially married or not. Plus, the kids getting close to your adult partner is not the only consideration. There is always the possibility that your kids may get close to your new partner's kids. They begin to gel as "bonussiblings" and then one of the adults decides to move on. It could undermine the ability of children to trust in their parent's judgment. Either way, the kids who depend on you to make solid decisions for their lives are looking to feel safe and secure, and you're just testing the waters. That's why it is best to wait until both your partner and you are confident that you know where your relationship is going and have a plan for your bonusfamily *before* you move in together.…

Step 2. Practice the *before* exercise: an exercise to prepare the new couple for what is ahead.

I have included a version of this exercise in just about every book I have written because I think it is so important that parents take moving in together seriously and have a plan in place before making the move. The key word here is *before*. The plan you set in motion before you move in together is the foundation on which your new family will be built.

Begin by having a goal in mind for each of the relationships you will create when combining families.

Ask yourself, "Now that we are a couple…"

Note: This exercise does not have to be done together, but after it is completed, the couple is intended to compare notes. (Have paper and pen available.)

What Kind of Relationship Do I Envision With My Partner When We Live Together "as a Family"?

Up to now, you were 2 autonomous people who made decisions for yourself and your children independent of each other. How will you approach things differently now that you are moving in together and combining your families? Your couple problem-solving method? What kind of relationship do you envision with your partner's children? This is important. What do you see when you think of each of your partner's children? Do you see a spoiled brat who drives you crazy, but you love this child's Mom (or Dad or caregiver), so you'll just make the best of it? Or do you see the potential for a loving positive relationship with this child?

What Can I Do to Foster My Relationship With My "Bonuschild"?

There's a particularly important component to this step—you must cultivate an individual relationship with your "bonuschild" that has nothing to do with that child's biological parent.

Case in point: So many times I hear parents tell me that they explained to their bonuschild, "I love your father (or mother), so of course I love you." In concept, these "bonusparents" are letting the child know how much they love the parent and that they accept the child because the child is part the parent, but think about what you really just told that child. Basically, you said, "My love for you is based on my love for someone else. You, as you, really don't mean anything to me. If your dad (or mom) and I break up, I will have no reason to talk with you again."

Look for ways to build a unique relationship with each child that has nothing to do with these children's biological parent. That may mean take walks around the block together or get ice cream, throw the football around, get a pedicure, or have heartfelt talks over a special outing for them. It can just be an hour, but demonstrate firsthand you are invested in these children because you like them, not because they come along with the deal.

What Kind of Relationship Do I Envision With My Kids Now That We Are a Couple?

Oftentimes parents attempting to combine families schedule all their time together "as a family" and forget to maintain that individual relationship with their own children that's really important to maintain the closeness all parents want with their kids.

What Will I Do to Foster My Relationship With My Kids?

Make sure you set aside one-on-one time with your children that does not include your new partner or your new partner's kids. It doesn't have to be a big excursion, but it has to be planned tactfully or else you could face favoritism issues. Most parents who share custody have enough downtime that they can spend one one-on-one time with their children when their bonuskids are with their other parent; however, there's a fine art to organizing that one-on-one time once you have combined your families.

Saying something such as "Honey, why don't you go out for pizza with Jason and Kylie, while I spend some time with Lisa and Greg?" sounds good in concept, but if the kids hear it, it can turn into "How come they get pizza!" and you've defeated the purpose. Plan the outings, consulting all the necessary parental figures first, and then tell the children the plan.

What about extended family? Will those kids call my parents "Grandma" and "Grandpa"? Aunts? Uncles? Ask the players. Will the kids feel comfortable calling your sister "Auntie Jeanne," or is "Jeanne" just fine?

Note: Sometimes kids don't want a "bonussibling" to call their biological relative, say, "Grandma" or "Auntie." I've worked with kids who have confided, "My parents expect me to share everything now—my room, my dog, and my friends. I don't want to share my grandma. She's MY grandma."

So have a heart-to-heart conversation with your family. Brainstorm together, "What will bonuskids call Grandma? How will Grandma refer to the bonuskids? What feels natural to everyone?"

How Will We Prepare Our Families?

Be honest and straightforward in your explanation and reasoning. The key here is to be matter-of-fact in your communication and maintain control. Try not to be swayed by judgments from family members who do not agree with your approach or final decision.

What Will I Do to Foster a Positive Communication With My New Partner's Ex-partner?

(Yes, your partner's ex…the kids are going back and forth between homes. *All* the adults will influence their lives, and you will influence each other's lives.)

Let's say your child is spending the night with a friend. Most parents would not think twice about calling their child's parents to confirm that their child is spending the night. They would most likely meet the other parent before their child goes to the home. They would explain that their child cannot watch anything more violent than PG-13 movies and is allergic to peanut butter. But no one reaches out when sharing custody of a child. Sure, the other parent lives there, but what if that parent decides to play 9 holes of golf in the afternoon or run to the store? Your child is left alone with someone you do not know.

Fostering positive communication means looking for ways to interact without being intimidated by each other. Your child lives with your new partner's ex-partner. Try and take time to get to know who that person is.

I often refer to my own growing pains while learning to co-parent, not only with my now ex-husband but with his ex-wife. It was a slow process for Sharyl and me, but, over time, we learned to respect each other's opinion. We actually agreed in our approach to parenting. She and my ex-husband did not.

One day, while on the phone, she was telling me a story about her daughter and how proud of her she was. In the next sentence, I shared something about my daughter as well. I, too, was proud of her. Back and forth we went until one of us pointed out we were talking about the same child. Sharyl was not intimidated or jealous. She stopped mid-sentence and thanked me for loving her daughter. If we hadn't fostered a positive relationship over the years, my referring to her daughter as *my daughter* would not have been accepted as it had been. But her daughter lived with me every other week, and Sharyl made it a point to get to know the woman with whom her child lived.

I know, I know. The *before* exercise sounds like a lot of work, but if you do it, you will be a success—or you will see it's too much work and decide not to go forward. The *before* exercise is designed to get you thinking and talking about what it really takes to combine your families. Falling in love is wonderful. Thank goodness after all the trials and tribulations of a breakup you found each other. But there is a whole new set of rules when you involve your children in your relationships. Finding someone new and combining your families can be the most wonderful thing in the world—or it can be torture for everyone. It's in your control. *It really is.*

Establishing House Rules

There is a fine art to successfully combining families. You see, the "parents" do not have the luxury of raising the children from scratch. It's a combination of different backgrounds, possibly ethnicities, developmental stages, likes, and dislikes. If you and your partner come from similar backgrounds, there's a good chance your lifestyles and approaches to parenting will be similar, but if you do not, your expectations for your children, your partner's children, and everyday living will be different. Without a meeting of the minds, you may have the following problem.

> **❝** *I thought it would be an easy transition to move in with Jerry and his kids, until everyone was gone one day, and I started to look around the kitchen. There was dust and grease embedded behind cookbooks just stacked all over the counter. The cabinets were gross, the floorboards had not been wiped down in years, and I was overwhelmed by the dirt. I wasn't used to living like that. Jerry didn't see it. So, while he was out running errands, I got on my hands and knees and cleaned the kitchen—after all, I was moving in a week. He called me from the post office to tell me he was on his way home, and he asked what I had been doing all afternoon. 'Cleaning the kitchen counters,' I said, 'and the cabinets, and floorboards, and bannister....'*
>
> *'What?' he asked. 'Should I be offended? You think I'm a pig?'*
> *'No,' I said, 'I just think we need to talk about what we both expect before I move in.'*
>
> *It made me realize we had never discussed what we felt were our responsibilities around the house—or what the kids' responsibilities would be. We were in love but not on the same page in terms of responsibilities to maintain a home. We got in quite the argument. In the middle of a heated exchange, he said, 'You know, that kind of stuff really doesn't bother me. I've lived in this house for 8 years. I never considered if it would bother you. I am sorry. I am going to have to make some adjustments.'*
>
> *The exchange was an eye-opener.***❞**

After you and your partner clarify what you want for your family, the next step is actually combining the households. Where will everyone sleep? Will the kids have chores? What time is bedtime? Is there a curfew for teens? What's the rule about homework and grades? Will you eat dinner together? The list is endless. Again, you have to put on your thinking caps, but first things first.

Getting Organized!

Because your children go back and forth between their parents' homes, ideally, both sides (biological mother and biological father) should be on the same page when it comes to discipline and rules, but if this is impossible, remember you can control only your own home, your 4 walls. So you begin getting organized by putting your own house into order.

▶ Assign sleeping quarters. Who will sleep where? Will the kids have to share a room? If so, what configuration?

▶ Split up household chores fairly. Discuss disciplinary tactics.
  – Will we coordinate efforts with each other's past rules?
  – Will we coordinate efforts between homes?
  – Will both of us discipline each other's children?
  – Demonstrate firsthand that you trust each other's judgment, and always appear as a united front in front of the children.

▶ Establish a daily protocol.
  – Homework times.
  – Meals. (Will there be specific times, and will you eat together?)
  – Establish bedtimes and wake-up times, so that kids can get to school on time.

▶ Establish daily house rules.
  – Can the kids eat in their rooms, or how about in front of the TV?
  – Can teens have their boyfriends or girlfriends or any other partners over without parental supervision?
  – Do they have to ask before raiding the refrigerator?
  – When and where are mobile phones to be used?
  – What are the repercussions for not following the rules?

▶ Establish a forum for family conflict resolution. How will you solve arguments or other family problems?

These are just a few considerations when setting up your household, and you will find others that are unique to your family. Let's take a look at how some of the organizational considerations look like in real life.

Assigning Sleeping Quarters

When parents combine families, those families grow exponentially. One parent may have 2 children; the other, 3. Add an "ours" child and this is now a family with 6 children. Rarely can families afford homes with 7 bedrooms—the parents need a bedroom as well, so it's imperative that some children share a room.

❝ *How do you decide who shares a room when you combine families?* **❞**

There are 4 things to consider when deciding who will share rooms.

▸ Gender

▸ Age

▸ How long the children have known one another

▸ How the children are related to one another

> **❝** *My 10-year-old daughter recently told me her 11-year-old stepbrother tried to get in bed with her the other night. His father and I have been together 6 months and only have a 2-bedroom apartment, so the kids share a room. My stepson admitted to it, but was very embarrassed, and my daughter is horrified. We aren't sure what to do at this point. My stepson goes back and forth between his mother's home and ours. I think he should stop sleeping at our home. My husband disagrees.* **❞**

Parents often see their children as innocent little ones and don't realize they are growing up and becoming interested in dating. At 10 or 11 years of age, a child's body is changing, and curiosity can easily get the better of these children. Many school districts initiate sex education at the fifth- or sixth-grade level, not to mention that kids are openly exposed to sexual content in movies and on TV. This does not mean that all kids will experiment, but it also doesn't guarantee that they won't. Having conversations with your children at this age is really important. Avoid putting children of the opposite sex who are not biologically related to one another together in the same bedroom. Experimenting with a stepsibling can affect every member of the family and lead to a breakup if not addressed properly. Children need clear family rules and boundaries to guide them in keeping from making mistakes—but parents can't set their children up for failure either. It would have been more appropriate to find a different home before combining families.

> **❝** *But, we can't afford a bigger home....* **❞**

If you must move in together right this second, a temporary change in the parenting plan that eliminates overnights may be in order. Ironically, the only time a parent would even consider putting a 10-year-old girl and an 11-year-old boy in the same bedroom and close the bedroom door is when their parents are involved with each other. Ask that question without the parental relationship component and most would immediately see it as inappropriate. Even children as young as 3 or 4 years may experiment when unattended, and allowing children with large age differences, say, a 12-year-old boy and a 3-year-old girl, to sleep in the same room is even more inappropriate. However, parents must be cognizant that experimentation is not exclusive to children of the opposite sex and is a normal part of maturing. Parents must be mindful that some children are more curious than others and will act on that curiosity. Many adults say their first glimpse that they might be gay occurred in adolescence. With that in mind, it is important that you stay available to your children and listen without judgment if they confide to you something they question or that makes them feel uncomfortable.

Leaving Children and Teens Unattended

How children and teens respond to each other has a lot to do with when they initially meet. For example, there may not be as much concern about leaving a 16-year-old boy alone with his 15-year-old stepsister if they have been raised together since they were 4 and 5 years old as there would be leaving alone a 16-year-old boy and his 15-year-old stepsister whose parents have been together for only 6 months. And remember, these concerns extend to all children no matter what their gender. But, for all scenarios, the house rules must be clear, and the children and teens must understand the consequences if the house rules are broken. Parents must anticipate any potential problems and put checks and balances into place that will guide their children to make good choices. Ultimately, as parents our primary task is to remain available to our children so that if they have questions, we can help guide them appropriately.

Chores

❝ *Each time my husband's daughter comes to visit, it's a fight. We live in another state, and she stays with us for the summer and during school breaks. With fall break coming up, I'm anticipating yet another problem. For example, during her last visit, I asked her to clean her bathroom. Her father overheard me and reprimanded me for suggesting she do some chores when she was visiting. He's very protective of his time with her and likes her to relax when she is with us. But we can't assign chores to the children who live with us full-time and not to those who live here part of the time. That doesn't seem fair.* **❞**

Something you will find in children and adolescents, particularly in adolescents, is an overwhelming preoccupation with fairness. They are constantly weighing what is fair, and if they perceive favoritism in any form, they will rebel or withdraw. At that point, one might predict the family break into factions—one side against the other—and, if that is the case, be prepared for the possibility of another breakup. It is rare once family members take sides that the newly combined family stays intact. Commitment to a new partner often wanes when moms or dads, for instance, think their child is being singled out or picked on.

Note how the father described his daughter's time with him. He said, "visiting." Noncustodial parents are often afraid that if things are too tough around the house, their child will not want to return. So, to ensure his daughter will want to come back, he likes her to feel as if it's a vacation when she comes to see him. In his defense, he's most likely motivated by guilt, because he realizes that he sees his bonuskids far more often than his own. He's trying his best, but what he's doing creates problems on many different fronts.

First, his relationship with his daughter can stay stuck in the visiting mode and not progress to the deep father-daughter relationship both would like.

Second, the obvious favoritism can cause animosity between a bonusparent and the other children in the home and between his daughter and her bonussiblings as well. The other kids will reject her because they perceive that her father likes her best, and they will reject him for the same reason. So, by acting as described, this dad is sabotaging his relationship with everyone—including his daughter—by openly favoring her.

For this reason, the parental figures must immediately get onto the same page and, together, form a vision for this family. Take a look at the *before* exercise described earlier, in Testing the Waters section of this chapter, to help get a clear picture of the type of relationships you want to have with each other's children, with your own children, and to reestablish your bond with each other. Establish house rules, assign chores, and treat all like family. Dad might look into counseling to help him conquer his insecurities associated with being a noncustodial parent. Again, the fair expectations will produce an equally fair outcome.

> **❝** *So should a child that only stays with us for a few months at a time be assigned household chores?* **❞**

Yes, a child who stays only temporarily at a time should be assigned chores and for a very important reason: perception. If children are to feel as if they are part of the family—and to be perceived as a family member—they should have similar responsibilities to each of the family members who live in the home.

Parents must remember when assigning chores that it is important to assign chores that are age appropriate and to stay flexible. This doesn't mean if a child balks at a chore assignment, the parents immediately give in. It means that both parents make it obvious to *all* the children in the home that they are listening to their concerns and making their decisions accordingly.

> **❝** *How come I have to clean up dog poop, and all he has to do is clear the dinner dishes?* **❞**

An important component to keeping it fair is to let the children in on your reasoning and why you have decided to be flexible within the framework of the previously established house rules. Consider the answer seriously, because it could set the stage for family division or family unity.

Do not say, "Because he is only here once in a while, and it's your dog."

Try, "Because you are older and can handle the responsibility. When he gets older, he, too, will have to clean up after the dog."

Should We Discipline Each Other's Children?

A crucial factor when successfully combining families is for the adults to decide on the rules and then put them into practice in a manner that will make the children feel safe, not intimidated, when they are enforced. If the partners contradict or undermine each other in front of the children, the children are less likely to listen to these parental figures. The children's defiance is simply a by-product of the parents' disrespect for each other—and once that happens, both parental figures will be ineffective at their job.

> **❝** *My son came home last night with a story about his stepmother yelling at him and putting him in time-out. He couldn't tell me why he was in trouble—only that he was. When I questioned his father, he knew nothing about it. Evidently, he wasn't home at the time. I don't think his stepmother should be disciplining him!* **❞**

Parents are the ones to establish policy and are the primary disciplinarians, that is true, but, as in this scenario, stepparents are often left alone as the caregivers of the children. Therefore, for the safety of the children in their care, stepparents must be empowered to make decisions, even discipline, but this is done by following the rules established by the parents, not by establishing policy on their own.

However, there is a caveat of sorts when considering this course of action. When the stepparent also has children of one's own and rules were already in place before combining families, parents and stepparents must put their heads together to ensure disciplinary consistency. A flat statement, "Stepparents don't discipline," is simply impractical under those circumstances.

Discipline: When Only One of You Has Children

66 *My son is 9 years old and has a lot of energy. Before my boyfriend moved in, everything was fine, but now that he lives with us, it's obvious my son irritates him. My boyfriend has never had children and gets short-tempered when my little guy does something he's not supposed to do. I find myself in the middle, defending my child to my boyfriend and explaining my boyfriend to my child. My home has become so uncomfortable, I look for ways not to come home. I love them both very much. How do I get them to respect and care for one another?* **99**

Lack of parenting experience is a common dilemma often faced by couples when one has children and the other does not. Both think the other just "doesn't get it"—and, in a sense, that's true. Both are coming from 2 completely different places.

Here it is in a nutshell: When a child with "a lot of energy" acts up, the biological parent may see the child's behavior as occasionally doing "something he's not supposed to do." Biological parents don't necessarily see a child's occasional misbehavior as critical and learn to analyze whether a situation requires them to step in. A partner who has never had children may see the same behavior as disobeying the rules and the parent's reaction as inconsistent parenting. Because of that, this new partner thinks being more consistent will solve the problem and inwardly believes it's the partner's job to get in there and save parent and child from themselves. But this new partner was never asked to fix anything, and when a newcomer tries to organize people who don't feel they need to be fixed, those efforts are often rejected. As a result, the new partner can feel unappreciated and become resentful. The parent and the child can feel misunderstood and become resentful as well, and the family can begin to pull apart.

Resentment blocks a family's ability to work together to find solutions. That's why patience and empathy are 2 important components included in the co-parent's communication toolbox. Without patience, we are more reactive than proactive, and without empathy, we have no insight into the other's point of view. A proactive approach coupled with an attempt to understand the other's point of view is key to healthy problem-solving.

Remember Your Communication Toolbox During Separation or Divorce

- Patience.
- Compromise.
- Empathy.
- Ask questions.
- Active listening.
- Reframe.
- Humor.

What Can You Do?

Backtrack and lay the groundwork for how you want your home to work. Refer to the *before* exercise mentioned earlier, in the Testing the Waters section of this chapter.

Get out of the middle. Stop running defense and allow the new partner and child to develop their own relationship that does not depend on your interaction to make it work. They may hit some bumps, and it may seem to worsen before it gets better, but they must figure out their own boundaries with each other—that's how they will develop respect and build a loving relationship with each other.

Parenting Style

You may have heard the saying "We parent as we were parented." That means we all have unique parenting styles that were derived, most likely, by how our parents parented us. If your parents were lenient, you will most likely be lenient. If you parents were strict, you will most likely treat your children in a similar manner. If you were brought up in an organized environment, as you raise your children, you will expect everything to be in its place. Unfortunately, if you witnessed abuse of any sort regularly, you may also perpetrate or be the survivor of abuse—the behaviors are familiar, and in times of stress, we fall back onto what is familiar as a reference—unless you make a concerted effort to be different.

This becomes a problem when you're combining families and your parenting styles compete. If you are lenient and your new partner is strict, the difference in approach can confuse and frustrate both the new partners and their children. The children's expectations usually line up with their parent's expectations, and that is why house rules and chore assignments must be clearly defined.

"You're Not My Parent!"

*Lindsay is a young lawyer with a 5-year-old-daughter.
She is married to Vince, a general contractor with a 13-year-old daughter named Bethany. The house rule agreed on by both parents was no eating in front of the TV, but Vince was tired one night and let Bethany grab a snack while she was watching* Modern Family. *He got an emergency call from a job and ran out to meet the owner. While he was gone, Lindsay came home. She saw Bethany munching in front of the TV and lost her temper. She chastised her for breaking the rules, and that's when she heard those dreaded words as Bethany stomped out of the room: "Ugh, you're not my parent!* 99

As a stepparent, don't immediately blame the child or teen when you hear those words; check yourself or how you and your partner have approached a situation. Most of the time, it's a signal that your approach is too direct, you are not being consistent, or, the most common reason, you are asking the child or teen to do something other than what the biological parent allows or has not asked to do in the past. It's a communication breakdown of the greatest magnitude—not between you and your stepchild but between you and your partner. Get onto the same page with your partner as fast as you can, consistently uphold the rules you have put into place, and you'll hear words such as "You're not my mother!" or "You're not my father!" less often.

Co-parenting tip. Using the best interest of the kids as your criteria for decision-making depersonalizes the issues between divorced parents and their new partners. The past is left in the past, and the children's present becomes the primary concern.

And finally, don't expect bonuskids to automatically respond the way your biological children do. Biologically related siblings don't necessarily respond the same way to teasing or discipline, and they have the same parents and background! Take the time to get to know your bonuskids and respect their differences. (Teenagers, especially, resent inconsistency and discipline that they perceive as unfair.) Establish rules and stick to them, taking into consideration that many personalities are fighting for their individual identities in this family.

Help for Combining Families With Teenagers

Parents who attempt to combine their families have observed that teens are the least willing to cooperate. If you think about it, the reason why is quite predictable. During the teen years, teens have their first sense of wanting to be an individual. The clothes they choose, or colored hair and possibly piercings, all say to the parent, "This is me! I don't want to blend in." (Except with their friends.) So, you see, a teen's distaste for blending into a family may not be about you or a desire to discount the family. For teens, it's more about their personal development and their need to exercise their own individuality at this point in their lives. If you respect that, *you* are more likely to be accepted.

Establish a Forum for Family Conflict Resolution

Families don't always get along, and when that happens, they need a plan to help problem-solve. Without a form of family conflict resolution in place that is fair to everyone, when conflict arises, bonusfamily members can feel singled out and ganged up on. When they feel that way, they begin to take sides, which usually splits along bloodlines. Once family members take sides, it's very difficult to resolve conflicts without prejudice. It's you and your kids against your partner and your partner's kids. And you don't want that to happen.

The most successful working "bonusfamilies" have a forum for conflict resolution in place right from the beginning. That way, each family member knows what to do when a problem arises.

Family discussions are a great way to resolve family conflicts—if they are done correctly. Family discussions are not a place for complaining and arguing. It's not group therapy or an opportunity to assign fault or blame. Family discussions, as a source of conflict resolution, work best when only one subject is addressed at a time and established rules are in place that everyone understands and obeys, like the parliamentary rules of order, so that everyone knows exactly what to expect.

Help With Organizing Your Own Family Discussion

Each family member should know that

▶ Anyone in the family who has a problem one would like to address can call a family discussion, from the oldest parent to the youngest child.

▶ When a family discussion is called, everyone *must* attend. No excuses. A date and time are set for the near future—and everyone attends, say, Sunday afternoon, 4:00 pm.

▶ Address *only one* problem at a time.

▶ The person with the problem opens the discussion. That person explains the concern and then the family members put their heads together to solve the problem. All may offer their ideas. The person who calls the meeting should come to the table with a suggested solution.

▶ Losing one's temper is not allowed. If someone does, the other family members ask that person politely to please calm down. No name-calling or blaming. The goal is conflict resolution, not additional conflicts. Look for solutions together.

▶ No one can leave the table until everyone agrees on the solution.

A successful family discussion is not a free-for-all. It is orderly, is good-natured, and addresses one problem at a time. The key to a successful family discussion is that all families establish their own rules. What works for you is correct for your family. Be open and flexible, and mold your method of conflict resolution to your family's individual needs.

Problem-solving With Children Who Have Experienced Domestic Violence in the Past

Children who have witnessed domestic violence may not perceive conflict the same as those who have not; therefore, it may take a while for them to see that disagreements during family discussions can actually be a vehicle to solve problems. They may be slow to participate for fear of recourse—possibly being yelled at or even hit. We now know that ongoing conflict after parents break up continues to affect their children, not only emotionally but physiologically as well. Current studies offer clinicians and mental health professionals additional insight into the long-term effects of domestic violence on the children who are exposed to it as they grow up. Brain imaging of sleeping children and fetuses in utero documents that exposure to domestic violence can reduce the size of parts of the brain, change its overall structure, and affect the way the circuits in the brain work together (see Chapter 8, Toxic Stress and Its Effect on Our Children). So if children witnessed domestic violence in the past as a younger child, it is imperative that as a parent you demonstrate firsthand calming ways to positively solve conflict within your new family.

Fighting in Front of the Children

Our first glimpse of how to communicate with a partner is by watching how our parents interact with each other. All parental figures are role models—including a parent's new partner. When disagreeing, if a parental figure screams, slams doors, or punches walls, or is verbally spiteful or insulting, your children mimic that same behavior in their relationships. Why not? That's all they have ever seen.

To worsen matters, children of divorce may develop a fear of normal conflict, afraid that even the smallest disagreement will end in yet another divorce or separation. That's why it's so important that arguments are solved quickly in a stepfamily—and that apologies are offered and accepted freely when disagreements occur.

> 66 *The day my daughter walked out of the room as I was talking to her, it registered. I was furious about the disrespect, but she was acting exactly the way I acted when I was angry with her father before we divorced—and, I suppose, the way I act now when I disagree with her stepfather. I realized I wasn't setting a very good example. I just thought I was mad. I didn't realize I was being disrespectful until I felt it from her.* 99

Even the coziest of couples catch themselves occasionally arguing in front of the kids, and when these couples realize the kids are watching, they often move to a bedroom, a bathroom, or possibly the garage to finish the argument and make up behind closed doors. Their kids don't see the concessions made to end the fight. They see only the final outcome—the parents are no longer arguing, but the kids have no idea how their parents got there. They were offered conflict as a model with no way to resolve it. That is why it is important that the children in your care see you make up as well. Saying, "I'm sorry," is a very strong tool to end an argument, but rarely used to the extent it should be.

There's a formula to a proper apology. It's a very easy one.

▶ Apologize: "I'm sorry."

▶ Take responsibility for your actions: "I lost my temper."

▶ State why you are sorry: "I shouldn't have yelled at you and frightened you that way."

▶ State how you should have responded: "I should have calmly said, 'Just ask me for help next time (or whatever you should have said).'"

▶ Reinforce the apology: "I love you. I did not want it to get this far out of hand. Will you accept my apology?"

So a full apology sounds like this: "I'm sorry. I lost my temper. I shouldn't have yelled at you and frightened you that way. I should have calmly said, 'Just ask me for help next time (or whatever you should have said).' I love you. I did not want it to get this far out of hand. Will you accept my apology?"

Co-parenting tip. "I'm sorry you feel that way" is not an apology. It does not acknowledge your part in the disagreement, nor does it convey remorse. Neither does following an "I'm sorry" with "but if," as in "I'm sorry, but if you hadn't (you fill in the blank), I wouldn't have gotten so angry."

Graciously accepting an apology in front of the children teaches them the power of forgiveness—perhaps the most important lesson we can pass on to make our stepfamilies a happy, safe, loving environment for our children.

Co-parenting tip. Make your co-parent your ally, not your enemy.

Facing the Common Problems

The Language We Use...

When talking with a family member, you may not realize that the specific words you choose or the labels you use to describe someone set the stage for a positive response or a negative response. You may think the disagreement you are having is over a specific problem, but it could be the way that you present the problem that places you into disagreement.

It starts with the labels we use to describe one another. Let's look at how reframing those labels will result in a more positive response.

For example, "My ex" becomes "My child's father" or "My child's mother."

So, rather than say, "I have to ask my ex what time he plans to pick up Samantha," try the more positive, "I have to ask Samantha's father what time he will pick her up."

This next one particularly hits home…and may cause a tinge of guilt when you hear it.

Rather than "Your ex," it becomes "Your child's father" or "Your child's mother," as in "Your child's father drives me crazy!" or "Your child's mother drives me crazy!"

So let's analyze that choice of wording. Exes drive us crazy. They have all made us nuts at some point, so the impact of that statement could get you a response such as "I know, honey. I'm sorry." But use the second choice, "Your child's mother," and now you are referencing the child with your anger—and you will probably not get the same response from your partner. "Your child's mother" connotes a type of respect, or disrespect, if used in a negative connotation, and subconsciously knowing that, you may check yourself before you even say it.

Another Important Label: Who Gets to Be Called "Mom" or "Dad" or Other Terms of Endearment for Parents?

In some situations, a new partner or stepparent is much more involved in a child's life than the corresponding birth parent. In my own case, my stepfather adopted me, with the permission of my birth father. We had been functioning as a family for 2 years already at that point, and my birth father had voluntarily excluded himself from my life completely. It still took me a long time before I felt completely comfortable calling my adoptive father "Dad," even though the words "I love you" came easily from the start.

In separation and divorce, it's natural for the birth parent to fear being replaced, especially if that parent remains involved in the child's life to a significant extent. It is therefore important to establish clear identities for the children involved. I think the worst thing you can do when introducing a new partner into the family is to insist that your children call that person "Dad" or "Mom" or another term of endearment for parents. Your new partner may love your children like a parent, and your children may love that person back, but unless those words develop organically over time as a result of the specific circumstances of your family, they should generally be reserved for the birth parents.

A few years back, I received an excellent suggestion from a reader, and I often use this story to demonstrate a thoughtful way of finding a suitable name for a bonusparent (stepparent).

> **66** *My fiancé and I went on a beach trip 10 months into dating. He has one child who was 5 at the time. During the trip, she started calling me 'Mom.' I assumed it was because we were filling mom-daughter roles while on vacation. In the mornings, I cooked breakfast and woke her up to eat. Afterward, I helped her dress and made her brush her teeth. I was with her all through the day, and then, at night, I tucked her in, and we stayed in the same room. I think*

this routine for the week we were vacationing became comfortable and she felt comfortable calling me 'Mom.' My fiancé and I didn't correct her, but 3 months later at Halloween, the child's bio-mom dropped her by so we could see her all dressed up for Halloween. While taking a picture with her bio-mom, she called out, 'Now I want to take a picture with my other mom.' It didn't go over well; however, I definitely understood her feelings and was content choosing an alternative name, but what name?

We struggled to find a suitable name. I didn't want to be 'Mommy Joyce,' because that's still calling me 'Mom'…and bio-mom didn't like that. I'm not her aunt or grandma, so the suggestions of 'Auntie' or 'Nana' seemed odd to me. We were getting increasingly irritated that we even had to deal with this issue, but I knew it was important. About a month later, my fiancé looked over at me and said, 'What about Mare? Mare (pronounced ma-ray) means "ocean" in Italian. She first called you 'Mom' when we were at the beach; it only seems appropriate.' The name and the meaning behind it touched me, and I told him it was even better than being called 'Mom'! The name has gone over very well, and although I hear the occasional 'Mom' that makes my heart flutter, we continue to gently encourage the use of my special name. **"**

This is a perfect example of how to approach this situation. The name you choose does not have to be a variation of Mom or Dad—just a special name that means something to the bonusparent and child. The reader reports that Mom was very grateful for their attempt and has just invited her to a "get to know each other" lunch. What better situation for a child than to be brought up witnessing the adults in her life openly respecting one another?

Along the same lines, I would like to mention that my youngest daughter, Harleigh, called me "Jann" for a while when she was 2 years old. My oldest biological daughter called me "Mom," but my 2 bonuskids, who went back and forth between their parents homes every other week, called me "Jann." My youngest daughter adopted the way my bonuskids referred to me, but this served as a means to explain why her older sister and brother went back and forth and who their biological mother and father were. By the time Harleigh was 6 or 7 years old, she was so used to her sister and brother's mother being around for special occasions that when we were planning a family vacation, she stopped the discussion: "Wait," she said, "Can Sharyl get off work?" It was explained that Sharyl would not be accompanying us on a trip this time.

" *How do I establish a new sense of privacy?* **"**

Privacy, or at least what you knew to be privacy, will be a thing of the past once families are combined. It's likely that your ex will need to come by your house sometimes to pick up kids or to drop off or pick up a forgotten item. Especially if yours is the home you shared when you were together, your ex may feel a little too comfortable dropping by and wandering around. When your children are home, impromptu visits can leave them feeling sad and confused about the state of their family, rekindling fantasies of what it might be like to all live together again.

> 66 *I came home from work early yesterday and found my ex and our 8-year-old son in my house. They were sitting in his room talking, but I think it was wrong that she was there. We have not been together for 2 years, and our son spends a week with me and a week with her. She does not have a key, and it's not even a house we have lived in together, but there she was, comfortably lying on our son's bed talking about his day. How do I handle this?* 99

In this scenario, most would think that you start with a conversation with the child, reiterating boundaries and reminding him of the rules. However, it's difficult to say, "Son, don't let your mom in the house." A better approach is to have a conversation with Mom. She's the adult and the one who needs to respect Dad's space and monitor her own behavior—not look to her 8-year-old son to make the proper judgment calls. Respecting each other's turf is an important component to successful co-parenting.

Two years is not that long after a breakup, and sometimes, parents have a hard time severing ties. If parents get along after they split, it's easy for the lines of demarcation to blur a little. Mom drops the child off at Dad's home after school on her designated week, no one is home for a few minutes, and it becomes, "Why don't you come in, Mommy?" Mom figures, "What the heck?" and the next thing you know, you come home to the ex and your son cuddled on the bed talking about their day.

But what if you had had your new love interest with you? It would have been an awkward first meeting. What if you had had a headache and didn't want to deal with all this? What if you had just plain wanted your privacy? *You* must be very clear about what you expect, or next time, you could come home to dinner on the table and your son saying, "Look, Dad. Mom cooked dinner!" It will be very difficult to explain to your son why you're so irritated with Mom when she was being so nice....

It's important to establish boundaries about visits early on. At a minimum, each parent should ask permission to visit the other house, rather than come by unannounced. Even when exes get along well, the kids might find that these visits really disrupt the new rhythm of life that they are trying to establish and maintain. It also forces the kids in these situations to address their feelings about the situation. If co-parents haven't given their children open permission to love their other parent and a parent shows up unexpectedly, they feel they must run defense for both parents' feelings. Having fun at Dad's? Mom shows up…the children wonder, *"Will it make Mom feel bad if she sees I'm having fun? What do I do?"* I've seen children go from happy to uncooperative in a matter of minutes, not knowing how to process their feelings when their divorced parents are unexpectedly in the same room or attend the same extracurricular event.

The following conversation points may be helpful to clarify boundaries in situations such as this, taking note that the child is *not* nearby when you are having this conversation:

1. "Please call first; do not just drop in."

2. "Please do not go into my home for any reason when I am not there."

3. "If you would like to pick up our son when it's not your week, please make arrangements with me, not our son."

4. Verify that child care is in place and there's no question who will be watching your son when he is scheduled to be with either parent.

Can You Be Too Friendly?

To be concerned about being too friendly may seem silly to co-parents who are at odds, but not all parents are combative after a breakup. Too much joking or even a casual goodbye hug that lasts just a little too long when you exchange the kids can give your children false hope of reconciliation. They may seem fine now, but once they realize there's no reunion in the works, you could, once again, be faced with a very disappointed little one dealing with the emotional turmoil of the breakup. Facing a breakup one time is bad enough. Facing it twice can be devastating.

> **❝** *My husband drove his son back to his mother's house this weekend. As he was saying goodbye, he told me his son asked him to hug his mommy. When neither responded, the child grew more insistent saying, 'Daddy, hug my mommy NOW!' Neither parent knew what to do, so they gave each other a hug. My husband said he called it to his son's attention by saying, 'Son, we're hugging!' Should requests like this be entertained or ignored?* **❞**

Neither. Both choices, "entertained" and "ignored," are reactive approaches. Consider a proactive approach, which means you anticipate this problem and have a plan in place so that you aren't caught off guard.

Divorced or separated parents inherently know not to fight in front of their children, but how much affection is appropriate?

It helps children to know that their parents don't hate each other after a breakup, but open displays of affection aren't necessary to demonstrate this. That's why when I am asked this question, I fall back on this easy rule of thumb—"cordial, not cuddly." This suggests the goal is a comfortable exchange when divorced parents are in front of their kids and that's it. Nothing strained, or contrived, and certainly nothing too familiar.

The most important thing for any children of divorce to know is that even though their parents no longer live together, both love them and will continue to love them. A good way to demonstrate this in this case might have been that when the child requested the parents hug, the parent who was leaving could have scooped the child up in his arms while saying something such as "Both Mommy and Daddy want to hug YOU!" Mommy could have then added an affectionate "You bet!" with a little hair ruffling for additional emphasis. As Dad continued to leave, he might have looked over his shoulder and said to the child, "Tell Mommy goodbye and that you love her!" and, as the child had said his farewells, Dad could have simply added, "Bye, Mommy!" and headed to the car.

This approach takes the emphasis off parental interaction and reinforces their mutual affection for the child. It also takes the control out of the hands of the child to reestablish parental control. The child knows Mommy and Daddy are united in their love for him, and a boundary has been set that is comfortable for all the players.

As time moves on, a more affectionate greeting, such as a casual hug, may become appropriate. The key is to always consider what your actions say to your children—and then act accordingly.

Adding Members to the Family

❝ *My daughter, Lily, aged 8, has had a wonderful relationship with her stepfather, Marc, for the 4 years we've been married. They've always been very warm and affectionate with each other. But ever since I gave birth to our son, 6 months ago, Lily has not been happy with my husband. I expected my daughter to be upset with the new baby but not with her stepfather. What's going on?* ❞

Any child-rearing expert—or experienced parent—can warn you about a child's standard reaction to a new sibling. But as you've no doubt noted, the changing dynamics of a bonusfamily are complicated and unpredictable.

This family is experiencing good old-fashioned jealousy—with a twist. Lily and Marc clearly share a strong bond, but Lily may think that this special bond is now being threatened. At 8 years of age, Lily is old enough to understand that

Marc is not her biological father but that he is the new baby's biological father. Lily worries that Marc doesn't care about her anymore, because he now has his "own" baby to love.

I had this problem in my own family when my youngest daughter was born. My older daughter was 9 years of age at the time. She had always adored her stepfather ("bonusfather"), but she became very short-tempered with him immediately after her sister's birth. My husband and I researched a lot and thought we had done everything we could think of to include my oldest daughter and his 2 children (from his first marriage) in the process of bringing another child into the family. But my daughter's reaction was not at all what we had expected.

One night, as I tucked my daughter in for bed, she broke down. Through a burst of tears, she confessed that she was afraid of no longer being special to anyone. Her 9-year-old reasoning told her that because I was no longer married to her father and it was obvious that my husband and I were happy, we would automatically love the new baby more than her. Some one-on-one attention and reassurance helped bring back her self-confidence, but her insecurity did not go away immediately. We had to revisit the subject on occasion as she got older.

When things such as this happen, it's important to continue to reinforce the unique relationship the stepparent had with the older child before the baby was born. Keep the lines of communication open, encouraging the child to talk with the stepparent about personal feelings, and allow them some time alone (without you or the baby). Try setting aside a special day or even a few hours together every week or so. Name the time so that they can refer to it when making plans. Something such as Bonus Time, or Fun Friday, or You and Me Time. It's their special time together and no one interrupts! This will help reinforce their relationship—and frequent hugs never hurt!

Co-parenting tip. Never undermine the child's relationship with the child's biological parent as a way to reinforce your stepfamily's importance.

Here's a quick checklist to help bonusfamilies prepare for an addition to their family.

Checklist to Help "Bonusfamilies" Prepare for an Addition to Their Family

- Include all the children in the planning for the baby's arrival. For example, include older children in the baby shower preparations and younger children by engaging them in conversations about the baby: "Do you want the baby to be a boy or a girl? Why? What color eyes do you want the baby to have? What color hair? What kind of things do you look forward to doing with the baby?"

- Make sure that the existing children don't feel like an afterthought, now that a new baby has been added. Look for ways to spend one-on-one time with them during your normal routine, such as asking them to help you bake cookies or wash the car. (The concept is this is something you do together, not a chore assigned to them.) If the older child is not your biological child, take turns with the biological parent for one-on-one time.

- Make any important changes before the new baby arrives. For example, everyone needs their private space, particularly the existing children. So if the new baby will eventually share a room with an older sibling, make sure the older child has an area of one's own—a special place to put personal stuff, such as a wall painted one's favorite color or a shelf for the knickknacks that belong only to that child and has nothing to do with that child's new sister or brother.

- Try not to make changes that the older child will equate with the new baby's arrival. For example, let's say you let the older child sleep with you. Kids love to sleep with their parents, and it's difficult to make the change once they get used to it. If you say things such as "Now that the baby's here, you can't sleep with me anymore," the older child could associate the change with the baby's birth and resent the baby for the change. You have contributed to the beginnings of sibling rivalry without even knowing it!

- Emphasize each child's individuality and your unique relationship with each child. Make sure they know that all your children are special to you and that the new sibling will add happiness to each of their lives. Explain that you may be temporarily busy with the new baby but that your love for each of them will never change.

- Don't automatically expect older siblings to babysit, especially if they are having trouble accepting the new addition. Until you are confident that your existing children feel comfortable with the baby, look for alternatives to the older children being responsible for the baby.

Who Do You Love Best?

The key to the successful introduction of a new baby is not compare each child but acknowledge each child's individuality. So if one of the children asks, "Who do you love best?" you can emphasize that you can't choose, because each of your children are so special to you, and then list what you see as unique in that child: "Honey, how can I compare? You are all so special and have your own unique gifts." But then bring it back to the child who is asking: "You have such a sweet smile—and you are so kind to everyone. I just love you so much." Watch out for saying, "I love all my children the same." This can make the child asking the question feel lost in the shuffle: "You don't see *me*. You love us all the same." After all, your child is asking because your child wants to feel special. By you lumping all your children together, they won't feel special at all—and that reinforces rivalry among the ranks.

Finally, although sibling rivalry is natural, at its core is that brothers and sisters have to share their parents' love and attention. They're also figuring out their place in the family and are concerned about who gets what and who is in charge. This is even more exaggerated when adding children to a combined family. Hopefully, the children become accustomed to one another and can comfortably share their parents, but being proactive in anticipation of the birth and in those early days after the new baby has been born can set the stage for the relationship your combined children have with one another and with their parent and bonusparent (stepparent) in the years to come.

12
Visualize Your Future

Every stumble is not a fall, and every fall does not mean failure.

OPRAH WINFREY

Putting Your Kids First

At every step in *Co-parenting Through Separation and Divorce,* we've talked about adjusting your mind-set and putting the kids first. Why is this a good idea? Because you know that one day, your children will grow up, and you want them to have the best possible lives when they do. And, just as important, you want to have the best possible relationship with them. There are so many details to consider when you're going through separation and divorce that it's easy to forget that a future is out there for everyone involved and that the pain, anger, and sadness of the moment is bound to fade, even if it never really disappears completely. Thinking about the future you desire now will form what you do at this moment and in the months and years to come.

As our kids grow older into teens and finally become adults, we may feel closer to them than ever before. As delightful as it is to nuzzle an infant or to have a preschooler crawl into your lap to read a book, it's truly amazing to hear your kids' more adult insights and experiences. This is a stage in life when they go from being our charges to becoming our companions, at least if we're lucky.

As you read through this book, we hope you realize now that co-parenting does not have an end point, at least as long as both parents are alive. In fact, events in your life and in your children's lives are likely to intensify the need to co-parent. As your children grow, they will probably form serious relationships or even marry. Their families may grow, and they may have children of their own. They will move into homes and start careers and build their foundation just as you once did. They may experience setbacks, including their own relationship problems. And hopefully, at each turn, they will still look to their parents for suggestions and direction. You will want to give them your complete support.

You, too, will be looking to share events with your children. You will hopefully have new relationships, professional achievements or setbacks, moves, and, yes, also illness and disability. With luck, your children and even your ex may be there for you to share in the joys and in the challenges and to help you celebrate and endure as a family. Your actions now and in the future can help determine how these events play out. Don't we all see the beauty in the following story?

> 66 *My ex and I were very young when we married. Actually, I was pregnant and getting married was something we thought was the right thing to do, so we did. Three years later when we divorced, it was not from anger but that we had just grown up and realized that the primary thing we had in common was our beautiful daughter. For the rest of our lives, she was the only child either of us had, and her kind and loving spirit kept us all close. I remarried and my husband never saw my daughter's father as a threat or disruption. He was respected as Terri's father and was in our lives as Terri's father. When he got sick, Terri was well into adulthood and had her own family at that point. It was the natural order of things to bring her father into our home, and my husband and I nursed him back to health. Did I ever envision this type of relationship? Absolutely not, but it's what is possible when love guides you to put your child first. There was never jealousy, no weirdness, just a general respect for the father of my child. Now that he is gone, I would not ever change a thing. I'm grateful he was the father of my child, and I'm grateful I met another man who was not threatened by love, caring, and respect.* 99

The Rules Still Apply

On learning the ages of my children, people often ask me whether I miss having younger children. I can answer, "No," in complete honesty. Beyond having kids who now, as adults, can jump into the car and run to the store for beer, there is the immense joy of relating to them as developing adults. Discussions of politics, economics, history, morality, and even sexuality grow deeper and more rewarding as we can look back and see how their childhoods and teen years might have informed their adult views. They bring to our lives the unique perspective of knowing us as parents, able to relate what is happening today to something that might have occurred on a family vacation 15 or 20 years ago.

In this deepening trust, however, lies a danger: you may let your guard down and forget some of the cardinal rules of co-parenting. It may be easy to remember how emotionally fragile a 6-year-old child is, but when that same child is a confident, self-assured 25-year-old sharing a drink with you at a bar, you may forget that that 6-year-old child is still in there. And nothing casts us back to our more vulnerable selves than the pain of a family separation. Let's take a moment, then, and review how the old rules still apply.

Keep Your Concerns to Yourself

As fun as it is to treat our kids as adults, it also opens us up to a new kind of vulnerability. As we get comfortable talking about adult issues and relationships, we may start leaning on them for emotional support, dredging up old injuries and finally unloading about what an awful person their other parent was. *Never make your child your confidant.* We may feel compelled to explain to them anew how the breakup was the other parent's fault and to defend ourselves against the anger and sadness they may still feel. It is still not the time for this. It is never the time for this. Your adult children will still feel loyalty to their other parent, and they will still see aspects of that parent in themselves. Feel free to share about how difficult or painful you found the process, especially if you can shed light on how they can overcome similar life challenges. But save your concerns about your ex for your friends and your therapist.

> **66** *I know my dad can be trying,"* an adult child of divorce told me during an interview for an article I was writing. "I always respected that my mother never said a bad thing about him. She would laugh and say, 'That's your father,' when I would come home with stories of his antics—some not so complimentary—but she never ranted or talked badly behind his back. I asked her one time why she didn't. She definitely had the right—and the ammunition. She just smiled and said, 'Where would that have gotten me? I knew you loved him too. I never wanted to take that away from you.' **99**

Now That the Kids Are Adults

Parents often feel that once their children are adults, they can handle "the truth," so parents may not be as cautious when discussing sensitive subjects or reflecting on the past. They may also continue to harbor animosity or dread confrontation with their adult children's other parent, so they look to their adult children to pass on information, thinking, *"They are adults now. It doesn't matter."*

It matters. Your children remain sensitive to both parents, no matter their age, and their allegiance continues to be tested when a parent asks them to relay a message, no matter how innocuous it appears. Adult children will shy away from a parent even faster than younger children, because they have the power to say no, and they will look for ways to avoid interaction if put in the middle.

It is also true that adult children have the ability to stand back, analyze, and add their own twist to the message, if they think it will be better accepted by the other parent—or they can simply refuse to pass on information. That then backs unprepared parents into a corner, and their relationship with their adult child is then affected. Let's look at an example.

Father (to his adult child still living at Father's home and attending college):
I know you were going to use the car to visit your mother, but I'm tied up at work and won't be home for an hour or so. Please call her and ask her to pick you up.

Child: *I'm trying to finish up a report. It's due tomorrow. Why can't you call her?*

Father: *I'm really busy, honey, and it will take me more time to get home if I break to call.*

Child: *You know she's going to lose it, Dad. She hates to have plans changed at the last minute. She's going to take it out on me, and I will have to deal with her telling me about what a flake you are.*

Father: *I can take it, son. Call her or else she's going to be really mad.*

Child: *You can take it, Dad, but I can't. I'm tired of this. You're the one who is late. You are the one who should call her.*

After years of being put in the middle, the adult child realized he now had the power to remove himself from his parents' destructive dynamic. He took a personal stand and took himself out of the middle. Simply saying, "No," put his father on notice—not disrespectfully—but required him to take responsibility for his own actions.

If you have some information you need to share with your ex, communicate directly, even if it's likely to be an unpleasant interaction, actually, *especially* if it's unlikely to be an unpleasant interaction. It puts your child or adult child into an awkward position, and anyone who has ever played a game of telephone knows how messages get garbled from one person to the next. Your ex is likely to have some sort of reply to whatever messages you've sent, and your child deserves better than to be a go-between for 2 warring camps.

Remind Your Adult Children That They Did Not Cause the Divorce

Young children use magical thinking, and they imagine that things they do and say have power over the world in ways that don't truly make sense. It's easy, therefore, to remind a 6-year-old that she did not cause your separation or divorce. What about when she is an adult? Shouldn't she know better by now?

In some ways, perhaps she does. But the child is still in there, and when issues arise from the separation or divorce, even decades later, she may still be feeling guilty, rehearsing a script of "If only…" scenarios. When you talk about what happened, remember to address those concerns even now. It's never too late to remind your children that they were never at fault.

You May Feel as if You Are Repeating Yourself

An adult child of divorce once confided that dealing with her parents' divorce didn't necessarily get easier as she got older. It just changed. It was a special kind of mourning—intellectually, she understood that the divorce was a long time ago, but in her heart, whenever there was a milestone for her own children, she still wished her parents were together. They did not have a comfortable co-parenting relationship as she grew up, and once she had children of her own, she longed for a comfortable holiday for her children where Grandma and Grandpa could be in the same room.

> **❝** *My biological mother and father were divorced when I was 4. My dad remarried, and over the years, we began to refer to him and his new wife as 'the parents' and my biological mother as 'Mom.' My mom and my parents developed a very close relationship and really raised us together as a committee, of sorts. Twenty-three years later, when I was in my 30s, my dad and his wife divorced. I was devastated and I remember telling my best friend, 'I don't remember my biological mom and dad being married, but my parents are divorced and I hate it.'* **❞**

With this in mind, don't think your job is done because time passes and your kids get older. You may have to revisit the divorce many times as both your memories and your children's memories are affected by time passing. The conversation will continue, as will the necessity to offer your children and their children patience, love, respect, and understanding.

Set a Goal for the Future

When your child was young, you were able to demand respect. If you didn't like the way she talked with you, you could send her to her room. Now, however, she has a whole house, or at least an apartment, and she probably likes it there. The best way to ensure that she treats you with respect is to model it yourself. Hopefully, for many years now, you've been showing your children how to communicate with others in a way that empowers them rather than demeans them. If not, you might be able to ask for a fresh start now, but no one is obligated to grant that request, so hopefully, you've lived in a way that you can say, "Please show me the same respect I show you."

One way to help your relationship to mature is to develop habits of mindful communication. Recall that the pain of separation and divorce never goes completely away; as big as she has grown, your child may still feel hurt and upset about what happened. Rather than try to deny this feeling ("You don't really feel that, do you? But look at how good things have turned out for everyone!"), just try and acknowledge it. When our children are preschoolers, we teach them to name their feelings (see Chapter 8, Toxic Stress and Its Effect on Our Children). We say simple things, such as "You seem really angry right now." That sentence is just as important for a 20-year-old to hear as for a 3-year-old. Simply demonstrating that you're aware of how your child feels and giving your child your permission to have those feelings is a strong start to an honest, open, and accepting conversation.

This step is just one way that you can use the same techniques that doctors, psychologists, and therapists use to help people open up to them. Don't just name the feeling but show that you understand what your adult child has said by rephrasing it: "It sounds like you're feeling a lot of stress about graduating college and wondering what you're going to next." Then wait for an acknowledgment or a correction: "I'm stressed, but it's not because I don't know what I'm doing next; I'm just not sure it's something I'm interested in." Then you have a perfect setup for a follow-up question: "Is there something you can think of that you'd rather be doing?" This process is called *active listening*, and, as formulaic as it seems on paper, it takes a lot of practice to get right. We are often so eager to air our own opinions or share our own stories that we forget this simple way to engage.

There is another easy way to engage in meaningful conversation that many people under-use, and that is not to engage in conversation. By that, I mean that when there is a space, especially when people are feeling uncomfortable, we often rush to fill that space with words. The words we choose at those moments often seem helpful but may do more harm than good: "I understand what you're going through. Everything happens for a reason." Instead of filling that awkward silence, just sit with it. Let your child be quiet for a while, to gather her thoughts. If you can avoid jumping in, the next thing she finally says is likely to be quite telling. And if she remains silent, you can always offer to help: "Can you think of anything I can do?" is almost never the wrong thing to ask.

Milestones Ahead

Whether you're just starting to consider separation or divorce or decades have passed since your breakup, it always helps to consider how your situation is going to affect major events in your children's lives. If nothing else, visualizing these moments can help remind you how important it is at every step to take the high road and to create the sort of working relationship with your ex that will make space for positive co-parenting experiences in the future.

Moving Out

Traditionally, one marker of adulthood has been moving out of the child-hood home. Whether to attend school, to take a job, or simply to gain privacy, many kids leave home once they are in their late teens or early 20s. This once-ubiquitous rite of passage, however, is evolving rapidly as extended adolescence and scarce economic opportunity combine to keep adult kids at home or return them to their parents' homes after they have left. Let's consider both scenarios.

As long as a child depends on you, you have quite a bit of say in where that child spends time. Within limits, you can create and enforce a visitation schedule, albeit with increasing input from kids as they mature into their teen years. If your teen can drive, transitions may actually become simpler, as she may be able to transport herself from one home to the other. Older teens may also have the right to choose which parent they live with. When a parent petitions the court to adjust the parenting plan for their 17-year-old who wishes to live with them, judges often agree, understanding that the teen is less than a year away from legal adult-hood and then could choose where to live anyway. If a custody change is granted, it is vitally important that the relationship with the other parent continues to be respected and that the parent's time with the teen is reinforced by the other parent.

Once teens or young adults move out, however, they're on their own. Your control over where they spend their time boils down to how much they con-tinue to rely on you for financial or logistical support. The move itself may require coordination with your ex. Moves usually require financial support and logistical support. Who is going to rent a truck or hire a mover? Do you plan to help carry boxes and furniture? Are there things to buy: linens, pots and pans, and electronics? Who wants to help with those, or are there spare items either of you can donate to the cause? Will your teen or young adult need a parent to cosign a lease or even serve as co-borrower on a mortgage? What about renter's insurance? Chances are good that this step your teen or young adult is taking toward independence will require substantial support from at least one parent, if not both, and strong communication with your ex can help everything go smoothly.

There are any number of reasons not to drop in on an adult child without warn-ing, but separation and divorce add another: When is your ex planning to visit? This sort of situation arises for our family during parents' weekends for our adult children who are away at school. We have to communicate ahead of time about who is taking the student and roommate to breakfast, who gets lunch, and whether all of us having dinner together will be fun or awkward. Is there a concert, an art show, or a sports event to attend? If so, will you save each other seats or work to minimize uncomfortable encounters?

If you're following the most important rule—putting your children (and now adult children) first—you can always ask them what they'd prefer: "I'd love to meet your new partner, but it looks like your mom has dinner planned. Can we take the two of you out for lunch?" At the same time, don't be surprised if your child grows tired of playing social secretary. "I don't care, why don't you and Mom figure it out?" is a perfectly acceptable answer and one you should be prepared to act on. A student facing the stress of move-in weekend, midterms, or graduation may not want to also juggle the calendars of various well-intentioned parents, "bonusparents," and grandparents, and the student shouldn't have to.

Moving Back In

According to the Pew Research Center, more adult children are living with their parents now than at any time since the 1950s. After reaching a nadir of 12% in 1980, "multigenerational families" are on the rebound, accounting for 20% of American households in 2018. The chances are fair, then, that at least one of your adult children will be living with your co-parent. It's unlikely in this scenario that you'll return to a visitation schedule, but there may be reasons that an adult child chooses to spend time at one home or another. These situations can work out well for the parents, as a responsible adult child may be able to care for the house, the pets, or even a grandparent when they're away. At the same time, these situations may require some extra thought in the setting of a separation or divorce.

Before an adult child moves home, you'll want to have a long, honest conversation about which home makes the most sense. The change is likely to be complex, regardless of what happens. You may be thrilled to spend more time with your child, but you may also have concerns about related costs, the presence of your child's friends or romantic partner in your home, or about how your own romantic and social life might be affected. If your child invites the other parent over, how will that feel to everyone? Would it be welcome or awkward? Could it lead to conflict? These may be some challenging conversations to have, but they are important issues to hash out before the furniture arrives. Setting clear boundaries will keep conflict to a minimum.

Weddings

Marriage rates are gradually dropping among young Americans, but there is still a fair chance that, at some point, your adult child will have a ceremony to formalize a relationship with a partner. Given the statistics, the aisle may be divided not into "bride's side" and "groom's side" but into quarters for each parent. This is yet another opportunity to have an honest conversation with your child and your ex. As always, put your child first. This may seem like a basic concept, but weddings bring out strong feelings about culture, religion, status, and tradition, and you may find yourself wedded, so to speak, to a vision of this event that has little to do with what your child actually wants.

It may help to have an officiant or wedding planner (if one is involved) offer up some different scenarios. Anyone who participates regularly in weddings has likely faced all sorts of situations and has had experience with a variety of solutions. If the bride is close to her father and her "bonusfather," for example, who walks her down the aisle? Both of them? Neither? There's no right answer to this question except the one that makes her the most comfortable. Given your own experience, you may have some very strong feelings about marriage and all the ceremonies around it. Your child's experience, however, may be very different from your own, and now is the moment to let children have it for themselves.

Grandchildren

Another step in many adult's lives is to have children of their own. Just as with weddings, this is likely to be an emotional process for all involved. First, there is the fear you may feel for the mother's and the baby's health. Beyond that, however, is the image you may have of how the birth should happen: who should be there, how soon you'll hold the baby, and even what the baby's name might be. Again, however, we have to go back to rule No. 1: "putting your children first." Start by asking your child how much she wants you involved in the pregnancy and the birth. Would she welcome a baby shower or see that as old-fashioned and intrusive? Does she have a birth plan, and, if so, do you play a role? Once the new baby is born, who will be allowed to visit and when? Does your adult child want both of her parents in the room, or would it be less stressful if you took turns visiting?

The questions continue after the baby comes home. You may have time, resources, and experience to share. But, then, so may your ex. How does your child envision your involvement? The other parents'? You can anticipate a whole new round of birthday parties, school events, and holidays that now must be shared not only with your ex but also with another parent's family members, however many of them there may be. Your best bet is to offer all the help you can provide while refraining from pressuring your child to allow you more involvement than makes her comfortable.

Holidays

Holidays can be delightful times to spend with your kids and stepchildren, but they can be especially stressful for grown children of separation and divorce. Imagine an adult couple with their own children facing Thanksgiving. If neither is a child of separation or divorce, they still must decide which of 2 families to visit or host for the holiday. Of course, if everyone lives in the same place, perhaps all sides of the family can gather together, but, even then, if both members of the couple are not only children, what about their siblings? Now let's imagine that, as often happens, both members of the couple come from separated or divorced families. Now a minimum of 4 different households might reasonably expect to see them for Thanksgiving and maybe more, depending on how many subsequent pairings each of the parents had. Of course, you're going to want to spend time with your kids, your stepchildren, and their families, but if you don't see them for any specific holiday or event, be understanding of the pressure they face to make everyone happy.

Jann Family Holiday: The key is to think outside the box. Fine-tune holiday celebrations to meet your family's needs. For example, my adult kids have chosen not to go to the "parents'" homes for Thanksgiving and Christmas (there are 4 different sets of parents and far too many places to hit on one day), but for the parents to go to their home. They have an open house and all who choose to go, do. There is no animosity among exes, no drama among new partners, and if all show up at the same time, the more, the merrier. We try to remember that holidays are only one day, and life goes on once that holiday has passed. We do our best to be accepting and nonjudgmental all-year round.

David Family Holiday: My kids aren't even all grown yet, and already we face these questions. My middle child attends a boarding high school in another city, and he is delightful to spend time with, so when he comes home for breaks, of course I want him to spend all his time with me or at least to divide his minutes evenly between our house and his mom's. At age 17 years, however, he also has friends he wants to see and things he wants to do when he's home, so, rather than count out the hours between his arrival and his departure and split them down the middle, we let his interests determine where he is and when. When any of us misses him too much, we get on the road and go buy him lunch.

Graduations and Other Milestone Celebrations

❝ *My daughter is graduating this weekend, and her father and I are at odds as to how to handle the celebration afterward. I want everyone to come over to my home for a casual BBQ, and he wants to take everyone out to dinner. My daughter tells me she would prefer the BBQ but understands her father might be uncomfortable at my home now that I have remarried.***❞**

You always begin by putting the children first, and that means the parent considers the child's feelings before one's own. But it sounds as if the young person in the scenario has become quite the diplomat and has learned to juggle her parents' preferences like a pro. She has told her mother that she would prefer to do what she wants, but she understands why her father may not want to attend under the circumstance—therefore, this implies that the only alternative is to do what Dad wants—but she's not picking sides. She's allowing her mother to make the choice by being empathetic to Dad's dilemma. Quite ingenious. That way, if Mother makes the concession, it's of her own free will, which will hopefully eliminate any animosity she might feel for not getting what she wanted. This young person has been in the middle of her parents for a very long time.

If it's difficult for both sides of the family to congregate at one of the parents' homes, the best alternative is a neutral place. Home is a parent's private turf, and it's not surprising that an ex might feel uncomfortable, particularly when one or both have remarried.

That said, it's not uncommon that divorced parents celebrate together—not even uncommon that they celebrate at each other's homes—but if one shares a preference not to, that's a cue that a neutral place is the best answer.

If a child truly prefers the more casual BBQ, a good alternative might be to have the graduation celebration at a local park where those attending can BBQ, perhaps bringing potluck offerings, but celebrate on more neutral ground. To appease Mom, she might be in charge of the meal planning—Dad gets his neutral place, Mom gets her BBQ. The child has both her parents near her at an important time in her life.

Just because your teen has turned 18 years old and is legally an adult doesn't mean the potential for celebrating with an ex ends. She will have many other milestones in her life—holidays, college graduation, and marriage—and wait until she has children of her own. Some parents of adult children say they have seen their ex more since their children have started having children than they saw them for years. When parents break up, they can throw 2 birthday parties for their own children, but rarely do their children throw 2 birthday parties for their children because Grandma and Grandpa or their other caregivers can't get over themselves.

> 66 *I really don't want both my parents to come...even after all these years, they still snap at each other and I really don't want to be around it.* 99

What if parents absolutely cannot celebrate their children's milestones together after a breakup? There's no tried-and-true rule that they must. There are those divorced parents that hold on to that animosity forever and that is their prerogative, but it is also proven in studies that holding a grudge can affect you mentally, physically, and emotionally; plus, it will be the example you are setting for your children about dealing—or not dealing—with stressful situations. Sometimes, if that has been the example shown, children would prefer not to have a special milestone spoiled by battling parents. That means that even as adults your children will have to opt for 2 separate celebrations, pick one parent to attend, or, in some cases, choose to celebrate without you. These are the children who don't come home for the holidays once they grow into adulthood. Their divorced parents' behavior continues to put them right in the middle and choose a parent, and rather than continue to check their allegiance, they walk away.

Health Care

We would love for our children and ourselves to be healthy forever, but as a doctor, I know that illness happens, often unexpectedly. When your children are juveniles, the custody agreement should spell out who pays for health insurance and how health care decisions are made. Once they are adults, however, everything is up in the air. Will they stay on your health insurance or get their own? Who would they like to have the health care power of attorney, in case they are unable to make a decision for themselves? If they have a chronic condition, such as asthma or diabetes, have they learned everything they need to know to care for themselves?

You'll also need to consider some of these questions for yourself. If you have not remarried, who holds your health care power of attorney? Have you talked with your children about what sorts of interventions you would or would not want done during a health emergency? Could health care professionals reach your children were something to happen to you? None of these are fun things to think about, and your children may even resist having these conversations. They are, however, critical conversations to have, but there may come a time when everyone is thankful for the clear guidance.

It's Complicated

Separation, divorce, and remarriage create new kinds of relationships that can require creative solutions, especially as life moves forward. My grandmother celebrated her 100th birthday last year, and she had been widowed and remarried and then widowed again. I knew that her second husband had adult children, but the only members of that generation I had ever known were my dad and my aunt. Suddenly, at age 50 years, I was learning the names and faces of people I had barely even considered as being part of "my" family. As it turns out, these "bonusaunts" and "bonusuncles" are also lovely and interesting people, and I enjoyed getting to know them along with "bonuscousins." Let's consider some scenarios.

Adult Stepchildren

Ideally, you developed strong relationships with your "bonuschildren" when they were younger. You undoubtedly hope that they value you and the special role you have played in their lives. That said, once they are adults, stepchildren are free to determine what sort of relationship they want with you or with anyone else. If you are still in a relationship with their birth parent, you are likely to see them often. In some cases, however, you may no longer be in that relationship, and what then?

That really depends on how they feel. They may have developed strong bonds with you and be eager to seek you out. Or they may be done with the phase of their lives that included you. Complicating matters further, their birth parent may discourage them from contacting you if things did not end well. Even if they don't feel close at this moment, remember that people grow and change, and the relationships they seek out change with them. There may be a special strength they recall you having—maybe you're especially calm in a crisis or know everything about taking care of babies—and when the time comes, they will seek you out. The most you can do is to leave the door open for contact.

Second Exes and Beyond

Personally, I feel as if I learned enough from my first marriage to make my second marriage last forever. I know, however, that the odds are against me. Whereas around half of first marriages end in divorce, the ratio jumps to 67% of second marriages and 74% of third marriages. These statistics mean that many family separations often affect bonusparents and bonuschildren as well. If negotiating adult relationships with natural children can be challenging, the complexity grows with the number of relationships that have formed and unformed. What sort of relationship will your children want with an "ex-bonusparent," and what say do you have in it?

Essentially, if you're putting the children first, the guidelines remain the same. Hopefully, your kids found something to appreciate and enjoy about anyone you have brought into their lives. How they want to extend that relationship really depends on their needs and desires, not yours. Let's look at a story to illustrate.

> 66 *Five years ago, my ex ended our marriage, but he has kept in touch with my youngest daughter (we married when she was 12 and she lived with us). She now has 3 children—my grandchildren— and wants her stepdad to play a role in their lives. He's been living with someone for the past 4 years. He has avoided any contact with me except for a few business issues, and I've never met his girlfriend. It was so difficult over the holidays when there were gifts from G'Pa Paul and the girlfriend. I trusted him to be a good stepparent, and he hurt all of us by divorcing me. I thought I was past being hurt, but hearing her name with the gifts was so very difficult, and Easter is around the corner. I'm anticipating the same thing, and I'm dreading the holidays.* 99

When we meet someone and decide to make a go of it, we rejoice when they take to our children. We promote the closeness, allow one-on-one time, and secretly celebrate each time they remember our children's milestones without our reminding them. We delight in their devotion to both us and our children, but then, as can sometimes happen, the relationship ends and we are devastated, not only for ourselves but for our children as well.

It's difficult to separate ourselves from the feelings of hurt, envy, or jealousy after a breakup, and the pain becomes even more acute if you have been left for someone else. It may take years to get back to normal, and you can feel stuck in a sea of emotions that are difficult to navigate. Plus, there may be other feelings to cope with, feelings such as "These are my children. I shared them with you once, but you chose to leave, so leave—and leave my children alone."

But that's from the parent's point of view, not the child's. In this scenario, from the child's point of view, she has done exactly what parents long for when they remarry. She has built a loving relationship with a stepparent. The breakup didn't change her devotion to her stepfather, nor does it seem to have changed her stepfather's devotion to her. They are maintaining a relationship because the child wants that relationship to continue—for herself and, now it seems, for her children. That doesn't make this mother feel any better. She's still stuck in her hurt, while her ex-husband continues to maintain a loving relationship with her daughter.

And it seems her ex-husband is conducting himself in an exemplary manner. He's not demanding to attend family get-togethers but looking for alternative times and places to maintain familial relationships privately. He's supplying presents when appropriate, and he attends milestone and holiday celebrations only when invited. He's maintaining a relationship with a child he's raised because she wants that relationship to continue and because his ex-wife has not found someone new; he's the most obvious candidate to fill the grandpa shoes. Again, everyone is happy but the child's mother. Her hurt and pain is real, and her question makes it obvious that she anticipates more pain in the future.

Although this situation may sound convoluted, it is really quite common. More couples break up than stay together, and, as a result, today's parents must be cognizant of what each relationship they have demands of their children and grandchildren. This hasn't always been so. When people broke up less often, they simply didn't have to face the fallout of breaking up and starting over. One could make a blanket statement, such as "A stepparent has no business continuing a relationship with a stepchild—when your relationship ends, the stepparent's relationship with your kids end too." But in today's relationships, that isn't what we ask of our partners and children when we are together. We want them to care for each other as individuals and build loving separate relationships, and then when they do and we break up, you bet it's hard, but—and this is not to be flippant—that's life. Life! You can do this and be stronger for it.

Here are some tips that may help.

Tips When It Comes to Dealing With Second Exes and Beyond

- Understand that your relationship with your child has not changed. Build on that.
- Let each relationship stand on its own and don't compare on any level. Not your relationship to your child, not your relationship to your ex, not your ex's relationship to a new partner, not how your ex responds to your child, not how "she" (or "he") responds to your child, and certainly not how your child responds to anyone. None of it. They are now all adults and make their own decisions—as do you.
- Don't rehash the pain. If revenge is important, know that the best revenge is to move on and truly be happy.
- Reframe sadness. Instead of, for example, "I thought I was past being hurt, but hearing her name with the gifts was so very difficult," try "I'm so excited to see my daughter and grandchildren!" Picture their smiling faces, not in relationship to "her" (or "him") but in relationship to you! Period.
- Stay focused on where you are and what is ahead of you, not what is behind you. If you don't like where your life is headed, change directions.

As difficult as it might be to continue to interact with an ex, even from afar, if a child accepted that ex as a parental figure in the past, it's up to the child if she wants to continue the relationship in the future. And from an ex-etiquette standpoint, proper manners dictate that the decision to invite anyone to a get-together, particularly if it is at your home, is up to the hostess.

> **66** *I was married to my 'bonuskids'' father for well over 20 years. Although we are on very good terms, if we weren't and my 'bonusdaughter' wanted our relationship to continue, that's the way it would be. She had a very difficult time with our divorce. I can't imagine how she would feel if I stopped talking to her because I was no longer married to her father. My relationship with her began when her father and I got married, but over the years, we have developed a bond that is not dependent on that marriage. That relationship continues to this day.* **99**

Final Thoughts

If anyone has ever told you, "Relax!" when you are upset, you understand how difficult that can be. This fact can become painful when your kids fail to share your affection for a new partner. As adults, in fact, they may be even more critical of your new partner than they were when they were younger. If you remember the first time they brought home a date and you were wondering whether this person was "right" for them, now it's your turn. If no one can be good enough for your kids, how can someone be good enough for their parents? You can certainly hope that with time, they come to appreciate your partner, but you cannot force the issue, and sometimes you'll just have to be content with the fact that you're living your own life, just as they are living theirs.

Our actions as our children grow set the stage for their relationships in the future. They watch every move we make, and if we have made mistakes, they watch how we correct them.

When all is said and done, if we lead with love rather than disdain, acceptance rather than judgment, inclusion rather than rejection, and respect rather than contempt, we offer our children a road map to more rewarding relationships on all levels.

Index